Growing in Faith Through Choral Music

by

SUE ELLEN PAGE

Based on the principles of
Ruth Krehbiel Jacobs, founder of Choristers Guild,
in her 1948 book,
The Successful Children's Choir

H. T. FitzSimons Company

One of the Fred Bock Music Companies

H.T. FitzSimons Company
a division of Fred Bock Music Company, Inc.
P.O. Box 570567
Tarzana, CA 91357-0567

ISBN 0-9646552-0-9   (Hard Cover)
ISBN 0-9646552-1-7   (Soft Cover)
Printed in the United States of America

Printing number
1 2 3 4 5 6 7 8 9 10

Photographs, pages 29, 39, 47 by Nancy Hodges.
Photograph, page 143 by Mark Czajkowski.

Quotations from *The Successful Children's Choir*, by Ruth Krehbiel Jacobs, © Copyright 1948, renewed 1976 by H.T. FitzSimons Company, are used by permission of the Publisher and the Arthur Jacobs Estate.

HEARTS AND HANDS AND VOICES
Growing in Faith Through Choral Music

*This book is dedicated to Robert W. Page and Joyce H. Page, who, during
forty years of music ministry, trained hundreds of young people, including
their own five children, using Ruth Krehbiel Jacobs' model.*

Acknowledgements

Dr. John S.C. Kemp and *Dr. Helen Hubbert Kemp* have, since we first met in 1966,
consistently provided guidance, opportunities, tutelage, and friendship. *The Rev. Dr.
Wallace M. Alston, Jr.*, Pastor of Nassau Presbyterian Church, Princeton, NJ, preaches
and teaches the importance of the life of the mind in the context of the Christian faith.
This conviction has provided fertile and challenging soil in which to develop the ideas
herein. I owe much of the opening chapter to him. My many other colleagues on the
staff of Nassau Presbyterian Church have participated in that growth as well: *The Rev.
Cynthia A. Jarvis, Dr. Kenneth B. Kelley, Joyce MacKichan Walker, Kathi Morley,
the Rev. Elsie Armstrong Olsen, the Rev. Sally Osmer, the Rev. Dr. Theodore Gill,
Mark Orten* and *Tina Blackledge. Maureen Franzen* assisted me with her fine
secretarial skills. *Steve Pilkington*, Head of the Church Music Department, Westminster
Choir College of Rider University, *Lindsey Christiansen*, Head of the Voice Depart-
ment at Westminster Choir College and Elder at Nassau Presbyterian Church, and
Marcia Wood, Administrative Director of the Trenton Children's Chorus have each
been helpful in the exchange of ideas about worship, the role of the choir in worship
and the choir as a representative of the church in the world. My friend and classmate
Donna Plaskett once challenged me to take my conducting more seriously and
Constantina Tsolainou, currently on the conducting faculty at Southern Methodist
University, helped immeasurably in the achievement of that goal. Countless other
professional colleagues across the country, especially *Michael Kemp* and *Rebecca
Thompson*, have in various ways contributed to this work over the course of many
years, through the exchange of ideas, by asking the right questions, giving advice and
encouragement. *Carol Wehrheim*, Christian Education Consultant, was most helpful
with her fine editing skills coupled with her enthusiasm for the work the church must
do with and for children. Two librarians were most supportive and cooperative: *Nancy
Wicklund*, Head of Reader Services at Talbott Library, Westminster Choir College of
Rider University; and *Carol Fagundus*, Assistant Head, Order Division, Princeton
University Libraries. Thanks to *Patricia M. Evans*, Executive Director of Choristers
Guild and to the *Arthur Leslie Jacobs Foundation* for their fervent endorsement of this
project. To *Fred Bock*, I express appreciation for the invitation and challenge to tackle
it in the first place, and for his patience and composure in awaiting its completion.
Lorynne Young and Linda Duffendack Mays, for FBMC, were superb in helping
prepare the final manuscript. The spouse and children of the author are often
acknowledged—I now understand why. *Eric, Amanda, Luke* and *Ben Johnson*—Thank
you. Finally, I must acknowledge with a grateful heart, the present and former
choristers (and their families) of *The Choirs for Children and Youth at Nassau
Presbyterian Church* and *The Trenton Children's Chorus* with whom it continues to
be my privilege to make music each week.

> *"You don't have to do great things. But the little things you are doing in
> your sphere of influence can be done with great conviction, great wisdom,
> great beauty, and great love."* —Ruth Krehbiel Jacobs

Foreword

In this "word before" the chapters of Sue Ellen Page's book based on the principles of Ruth Krehbiel Jacobs as documented in *The Successful Children's Choir*, I would like to share personal glimpses into the colorful background of the original publication.

Soon after the death of Ruth Krehbiel Jacobs on April 30, 1960, I received a large box of materials from Ruth's husband, Arthur Leslie Jacobs. I was deeply touched and enormously challenged by the letter which accompanied these books, articles and unfinished projects. Leslie Jacobs wrote, "Ruth's mantle has fallen on you. I want you to have her Lecture/Notebook with the hope that you will embrace the work which Ruth began and nurtured . . ." This was a big assignment for a busy mother of five children!

Ruth's notebook is mostly hand-written in very small distinctive script, sometimes in ink, sometimes in faded pencil. Longer articles are typed with the same old typewriter that tapped out the original CHORISTERS GUILD LETTERS, which began to be distributed to charter members in 1949. At that time, Ruth's office was her Santa Barbara, California kitchen, and her editor's desk, her kitchen table. From her notebook came much of the content of *The Successful Children's Choir,* published in 1948, with its tenth printing in 1995.

Three decades have passed since I received that box with its treasures and challenges. Since then, I have worked with children, teachers and directors in all 50 states, in most of the provinces of Canada, in Sweden, Germany, Japan and other countries. I found myself using not the words nor the methods contained in Ruth's notebook, but the wisdom of her vision and the simplicity of her approach.

One of Ruth's ardent goals was to have university level courses taught in colleges and seminaries, where students could prepare themselves as responsible and dedicated educators and musicians who take seriously the great art of teaching children in churches, schools and communities. This is happening, and often the required text has been *The Successful Children's Choir.* I learned during these 30-something years that every leader must carry the flame with individuality and personal authority which grows out of experience and love. Sue Ellen's expansion of Ruth Jacob's early publication is a shining example of the "growing up and moving on" of leadership.

Although I am still actively involved carrying out my "assignment," it gives me great satisfaction to know that the next generations have superb leadership continuing the Children's Choir Crusade with renewed fervor, knowledge, expertise and an on-going commitment to excellence.

Helen Kemp
Professor Emeritus, Church Music & Voice
Westminster Choir College, Princeton, NJ
June 26, 1995

Preface

A friend, whom I'd asked to read a late draft of this book, asked, "Is this to be your *magnum opus?*" Questioning a first-time author as to whether or not she has another book in her just as the material is going to press is a bit like asking a first-time mother, within moments of giving birth, if she wants to have another baby. "If you don't plan to write another," he continued, "then there are some omissions you may want to explain." Among his perceptive observations was that a preface should be written about what this book purports to do and not do. I have taken his advice.

This book recognizes and recommends the many extraordinarily fine materials that currently exist in the fields of music education, choral conducting, church music, theology and liturgy. Many of these have been published within several years of this copyright. No doubt many more will follow.

In this light, a conscious decision was made to explore in *less* depth those subject areas for which excellent, readily available materials already exist. In such cases, little if any words of value could be added by my placing cursor to screen. An example is the question of score study. In the chapter on conducting, one might expect to find a lengthy segment devoted to this critical aspect of preparation, complete with analysis of a variety of anthems for children's choir. I have chosen to treat the subject in less depth because so much worthy material has already been written on it. The reader is referred to the bibliography where numerous conducting resources are listed that address the topic in depth.

Likewise, a conscious decision was made to include and explore extensively, those particular areas of church music which, in my judgement and through conversation with colleagues, need to be visited again and again. These topics and issues are those about which I felt reasonably hopeful that my particular experiences might shed a small, but perhaps useful, light. The discussions in Chapters 1, 2 and 8 about the challenges facing the church, the nature of the church in the world, relational issues between pastors and musicians, staff and congregation, and the impact of the popular culture on worship styles is, to my knowledge, not treated at length in any existing book geared specifically to children's choir directors. I know that these issues are of profound concern to readers. A long time acquaintance who is the director of music in a large, Southwest congregation recently said regarding the current state of the church and church music: "I am glad that I am within ten years of retirement." He went on to say, "I could not recommend this field to anyone right now." It is my hope that through thoughtful discussion of our discouragements and our successes, we may be bound together in order to support and encourage one another.

The Appendices are unusually lengthy. This is an attempt at organizational expediency and in no way suggests that the material has been "relegated" to an Appendix. Rather than being placed in the body of the book, materials in the Appendices are grouped by type in order to be located more quickly, rather than wading through entire chapters.

Without apology, this book is Presbyterian through and through. Since it is not possible to speak with any authority beyond one's own experiences, readers from other denominations or from secular choral organizations are invited to glean whatever can be universally applied to choral situations with children and youth. Finding the child's true singing voice, for example, is done the same way in a Methodist congregation as it is in a public school or in a Catholic parish. The same premise applies to issues of interaction between people, and to decisions regarding standards of excellence in selecting and preparing repertoire.

The church I have served since 1982 has been described as *staunchly* Presbyterian, historically linked to one of this country's great universities. Its emphasis on the life of the mind and the necessity of bringing our finest fruits to worship and to our work in the world, celebrate and acknowledge God's "countless gifts of love" to us. This congregation serves as the context for exploring the ideas herein. It was suggested that I remind the reader that the building of the choral program for children and youth in this "staunchly Presbyterian church in an east coast college town" did not happen overnight—that patterns for program growth and for establishing a tradition of excellence took time here, as they will anywhere. Our young people and their parents are every bit as busy as other families across the country. Our singers are not inherently more musical than other children, although they do have many opportunities outside of the church in which to nurture their talents. Not every young person who attends this church participates in the music program, but most of them do, and they come back each fall.

In the early years, some staff members and church officers needed guidance in order to understand the inherent power of an effective music program for children and youth in the church. Persistence, persuasion, patience, and a passion for this work—coupled with God's grace and the gift of time—have made possible whatever success we now enjoy. As a staff, we have tried not to make excuses when confronted with circumstances which could potentially limit success. Instead, we asked the question "What if?!" "What if money and time and staffing were not a problem? What could we do???" Looking at even the most remote possibility has led us down paths we are grateful to have had open to us.

The "What if?!" attitude applies as well to long range planning for rehearsals and for selecting worship resources. For example, in most communities, the teen-age mind-set is so centered in the popular culture that it has become the criterion that determines the repertoire a senior high choir can and will sing in worship. "What if" the director sets as a goal, from the children's earliest days in the music program, "growing them up," in faith and in song, into competent young artists within the context of their faith community, by continually selecting fine choral repertoire instead of choral fluff? Plant healthy seeds and tend them well. They will grow.

Ruth Krehbiel Jacobs' beliefs and vision are at the heart of this ministry of music. If the philosophy and techniques chronicled here assist in the achievement of these goals in other churches, I shall be glad for the time spent in recording them.

Sue Ellen Page
Princeton, NJ
June, 1995

"Be careful about calling yourself an 'expert'. One definition is that an 'ex' is a has-been, and a 'spurt' is a drip under pressure."
—*Ruth Krehbiel Jacobs*

Introduction

In 1948, Ruth Krehbiel Jacobs, one of the outstanding church musicians of her day, published a 64-page book called *The Successful Children's Choir*. Reflecting on the particular challenges and problems of working with children's voices in the church, she recorded the results of her successes with children in choirs over a period of 20 years serving congregations in Worchester, Massachusetts and in Los Angeles, California.

Ruth Jacobs recognized the need to address issues relating to the quality of work with children's choirs. The United States was seeing an upsurge of interest in building what was often termed the "Junior Choir." Mrs. Jacobs attributed this increased interest to a very practical reason: *"Church musicians, dealing with the eternal problem of finding recruits for the volunteer choir, stumbled upon the idea that a children's choir might eventually create a more adequate supply of adult singers."* (p. 7)

Similarly, she recognized that *"very few schools of church music include a course in children's choir methods, and literature on the subject is practically non-existent. The leader is forced, if he has the courage to venture out on the project at all, to stumble along by the trial and error method."* (p. 7)

Mrs. Jacobs used as her basis two related fields: for a model of tone quality, the professional boy choirs of Catholic and Episcopal churches; and for a model of teaching methods, the public school music teaching of the day. But again she hastened to add that *"for the most part, we will have to learn by the hard method of actual practice."* (p. 7)

In 1949, the year after the publication of this little book, Ruth Krehbiel Jacobs and her husband Arthur Leslie Jacobs, along with 123 charter members, founded an organization they called Choristers Guild. Arthur Jacobs took care of administrative details. Ruth Jacobs wrote articles for the new organization which contained a wealth of practical suggestions. Additionally, she solicited success stories and practical tips from other church musicians, and published them along with her own material in a series of letters to the small but growing membership. The magazine of today's Choristers Guild takes its name from these early "LETTERS" in which members shared ideas to support one another's work. It is difficult now to believe, but a number of Christian educators of the day openly resisted Ruth Jacobs' efforts to establish well-trained children's choirs. They considered her ideas a detriment to the overall program of the church!

A second method of sharing knowledge was used by Ruth Jacobs and it too continues today—the Festival of Singing Children. Often combined with a directors' workshop, Mrs. Jacobs would travel to various cities where children's choirs from churches in the area would gather to sing agreed upon anthems in the context of a worship service. Many of us who grew up in the fifties remember such festivals with Mrs. Jacobs as the guest conductor. Indeed in 1960, while in Oklahoma to conduct a Festival, Ruth Krehbiel Jacobs died a month before her 63rd birthday.

At the time of this writing, Choristers Guild has a membership of 8,200 across the United States and in 28 countries. Local, state and regional chapters have been organized in order to create greater opportunities for collegiality among directors of choirs for children and youth. The national office of Choristers Guild sponsors summer seminars, teacher workshops, and publishes a wide variety of anthems for children and youth, and music for handbell choirs. Organizational and promotional materials abound, as well as recordings, videos, and other teaching aids.

The Successful Children's Choir has been on my bookshelf for many years. This same book provided the model my parents used for the multiple choir program they began in 1955 at First Methodist Church, Montgomery, Alabama. There, as a chorister, I experienced Mrs. Jacobs' principles firsthand. As a choral director and teacher in the church, *The Successful Children's Choir* has been a primary source for inspired words and fundamental truths. Ruth Jacobs' talent for succinct and beautifully crafted expressions of her faith and of her philosophy is truly remarkable. This book begins each chapter with a quote from Ruth Jacobs' pioneering work. (The page number following each quote refers to the page where it may be found in *The Successful Children's Choir.*)

My own contribution to the church musician's bookshelf attempts to address the particular challenges we face as we approach the 21st century, at the same time re-visiting fundamental truths about children, youth and our Christian faith, and how we express that faith today. The discussions of the Church in Chapter I and the Director in Chapter II serve as a foundation for the "trade-school" topics found in further chapters. The final chapter, "The Choir in Worship," attempts to fuse the previous segments into a whole.

What is offered in these pages is based largely upon sensations and perceptions from childhood experiences as a chorister: *"effort, cooperation, regularity, loyalty," "fine music, high ideals, and participation in public worship," and "consciousness of the presence of God, and active response to that presence." (p. 8)* While much has changed since Ruth Jacobs' time, much has not. Her "Director's Creed" is printed here. It is as valid today as when it was first published in 1948.[1]

A Director's Creed
by Ruth Krehbiel Jacobs

1. *I **believe** that the children's choir is potentially one of the greatest agencies that the Church possesses for rebuilding its waning strength. No other organization has greater natural opportunity for training in those qualities that characterize a strong Christian faith. Other children's organizations are character-building, but the children's choir offers the opportunity of responsibility for the worship attitudes of the entire congregation. When they enter the chancel as a choir, the children become **ministers** of music, and the effort to meet that obligation creates a consciousness of worship to a degree that is otherwise difficult to attain.*

   A well-trained choir is a regular choir. No honest director will tolerate irregularity, for he knows that regularity is the cornerstone on which all other virtues must be laid.

   Cooperation, too, is inherent in choir work. No choir can be successful unless the individual can learn unselfishly to work for a common goal. And, in turn, the personal satisfaction in achievement is multiplied by the satisfaction of all others in the group.

   Effort, too, is one of the qualities that choir membership develops. In many organizations one can be a member without contributing to the total effort. In a choir, there is progress only when every member carries his full share.

   The Protestant Church[2] is alarmed about the large percentage of loss of children at the high school age level. But those churches that maintain an active progressive choir system have proven that the boys and girls trained in habits of worship and participation in the children's choir, in large numbers carry their interest through the dangerous years of adolescence.

   For its unique opportunity for training in effort, cooperation, regularity, and loyalty, and for its ability to carry this training through progressive stages of active participation into maturity, the Protestant Church would do well to give its children's choir full financial and moral support.

2. *I **believe** that what the children absorb unconsciously from their assimilation with fine music, high ideals, and participation in public worship may have greater value than what we consciously teach them.*

3. *I **believe** that the greatest ultimate purpose of the children's choir is worship: consciousness of the presence of God, and active response to that presence. There are too many nominal Christians: the children's choir must help through worship to create a generation of Christians who accept the principles of Christ and have the fortitude to live by them.*

4. *I believe* that our emphasis must be on the child, not the subject. *Great music has no value in itself; only when it penetrates the personality and has its influence there does it really live. Attitudes of worship are only a means to help to create the experience of worship. In the children's choir we have powerful forces at our command - music and worship and discipline; those must be used to develop cultured, disciplined and devout individuals.*

5. *I believe* that if the children's choir is to achieve the maximum of its *potentialities, it must have thoroughly trained leadership. And it must be recognized by the Church at large as a legitimate and integral part of its educational program. In the last several years, the quality of children's choir work has improved conspicuously, but before this improvement can become general there must be opportunities for sound leadership training. It is true that numerous summer institutes offer short courses in children's choir techniques, but a sound working knowledge can hardly be acquired in two days or two weeks. Children's choir methods must eventually become an integral part of the basic training for the professional church musician. With that training he will not be so prone to shift his responsibility for the children's choir onto the shoulders of some willing but untrained young assistant. And with that training and its resultant authority, the Church will eventually be forced to recognize and support the movement that is such a great potential in the revival of vital Christianity.*

Using these principles as our foundation, let us attempt to build a children's choir program that will be of interest to the child and of abiding value to the man. (pp. 7-9)

Endnotes

[1] No attempt has been made to update (make inclusive) the language style common to Ruth Jacobs' era.

[2] Jacobs was writing pre-Vatican II. The programmatic differences between Protestant and Catholic congregations today are much less, due to papal, ecumenical and societal changes.

Chapter 1

THE CHURCH
AND ITS MUSIC:
WHAT ARE WE TO BE?

"I believe that the children's choir is potentially one of the greatest agencies that the Church possesses for rebuilding its waning strength. No other organization has greater natural opportunity for training in those qualities that characterize a strong Christian faith." (p. 7)

When Ruth Krehbiel Jacobs wrote *The Successful Children's Choir* in 1948, she was writing to an audience that was in many ways vastly different than that of today. Her first readership was essentially operating from a World War II frame of reference, yet she drew upon ideals which are of enduring value and truth: children like to take pride in their work; music can be of profound influence in the worship life of a congregation and in nurturing the faith of the singer and the listener; a quality music program is an investment, not only in the present but also in the future, since it keeps children and youth involved in the church and prepares them for church leadership as adults.

Ruth Jacobs' insight not withstanding, she could not have predicted the extensive technological advances which would radically transform the world by the end of the 20th century. Word processing, spread sheets, desktop publishing, e-mail, etc. are facts of life in communities large and small. These capabilities simultaneously simplify our lives and expand our horizons. A potentially negative technological challenge for the church musician, however, comes from a theological shift: the music of choice in many congregations now demands little more than finding the correct place on the accompaniment tape. The church musician of today has at once more options and more potential limitations than generations before.

Similarly, who could have predicted in 1948 the many challenging social changes that professional church workers would face: the gradual dissolution of the traditional two-parent family as the norm in American homes; families in which both parents are working outside the home; neighborhoods that are no longer occupied by families involved in the local church; congregations who choose to drive miles from their homes to their houses of worship; church members who have not been trained to give sacrificially to the programs of the church.

Indeed, the culture in which we find ourselves as we enter the 21st century is very different than the one many of us were familiar with as children and youth. For churchgoers who grew up in the 1950's and earlier, it was commonly assumed that not only would we attend church school and worship each Sunday morning, but that we would be there again for the hymn sing and worship service that evening. Then on Wednesdays, we would come for choir practice followed by the all-church supper and Bible study. Such attendance did not guarantee faithful, life-long Christians, but it did at least provide the Church with a regular and systematic opportunity to convey and reinforce its message week after week, year after year to large numbers of people.

While still the norm in a few places, the church's attempt to witness in and to a secular world is meeting challenges unimaginable a half century ago. We have already noted the technological advances in communications and travel that have yielded a rapidly shrinking planet and world community; the changes in the American family structure are significant. But there are more challenges still: knowledge is said to double every ten years; the number of people living and building careers in countries other than that of their birth will continue to expand, bringing increasing multi-culturalism to cities large and small; the Sunday morning profusion of extra-curricular activities for both boys and girls, coupled with compelling television news magazines for adults, attest to an increasingly *secular* society; alternative religions, cults, and secular humanism are popular options for people who prefer a "new age" theology to old fashioned Christianity.

The Disappearance of the Sabbath

In his book, *The Gospel in a Pluralist Society*, theologian Lesslie Newbigin defines a pluralist culture as one in which there is "no officially approved pattern of belief or conduct...a free society, not controlled by accepted dogma but characterized rather by the critical spirit which is ready to subject all dogmas to critical (and even skeptical) examination."[1] The Gospel, as presented by the church, has not been exempt from the examination. Indeed, in this increasingly multi-cultural, humanistic, and pluralistic world, the church is no longer the center of family life it once was. And for many of the families who choose to make church a part of their lives, participation is very limited. Sending the children off to church school while the parents attend the worship service is "all our family can manage after a hectic week." For this family, adding a Christian education class for the parents and a worship service for the children would double the length of their morning. Church professionals find themselves shrugging their collective shoulders in despair as Sunday morning competition results in such anomalies as hockey uniforms underneath choir robes or families gathering at the soccer field rather than in the sanctuary for worship.

Nominal Christians

"There are too many nominal Christians: the children's choir must help through worship to create a generation of Christians who accept the principles of Christ and have the fortitude to live by them." (p. 8)

We may be dealing today as never before, at least in modern times, with what Ruth Jacobs called "nominal Christians." The first two centuries of the church knew a similar world—polytheistic, pluralistic and officially secular. As in the first century A.D., there are many competing religions and gods. Christianity today is clearly in a minority position.[2]

Nominal church membership manifests itself in a variety of ways, all of which God may well be able to use ultimately, but all of which can be disheartening and difficult to deal with for a church staff. A frequent manifestation of this nominal church membership is the family who participates in the life of the church as *one of many things they do for a time*, in order to be "well rounded." Two common examples are the child who attends choir enthusiastically, but only for a year or two; or the young person who becomes confirmed, then drops out completely, often taking the parents as well. Sometimes, the family or individual gets involved because of a burst of newly found interest, usually centered around a charismatic personality among the church leadership, or around a stand a particular church takes on a social issue. While in both cases there is always the possibility for a genuine faith journey, there is also the possibility that there is little in the way of an intentional, personal, thoughtful, growing connectedness to God in Christ. This is as true in mainline denominations, both liberal and conservative, as it is in the more fundamentalist denominations.

Another sign of nominal church membership is to be seen in *giving patterns*. In many churches of the Protestant mainline, the days of tithing as a matter of course are gone, and, as long-time church-goers who have led a life of serious stewardship pass away, congregations are left with fewer givers at those levels to take their places. Even though the incomes may equal or surpass that of their elders, the giving patterns of many contemporary church-goers are far from sacrificial. To be sure, some of these families may well be giving amounts equivalent to those who have gone before, but there are more requests for charitable contributions now than ever before. The church, for many, has become just one more "charity," along with the United Way, the Heart Association, and the local theater guild. Furthermore, in some churches, non-pledging parents enroll their children in the choral program and/or church school but do not voluntarily give financial support.

Contributing to the issue of nominal church membership is a second effect of the secular world: that of *transiency*. People may move many times during their working years. Increasingly, the church-goer shops around before deciding upon a particular congregation with which to affiliate, then chooses a church that meets individual or family needs irrespective of denomination. This differs from past generations when "Protestants knew what distinguished them from the Roman Catholics. Roman Catholics believed in the authority of the Pope, went to confession, and ate fish on Friday. Quakers and Christian Scientists had no minister, Baptists held revivals and Methodists signed temperance pledges. Presbyterians simply looked like Presbyterians. They went to Sunday school and believed in predestination."[3] This "grass roots ecumenism"[4] is healthy in many ways, but it has at least two problems: first, it tends to create church-goers who are untrained in the tradition with which they affiliate; second, this mobile life takes a toll on programs of the church. A healthy music program for example, depends heavily upon the building of skills year after year, in order to establish a tradition of excellence.

Still another effect of the secular culture is the *move out of cities*, largely by the white population, into the suburbs. This has left many once vital, active congregations struggling to survive. A growing number of them have actually ceased to exist as a church. Often their magnificent buildings are turned over to other useful purposes, sometimes through the larger church and sometimes through secular agencies. Although there are urban congregations which have large endowments as a result of the stewardship of previous generations and the wise management of those assets, they often find that few people are willing to drive into the city when there is a neighborhood church near their home. A number of inner city congregations which do not have the benefit of healthy finances, often share ministers and a skeleton staff. They may find that their constituency is culturally different than the one that originally occupied the building, and frequently not of the denomination posted on the church door. The drying up of the large downtown church in many communities may have done something to the mentality of the church and its expectations both programmatically and artistically.

How is the church to be a potent force in this secular, pluralistic society? What is our role? How are we as church musicians called to minister to young people who may consider themselves too busy even to try what we have to offer? How do we minister to children of parents whose own church membership may be "nominal" at best? How do we run a sufficient program with insufficient funds? How do we garner a support system of parents when many appear to be overworked from the dual responsibilities of running a home and keeping a job? Clearly, the church (and thus the church musician) is in competition for people's minds and hearts, time and treasure.

Some might argue that the church is healthier when it has to "sell" its program along with everyone else—the YMCA, the ballet society, the music conservatory, the tennis center. It is possible that the days of getting a good turn-out on Sundays, simply because people felt obligated to come, may have ultimately contributed more to the loss of members than to the genuine claiming of souls. Surely the church itself must bear responsibility for the disenchantment of so many. So the question becomes, "How might we, engagingly and compellingly, 'sell' what we believe to be the news the world needs most of all and not 'sell out' to the secular world? How might we try to do the work of a God who is in this world, but not of it?"

A Parallel To Popular Culture?

Historically, the church has often borrowed from the culture of the secular world. A most notable example for musicians, of course, is Martin Luther. Although an accomplished musician who wrote both words and music, he frequently took common street tunes as the basis for his hymns. These were melodies that the average person could pick up after a couple of hearings. Luther used this technique in order to bridge the gap between a liturgy in which priests and professional singers "did" worship for the people, and a reforming liturgy, in which "the priesthood of all believers was reaffirmed" through congregational song.[5] Several of our most famous hymn tunes came into use in this way.

During the media-oriented second half of the 20th century this practice reached new, and potentially problematic, heights. At virtually any time of day or night we can turn on the television and view one of the following in the comfort of our living rooms: a plush set replete with attractive Christian talk-show hosts discussing the good news, slickly produced televised worship services, "Christian" soap operas and "Christian" sit-coms. Only the game show and sporting event formats have, at this writing, been left still to produce.

Undoubtedly, the most notable example in the twentieth century of the church's penchant for borrowing from the popular culture is musical: Christian rock bands, balladeers, and crooners abound. In his book *Contemporary Christian Music*,[6] author Paul Baker includes a column called "Sounds Like..." in which he systematically names a popular performer and then gives the name of his/her "Contemporary Christian" counterpart. Baker says, "The main thing to remember in using the chart is what it suggests. If you like artist 'A' in secular music, then there's a good chance you'll like some of the music of 'B' in Christian music." Indeed, this borrowed musical style has given itself the official name "Contemporary Christian."

Attempts at sincere evangelism notwithstanding, the motivating impulse is one of marketing: if it sells in the popular culture, clean it up and it will sell in the religious culture too. Kenneth A. Myers, who includes himself among evangelical Christians, writes compellingly about this in his book, *All God's Children and Blue Suede Shoes*:

"Achieving popularity by 'sounding like' establishes a curious pattern for people striving to avoid being conformed to the pattern of this world. The implicit message of such celebrity is that Christians are successful to the extent that they mimic the models established by the world...Such a strategy is a sad reminder that most of the Christian criticism of popular culture has focused on content while ignoring form. A generation after Marshall McLuhan, the Church still behaves as if the forms of mass media and the role they play in our lives, are value-neutral."[7]

We will explore this issue as it relates to musical choices for worship more thoroughly in Chapter 8. For our purposes here, it is enough to remember that *forms communicate values*[8] and that church workers must be diligent in monitoring those forms. A particular musical style, for example, is not necessarily appropriate for worship or for "selling" the church's message simply because it is popular. So once again, we ask the question. "How might we worship and do the work of a God who is in this world but not of it?"

What the Church Is and Is Not

We might do well to discuss what the church is and what it is not, before we try further to define our role in it or set out to accomplish it. First, *the church is not its institutions and activities*, as important as they are.[9] These are the ways and means the church goes about its life in the world: the building where we worship, where couples are married, where groups meet, where funerals are held, a place where we give money. None of these social and cultural characteristics correctly defines what the church is, although few would argue their importance.

Second, *the church is many things to many people*. For some, it is an agent of social change, for others a source of comfort in a troubled world. Still others claim its importance is its ministry of outreach, while for others the concern is primarily for the individual's relationship to Jesus Christ and how the church provides for a personal faith journey.

Church leaders, in an earnest effort to identify how the church is to be the church, have held round table discussions, brought in management specialists, enlisted experts in volunteerism and stewardship, chosen priorities, and set goals. The laity has been included in these discussions. Worship forms have been altered, liturgies renewed, lay readers trained. Political agendas have been set, votes cast, demonstrations organized. Countless denominational aids have appeared to help congregations in their varied tasks as they try to be the church.

Amidst all of this effort, all of the daily agendas set by the world, the church is sometimes tempted to forget that *"it exists solely for the purpose of bearing witness to Jesus Christ.* [emphasis mine] *The church may do many useful things in society, but if it does not bear witness to Jesus Christ, it is not the church....It is called to do no* less, and no more, than to bear witness to what God has done and is doing to renew creation, according to the faith and knowledge that has been granted to it."[10]

Bearing witness to God's work among us and God's faithfulness to us in a pluralistic world is clearly what the church is to do. *This is not a new challenge!* Each generation has had to find ways to deal with the particular faith crises of its day. It is no different for us than it was for countless church leaders before us. How to go about it in *our* time is the issue before us.

Rebuilding the Church's Waning Strength

Responding to the obvious signs of grave trouble within modern society and how these crises bear upon the church's attempts at proclamation, theologian Lesslie Newbigin asks a radical question: "What could it mean for the church to make once again the claim which it made in its earliest centuries, the claim to provide the *public truth* [emphasis mine] by which society can be given coherence and direction?"[11]

We might respond initially with skepticism. After all, we ourselves are products of this secular, pluralistic, multi-cultural world. As reasonable people, we are taught to be tolerant of others' religious views or lack thereof, and that to be intolerant and exclusive is to be a fanatic or reactionary.

Needless to say, Newbigin does not suggest intolerance, and only secondarily does he recommend challenging public life with the gospel through such avenues as literature, evangelical campaigns, etc. His primary vehicle for a Christian impact on public life is *through the Christian congregation itself.* What hope could this claim give our generation's particular challenge, especially in a time when many denominations are losing members, not gaining them?

In the 1940's, Ruth Krehbiel Jacobs referred to the necessity of the church to "rebuild its waning strength" (p. 7). Her basis for accomplishing this was the building up of its young people through the children's choir program and, in turn, empowering the entire church to greater faithfulness. Ruth Jacobs' focus on the children's choir and its director as a community of believers committed to discipline, excellence, and leading the people of God in worship is analogous to the writing, 40 years later, of theologian Lesslie Newbigen.[12]

The heart of a Christian community is the remembering of Christ's life. The community exists in Christ and for Christ and becomes the place where its members find that the gospel gives them the framework of understanding, the "lenses" through which they are able to understand and cope with the world.[13] This community is by no means perfect, since it is made up of imperfect human beings.

Still, the church has been chosen as the earthen vessel for God's renewing work in the world. Inadequate as we are, we are asked to bear witness to God's word through the *proclamation* of the good news, the *explication* of the good news, and the *application* of the good news.[14] We are asked to be a living testimony to the fact that God, taking the initiative, begins again with us, as God has since the beginning of time, and is with us, working in the world today.

Selling What the Church Has to Offer

But the fact remains, in order for the congregation to be the primary vehicle for a Christian impact on public life, church leaders must "sell" what it has to offer to a pluralistic, secular world. By "selling," of course, we do not mean the crass hawking of the gospel. We use the word advisedly in this context to refer to how the church makes its appeal - effectively and engagingly, to people who must *become motivated* to want what the church has to offer.

Studies indicate that no matter the size of the church, *growing congregations are those which offer varied points of entry for various ages and interests.* A vital music program has the potential to be one excellent vehicle for realizing this goal. There are many other points of entry: the church school, the worship service, social action opportunities, various fellowship groups, caring for the sick, and so forth. All of these points of entry have in common a three-fold demand in order to "sell" with integrity what the church has to offer: *proclaiming, explaining and applying the gospel.* Only then will the congregation have the tools to carry the good news out into their daily lives. In so doing, it is important to remember that neither the explication nor the application of the gospel can ever replace the simple declaration, or proclamation, of its truth.[15] When the gospel is consistently and clearly proclaimed and explained, contemporary people, through God's grace, come to see its application as relevant to them and are summoned to a life of faith and service.

That being said, an essential implication in this challenge is that *those of us in leadership positions within the church must first and foremost be believers.* The building of the community of faith as the primary vehicle for God's renewing work, will require more than people who view the church as merely a place of employment. (This is a particular danger for musicians, so many of whom need to look for a steady "gig.") Church workers must practice their craft out of a sense of vocation or "call" to this particular field (from the Latin *voco, vocare* - a vocation for which one is fortunate enough to be paid.) For the musician's part, we are Christian educators, and music is our tool.

> *"One might have all the qualities of personality and education...and still not be able to meet the supreme test of the honest choirmaster, for his greatest obligation is to establish habits of vital worship and active allegiance to the teachings of Christ. All other motives are distinctly secondary. But this greatest of all objectives is impossible of achievement if the leader is not devoutly and actively Christian." (p. 11)*

A particular congregation will be better able to do its job in the world if it is first *nurtured by a staff made up of mature Christian men and women,* all of whom look at the Big Picture, rather than only their individual piece of it. This attitude, of course, best begins with the senior minister and therefore is expected of everyone else. Second, if the congregation is to be the vehicle for living the gospel in a secular world, then it follows that *church leaders must nurture and care for the members of the congregation in many ways and on many levels.* More will be said about these issues in Chapter 2.

There is always the danger that in our zeal to bring people into the fold, the church will over-program its program. If what we are offering our members becomes more of a burden than a blessing in terms of the schedule we set up, or if we, in whatever ways, force programs to compete with each other due to poor planning or selfish 'empire building,' then we need to begin again. In too many instances, a youth minister, for example, jealously guards "MY kids," or a children's choir director refuses to consider another rehearsal time or a different age grouping. Not uncommonly, a minister is insensitive to the need of the staff to talk about coordinating program, or to know in advance such basic information as sermon topics.

If a church staff (and this may be particularly true in large churches) does not look at the whole ministry, programs tend to become extensions of particular personalities, even though the personnel involved may be diligently trying to be servants of the church. The staff which places as a priority talking together, studying together, praying together, having fellowship and playing together, caring for one another, exemplifies the ministry of the church and thus, is better able to re-examine what it is trying to provide in all areas of ministry for the members of the body.

Program Builds Outreach

Recently, at a meeting of inner city and suburban pastors, an interesting theory was developed as a possible solution to the common problem of not enough money to go around. Especially in the smaller churches, the pastors noted that once the overhead bills are paid (such mundane items as heating, electricity, water, paper, postage, etc.) and staff members' checks written, there is precious little left to divide between program and outreach, let alone expand the work in any area.

After some discussion of how the church "used to be," the pastors agreed that in former days, money for mission beyond the church walls and for denominational giving had been somehow easier to come by. In the days when the church had played a more central role in the community, when it was assumed that most people would choose a church home, money had come forth for local outreach and for domestic and foreign mission as well as for support of the national offices of the various denominations.

The discussion continued, much of it centering on the issues we have covered earlier: the secular, pluralistic world in which we find ourselves living. They noted the demand on people's time, and on their money and the difficult financial times in general. It was mentioned in this connection that many secular organizations are now involved doing the kinds of "good works" that were at one time the sole province of the church.

They noted that the statistics indicating a declining membership in the Protestant mainline may be a warning sign that serious steps must be taken to reverse the trend. *There can be no mission to others if the church itself is not vital and healthy.* If there is no church, there is no outreach.

With this in mind, one of the pastors ventured the following: what if congregations, no matter their size, concentrated heavily for a time on building their *program* in an effort to draw more people into the fold, hiring the necessary staff and equipment to do the job properly as the support base grew? Building the program of the church: choirs, Christian education for all ages, fellowship, pastoral care, even repairing and expanding the structure of the plant, if necessary, would be the immediate priority, not to the exclusion of traditional mission, but in advance of it. In this scenario, "outreach" takes on perhaps a wider definition than traditionally it may have had. The local congregation *reaches out* to those with no church home in order to include, support, and nurture them, inviting and encouraging them to show their gratitude for God's good gifts through their time, talents, and stewardship. The old fashioned word is, of course, *evangelism*. The processes of *proclamation and explication* would be used to lead the congregation towards *applying* more generous resources not only to the program within the confines of the building itself, but outside the church walls, namely in the local community and in national and international mission. With God's grace, a more educated and faithful congregation would be built, and, perhaps the pendulum would begin to swing once again towards those activities and habits (Wednesday night suppers, Bible studies, faithful giving patterns) that build and sustain churches.

Although not touted as a cure-all for every congregation, this concept has proven effective in a number of churches. The equation between "in house" and "out of house" may never be as balanced as it might be, but those congregations who have struggled with the issue of program as outreach know it has tremendous potential. Building the congregation's resources, especially as it involves staff, is a wise use of church funds. In a day when we are competing for people's hearts and minds, time and treasure, it is increasingly important to offer them the very best in terms of substantive, quality ministry, for, as we have discovered, people are no longer coming to church out of a sense of obligation to the institution.

The Capturing of Hearts and Minds

But in order to "appeal" to both the churched and the un-churched, the pressure is great to give in to the mind-set of the contemporary lifestyle and popular culture in which we live. Because the popular culture is so pervasive it can be difficult for churches to maintain integrity in terms of their theology, and consequently, their worship resources. Kenneth Myers notes, "The *consciousness* of popular culture, the manners and emotional habits it encourages us to take for granted, will become the consciousness of the society at large, the environment in which we are striving to be and to make disciples."[16]

A fuller discussion of the effects of popular culture is found in Chapter 8. For our purposes thus far, we simply note that one of its many appealing hallmarks is to give us what we want, and to tell us what we already know. In popular culture, few, if any, demands are placed on us to think in terms of the transcendent, or to encourage our understanding of things beyond where we are.

"Popular culture...emphasizes the self and the present. Its perspective is that of here and now, and you and your experiences are the arbiter of all things....At root, popular culture's dynamics tend to encourage a self-centeredness that Christians ought to avoid."[17]

And thus, increasingly, people join a particular congregation because of the demands *not* placed upon them. As one pastor said in partial jest, "You may park your mind along with your car, or leave it with an usher at the door." This phenomenon occurs in every denomination for what may seem different reasons but which finally comes down to an unspoken word that says, "You don't have to think to be a member of this church." The concept of the church as the primary vehicle for carrying the good news into the world, for proclaiming, explicating, and applying the gospel in ways which capture the *mind* as well as the heart, is dwindling.

And thus, increasingly, people are attracted to congregations which place few demands upon them. The preaching makes them feel good, and so does the music. One can join without ever attending a class to discuss with pastor and staff, what, *in the name of Jesus*, faithful church membership means. Indeed, the campaign of the church to be the primary vehicle for carrying the good news into the world, for proclaiming, explaining, and applying the gospel in ways which capture *minds* as well as emotions, must be waged within and despite a culture that "emphasizes the self and the present," a culture that gives us what we want and tells us what we already know.

The battle for hearts and minds is not limited to churches identified by one polarizing label or another. (Such labels as "liberal," "fundamentalist," and "conservative," believed preacher Harry Emerson Fosdick, were created for the convenience of people who needed something to say but are too lazy to think about it themselves.) All churches that take seriously the life of the mind must finally address the same issues of congregational nurture and thoughtful spiritual growth.

Despite the temptations to succumb to secular marketing maneuvers to attract congregants, there are healthy, growing congregations of all sizes and labels that take great care, through their worship and music, Christian education, new member classes, and outreach programs to encourage experiences that deepen awareness of the timeless and the transcendent. They challenge the minds and hearts of their people. They acknowledge, to be sure, that the only *requisite* for church membership is declaration of Jesus Christ as Lord and Savior but understand that *discipleship demands growth*, never satisfaction with one's place in the faith journey. For example, to a new member class: "Here is a list of every way we on the staff could think of for new members to give of their time in the service of their church. What will you do? Something from this list, or is there something we haven't thought of?" or, "Here is where our money goes. We need you to be a part of this effort. Someone from the stewardship committee will come to talk with you about what giving means to them." To a young person nearing confirmation age: "Joining the church is your decision, not your parent's or your pastor's, or your friend's. This Inquirer's Class is exactly that—an opportunity for you to inquire about discipleship. If and when you are ready to say that you want to try to live a life like Jesus did, then you may want to join the church. We will be with you and for you as you make this journey."

To a young couple upon the baptism of their child, the church presents a tape of hymns of the faith, perhaps sung by choristers of the church as part of their promise to help raise the child in the faith. An accompanying letter talks about the importance of the music of the church in the home, and of the choirs that await the child when s/he is old enough.

During "Know Your Church Sunday" each September, following the worship hour, all of the committees of the church, from Christian Education to Social Action, and from Choirs to Clean Up Crews, recruit their workers, in the name of the One who brought us together, to do the labor of the church in the year ahead.

Preaching that challenges the mind as well as captures the imagination...music that does the same and involves the congregation as much as the choir...adult Christian education classes that bring together divergent viewpoints, or tell a narrative history of our faith, or support the family through a myriad of life stages...a vital church school and a choir program to train up children with hearts and hands and voices secure in the knowledge of their faith tradition, their minds set on an ever growing spiritual journey...these are but a few of the many ways the church nurtures its people so they might never want to disconnect. Although individually small, each piece is an investment in the present and future of the church, even as they attest to all that has gone before. Opportunities such as these give people regular glimpses of what they can become. Congregations such as these will not be a sanctuary full of pew sitters who merely echo a party line.

As we seek to be the church in this time and place, I am often reminded of a particular "Pogo" comic strip by the late Walt Kelly. After several wordless frames full of exasperated expressions, comes the following: "This situation is full of insurmount-able opportunity!" Indeed, we are called by God to witness to God's ongoing renovation of the world. We are given hope to be the church precisely because, despite every error humans have made in its name, the church continues. God has not given up on the church. God renews the covenant with us again and again, despite our faithlessness. We do well to remember that:

"the God who establishes the church is also the God who sustains the church from generation to generation. We need not fear for the future of the church, nor are we called to bear the burden of its success or failure. We are called to faithfulness: to worship God, to live together as God's people, and to serve God's purposes in the world. The future of the church, however, is in God's hands and not our own."[18]

Endnotes

[1] Lesslie Newbigin, *The Gospel in a Pluralist Society.* (Grand Rapids: William B. Eerdmans Publishing Company, 1989), 1.

[2] From a conversation with the staff of Nassau Presbyterian Church, Princeton, NJ.

[3] Wallace M. Alston, Jr., *Guides to the Reformed Tradition: The Church* (Atlanta: John Knox Press, 1984), 2.

[4] Alston, 3.

[5] Brown, Robert McAfee, *The Spirit of Protestantism* (New York: Oxford University Press), 1965.

[6] Paul Baker, *Contemporary Christian Music: Where It Came From, What It Is, Where It's Going,* (Westchester, IL: Crossway Books), 1979.

[7] Kenneth A. Myers, *All God's Children and Blue Suede Shoes: Christians and Popular Culture* (Crossway Books, 1989), 21.

[8] Myers, 187.

[9] Alston, 51. I am indebted to Wallace M. Alston, Jr., and his book *The Church*, for the discussion on defining the church in this chapter.

[10] Alston, 125-126.

[11] Newbigin, 223.

[12] See also the contribution of H. Richard Niebuhr (1951) *Christ and Culture*. In it, he classifies theology, doctrine, Christian history and social theory into five areas: Christ *against* culture, The Christ *of* culture, Christ *above* culture, Christ and culture *in* paradox, and Christ *transforming* culture.

[13] Newbigin, 227.

[14] Alston, 126.

[15] Alston, 127.

[16] Myers, 59.

[17] Myers, 101.

[18] Alston, 14.

Chapter 2

THE DIRECTOR

"It would be next to impossible to make an all inclusive list of qualifications for the perfect leader, but certainly early on the list should come knowledge, sincerity, a social sense, good judgement, organizational ability, originality, and initiative." (p.10)

Who Shall Teach Them?

A number of years ago, I was a thirty-something mother of an infant and a pre-schooler. Having taken some time off from my career, the time had come to take on a limited amount of work. The small church where our family worshiped had no children's choir, so I offered to start one. After getting the go ahead from the pastor and an enthusiastic response from the organist, recruitment began.

There were about 100 members of the church, with perhaps eight children, pre-school through middle school. I knew it would be essential to excite the congregation enough for all eight of those children to join the choir, *and* for all eight to go out and bring in friends who were without a church home.

One Sunday morning I was given time to talk about the children's choir we would begin in the fall, its goals and some initial projects. Afterwards, a woman came to me and said, "You sound so excited about this children's choir and I'm so glad *you* are doing it. Sometimes I think a dedicated volunteer can do a much better job than a highly trained professional!" It took me a moment of what I am certain was a blank stare, for me to grasp what she was saying. Clearly she did not know what I had been trained to do or she would not have said what she did.

What possible negative experiences had she had with a highly trained professional? What qualities, by definition, does a "dedicated volunteer" *have* to bring to the job that perhaps a "highly trained professional" does not? Surely enthusiasm, love of children and teaching top the list. I began to see the wisdom of her words.

I was a dedicated volunteer for two years before leaving to be part of the music staff of the large church where I continue to serve. Each year, now that I am considered a "highly trained professional," I evaluate the program from this woman's perspective. Would it meet her criteria of a job well done?

On the other side of the issue of directors' qualifications comes a second anecdote. A man (no doubt a highly trained professional) attended the reading session on children's choral literature at a summer workshop. Afterwards, he remarked, "You really know how to conduct. Why do you work with kiddy choirs?"

Over the years there has, unfortunately, been the assumption that "real conductors" (or "highly trained professionals") would only want to work with at least high school age singers. Typically, people have viewed moving to a high school vocal director position as a promotion from the elementary level, rather than a change of focus. Often, the person in charge of the high school or adult choir is assumed to have better musicianship skills than the person who works with the children, whether or not this is actually the case.

The traditional male vs. female roles have prevailed in our field, men taking on the more "professional" image, with women assuming that of "nurturer." Fortunately, this has changed dramatically over the last half of this century, and now, women are working on a nearly equal par with men, choosing whatever age groups and settings are most appealing. Many more men now enjoy working with children's voices than ever before and the number of women conducting adults has increased dramatically. In assessing qualifications then, we come to at least five considerations:

1. Men and women who choose to work with youth and children's choirs should be trained choral musicians.
2. The best trainers of young voices will be people who combine the "dedicated volunteer" with the "highly trained professional."
3. Church musicians must be skilled administrators.
4. Church musicians must practice their craft out of a sense of vocation or "call" to this particular field.
5. Church musicians must develop their knowledge as theologians and seek opportunities for their own spiritual growth.

Let us look more closely at each of these areas.

Men and women who choose to work with youth and children's choirs should be trained choral musicians because young singers can become a fine choral ensemble only if the director has the necessary skills. It is important to point out here that the type of singing we are talking about with young people in this context is "choral singing," as distinguished from what might be termed "recreational singing." These are decidedly different approaches. The skills necessary to build a choral sound are much more sophisticated than the skills used to strum a guitar and sing "Kumbaya" around a campfire, or be a song leader for church school. The choral musician standard should apply equally to those teachers who work with very young children in preparatory groups, for it is at this age (six years old and younger) that the ears are the most perceptive. Ideally, it is here that the ground work is laid for beautiful tone.

The best trainers of young voices will be people who combine the best of the "dedicated volunteer" with the "highly trained professional." People who fit only one category to begin with, usually have the potential to grow, with at least some success, into the other role as well. Opportunities abound for training in choral music and teaching skills. Acquiring the qualities of a dedicated volunteer is not as simple as taking a course however. Suffice it to say that if the musician really does not want to work with children, it will be impossible to have the necessary qualities of enthusiasm and commitment.

Church musicians must be skilled administrators. Three areas are equal in importance:

1. the ability to work with people, to recruit, to organize oneself and others, to delegate responsibilities;
2. the ability to *articulate a vision* of the music ministry both orally and through the written word, and to plan a curricula containing (at least) long term goals for each age level;
3. the ability to develop a budget and the wherewithal to live within it.

Additionally, the good administrator will also be aware of and make use of opportunities in timely and judicious ways. In this regard, Ruth Krehbiel Jacobs wrote:

"The natural leader is both an originator and an administrator. He not only has good ideas, but can carry them out as well. The originator sees the applicability of the material that comes into his hands, the administrator keeps it at hand until the time is ripe for its use." (p.13)

Church musicians must practice their craft out of a sense of vocation or "call" to this particular field. Implicit in this "call" is a continual commitment to it. A month before her death, Ruth Jacobs reflected on this matter in her monthly editorial in the Choristers Guild LETTERS.

"I wonder how many of us are totally committed....When I hear of music directors at odds with the Christian education director it is difficult not to doubt their commitment to anything beyond their own program. The director who binds his choirs to himself with a blind loyalty that makes progress impossible for his successor, what is his commitment? The director who gets by with as little preparation as possible, the director who makes no effort to improve, the one who sees only the flaws in his associates, what would happen if they should experience an unmistakable sense of commitment?

"...The price [of this calling] is a different one for every person. The price is relinquishing of those very habits, desires, ambitions that stand between us and total commitment....Most of us spend our lives making small token payments, never coming into possession of the treasure. And how we envy the courageous few who ventured everything, and gained everything.

"Either Christ is God, and Savior and Lord, or He isn't. And if He is, then He has to have all my time, all my devotion, all my life. And once having accepted this commitment, He directs our work. Life is a complicated mass of interrelated people. Every one of us is affected by the lives of many people. We cannot determine arbitrarily the lives that will be influenced by ours, or how or when. But only when we permit a spirit greater than ourselves to express itself through us are we fulfilling the specific purpose for which we were created.

"Christianity needs that kind of leadership. Nothing else is good enough. The church needs it in every area of its efforts. Church music needs it."[1]

To practice their craft with this sense of calling and commitment, a fifth qualification becomes evident: church musicians must develop their knowledge as theologians, and seek opportunities for their own spiritual growth. Theology (*theos*-God, *logos*-word or knowledge) is the study of our knowledge of God, the attempt to serve God with the mind.[2] Anselm, an 11th-century theologian, defined theology as faith in search of understanding. Believing in God is not enough. If it is to grow and last, faith must *seek* understanding.

Another reason church musicians need to study theology is to acquire a working knowledge of the Bible and its interpretation, history and thought. There are many occasions when church musicians are called upon to teach: to "explicate" the texts presented through anthems. But a working knowledge of the Bible is not enough: thinking men and women have to struggle with the inconsistencies of a book whose most recent chapters were written nearly two thousand years ago. We are teaching children who live today, not those of ancient times. We need to be interpreters of what the Bible means.

"Every human experience is interpreted by the experiencing person or it is not passed on. It is always interpreted within the framework by which that person comprehends what is real. When knowledge expands, it renders the interpretive framework of ancient people inadequate, and it reveals the ignorance of the past. For people living in one age to try to cling to the objective truthfulness of the concepts of another age is to participate in a doubtful enterprise."[3]

Interpretation of the scriptures must be rooted in the research of modern theologians who have studied the world of the ancients and who attempt to put the language and customs of the Biblical people into context so that people of today might better understand them. In this way, the Biblical message becomes the means through which we "hear, confront, and interact with the Word of God."[4] Church workers must be thoughtful in the pursuit of religious truth or risk disillusioning young people with the organized church altogether.

Additionally, in a day when the standard for repertoire is poor in many congregations and when pastors and worship committees may be untrained in how to think through guidelines for selecting worship resources, the musician must be able to speak theologically in order to articulate why certain popular or familiar styles of musical expression may not be appropriate. We will discuss this issue in Chapter 8.

Finally, a knowledge of theology applied to our daily lives will better enable us to minister to our singers and to one another. We need to be able to analyze from a theological perspective and not be bewildered by things which happen both to us as individuals and in our world. We need a context in which to defend the faith against competing points of view as we live in this secular and pluralistic culture. Children need adults with words of assurance based on the evidence of God's renovating activity in the world today in order to counter the turmoil they see around them and in the media. Furthermore, the witnessing of a faith seeking understanding (that of their choir director) can be a source of inspiration and confidence to young people as they continue on their own spiritual journey.

Where to Labor? Recalling the Human Nature of the Church

A question arising for the church musician is that of where to labor. Which particular congregation? Too often the answer is reflective of a difficult economic climate and insufficient employment opportunities. Still other considerations have to do with the location of an existing full-time job, either one's own, or that of a spouse, since making music in the church is often a part-time proposition. Therefore, the choice of congregation may be a simple matter of what is available at the time in a particular area.

When choices are possible, however, there are a number of factors that have much to do with how we go about building the congregation through our particular call as church musicians. It is crucial to actively seek a place of employment that supports the talent and vision of the church musician, particularly, in our case, as regards the director of choirs for children and youth.

In the last chapter we explored some of the traits of those churches that go about their work with care, taking seriously the proclamation, explication and application of the gospel to their own congregations and to the world. These congregations are usually, though not always, led by a senior minister who has at least two of three gifts:

effective administrative skills, a genuinely "pastoral" manner, and effective, substantive preaching. A church that has all three characteristics in a single pastor is fortunate indeed. But even when the minister has all of these skills, problems often exist between pastor and musician.

It is lamentable that few seminaries give any attention at all to the area of church music. Some seminaries do not even train their students in the matter of administration. Beyond courses in church polity and perhaps building a budget, such sensitive areas as personnel skills, group dynamics and management techniques are often ignored. The effectiveness of a particular pastor as he or she deals with the staff is left largely to chance, and will be successful or not based upon personality, whatever techniques the minister happens to develop through trial and error, and any luck he or she may have in choosing a staff of people who can work together.

Discussions with musicians about their pastors have been, possibly since Bible times, most revealing and lively. Among frequent complaints are the following:
The minister at the church where I work:
- doesn't know anything about music.
- only wants to hear what s/he likes.
- wants me to use only the music that the congregation likes.
- always chooses all of the hymns.
- never wants free accompaniment for the hymns.
- allows us to sing only in English.
- wants the children to sing every week (or every two weeks) and then complains that they don't sing *loud* enough.
- doesn't want a "spectacle" made, so we can't move the choir into a position for them to see me conduct, or to hear each other sing.
- rarely gives me sermon topics in advance.
- is afraid that I will become more popular with the congregation than s/he is.
- shows favoritism among staff members.
- takes advantage of the hours I put in beyond the ones I'm paid for.
- doesn't see the need for me to have secretarial support (a larger rehearsal space, a bigger budget, robes for the children, etc.)
- doesn't back me up.

Furthermore:
- I am not included in staff meetings or on staff planning sessions.
- I have no health or retirement benefits package.
- I have no job description.
- I have no one to whom I can express my concerns.

The list of course goes on, customized by denomination and particular personality quirks. At a seminar for musicians and pastors on the same staff, the pastors went into one space and the musicians into another. They were given identical anonymous surveys to complete, identical save one feature: the pastors were to answer questions regarding their musicians, and the musicians were to answer the same questions, but regarding their pastors. When compared, the surveys revealed that the complaints about one another were virtually the same. Many of the pastors thought the musicians had big egos, and the reverse. Many of the musicians felt the pastors didn't appreciate their expertise, and the reverse, and so on down the list. Another interesting feature of the survey asked each pastor and each musician if they read articles or books in the other's field. The answer in most cases was never, or rarely.

We would do well, before despairing too long about this all too common reality, to remember the humanity of the church. That is to say, the church is given by God to imperfect human beings. It should be expected that relational problems will develop as they will in any "marriage." That being said, what can we do to avoid potential hurts and frustrations, or to deal with them when they arise?

The first answer may lie in the earlier question of where to labor. Musicians need to hone their interviewing and assessment skills. Not every church will be right for every musician. Crucial questions to ask oneself before deciding to accept a position might include:

Do I feel at least some level of comfort with this person who might be my boss?

Is there the potential for being seen as a colleague by him, or has he raised the importance of the clergy to such a level that non-ordained staff members are viewed as less significant?

Do I sense that she is capable of change?

Will I enjoy being around her for any length of time?

What have I sensed about her interpersonal skills?

Is he a team player or does he essentially want to be left alone to do his thing while I do mine?

Is the chair of the personnel committee accessible?

How much latitude do I detect they feel free to give? How much do I need?

How well thought out are their goals?

Is their vision of what this program can be compatible with mine?

Other questions need to be asked of the search committee and pastor. Note that most of these questions should be phrased as *expectations* on the part of the musician.

What about the issue of regular meetings with the pastor and other members of the staff?

How is worship planning done?

What is the role of the personnel committee?

Is there a protocol for discussing issues pertaining to one's employment should that become necessary?

What do they perceive the role of a music committee to be?

How is job assessment done?

Is there a benefits package for non-ordained church workers, and if not, is there some work being done to rectify that situation?

Just as pastors' seminary training is woefully lacking in some areas, so is the training of the church musician. As artists, many of us tend to live in ivory towers, full of creativity, and/or nurturing skills, but lacking in survival skills. A good search committee will have at least one business person on it. The musician who interviews with even a brief list of *brass tacks issues* will be a step ahead of one who doesn't have any list at all. As budgets tighten and demands for skills beyond musical brilliance grow, there is less and less room for the "creative oddball."[5]

There are occasions when even with the most careful selection, the "marriage" becomes difficult to maintain. Sometimes we try to deal with the problem by "whining." It is almost as though if we whine and sigh long enough, the problem will go away in time. But whining and sighing ultimately have diminishing returns, taking a negative toll on one's energy level, outlook, and relationships. Carrying anger for any length of time will have similar results. The problem is best dealt with directly. Hopefully, the church is the place above all others where mutual correction, expression of frustration, and confession of personal failings can take place without fear of recrimination, judgement, trivialization, or bitterness.

Too many times in an attempt to please, we simply grin and bear it and keep on trying harder. This is also an avoidance technique and as such, does not get to the root of the problem.[6] For example: the tradition in your church allows you a 20-minute block of time for music on Sunday mornings with a group of children as part of the church school. You are expected to produce an anthem for worship every two weeks. Rather than spin your wheels at something you know is non-productive, *your job as the expert* is to say, "This won't work." Explain then, using what is termed the "reframing technique:" "We can do one of several things here: expand this group to become a real choir rehearsing an hour once a week after school and singing in worship every four weeks or so; or, continue with the current structure and schedule and have the children sing once every two months." The church musician's job is to help the non-music professionals realize that the product they want produced in the current framework is not possible to do with any sense of artistry or confidence from the children. When this is the case, the children cannot be prepared to be worship leaders.

Too often, we don't take time to articulate to ourselves, let alone others, the possible solutions. We just continue frantically trying to please, and gripe or whine about it to friends and family. A critical administrative skill is the ability to recognize that some situations don't work and that whining or wishing it was different won't solve anything. Being able to give viable options is a useful skill.

As we see in the above example, taking the initiative is often the wisest course of action. Taking the initiative before troubles begin is even wiser. As Christian men and women, we are called to support one another, to look out for one another, to befriend one another. A note to the pastor after an especially fine sermon; a mention in passing to a member of the congregation or staff about the fine work of a colleague; reaching out in creative ways to the committees of the church; offering to help with mundane chores when another staff member has a major project underway. These genuine expressions of devotion to one's church, one's work, and one's colleagues do much to cement relationships and avoid, or at the very least, help us through difficulties when they arise. Actions done as a part of one's faith commitment are very different in tone than those done for "political" reasons.

One of the difficult things for eager, enthusiastic people to accept is the premise that, finally, "you can't do more than you can do."[7] If earnest and good faith efforts have been made to go around, over and through a problem and those have failed, maybe what is left is leaving the situation entirely. When this happens, it can be painful. After all, this may be seen as a kind of "divorce."

Servants of the church need to be reminded from time to time that the promises proclaimed, explained, and applied to our "flock" are true for us as well. The God who made us and first loved us is caring for us in ways we may never understand, and will never let us go. Acceptance of these promises for one's own life can be the path to healing and beginning again.

Be Prepared

After recounting for undergraduate church music majors the "dedicated volunteer and highly trained professional" stories cited earlier in this chapter, the first session's lecture ended like this:

We assume you will leave this college a highly trained professional. But we hope to help you find within yourself a love of this work, which when coupled with your well-honed skills, combine to make your labor one of extraordinary ministry. Creating the environment for exciting and meaningful things to take place requires enormous preparation—first in the training of your musical skills. You must know how the voice works, especially the developing voice and how choice of repertoire has everything to do with that development; your conducting skills for children should be no less than those you would use with any other age group.

Additionally, and especially for this work, you must be a teacher. You will need to learn how to manage a roomful of wiggly youngsters or "sophisticated" middle schoolers, or questioning teenagers. You need to know how each of those age groups thinks, what skills they bring to their learning at each stage of development. You will need to know how to work with those for whom pitch matching does not come easily. You must commit yourself to teaching the language of music literacy so that your singers may become readers of that language. You must learn how to sequence the teaching of the material to be taught so that the pathway is anticipated eagerly and understood clearly by your singers.

You need to develop a working knowledge of basic tenants of the faith in general and the specific tenants and polity of the particular denomination in which you will work. You will learn about working as a team with others on the staff and you will carefully avoid stepping into traps which could result in accusations of "kingdom building" for the music program.

As if this weren't enough, you will need to be a top-rate administrator and people person, with skills to build the program and keep it running well. You will learn to punt, for few things when working with children are completely predictable.

A Director's List of Ten Things to Remember

A list format, dealing with concepts in broad strokes, is often handy as a reminder and thus is given here. Some of the following points will be dealt with in depth in subsequent chapters.

Personal Readiness:

1. A positive self image is necessary to be creative and spontaneous. This is true for children and it is true for their choir director as well.

2. A corollary to the above: dress for rehearsal with attention to color and style. This is not solely personal vanity. It is harder to present an enthusiastic countenance if the appearance is drab or frumpy. Ask, "Would I like to come to a choir rehearsal directed by me?" Just as the room must be orderly and attractive, the director should at least *appear* fresh and glad to see the choristers at the beginning of each rehearsal.

3. Efficient, effective directors bring their best selves to rehearsal. Leave problems, frustrations, and any pettiness outside the rehearsal space to deal with later. Our work is more important than those things at this moment.

4. Know the music before teaching it! This is surely self evident, but there may be times when other demands get in the way of proper musical preparation. Study all musical aspects of the anthems, read the texts aloud as poetry, look for ways to troubleshoot potential problem spots, etc.

Administrative Details:

5. There are many valid ways of leading music. When in the position of choosing teachers for various music activities, evaluate the talents and skills of those involved and seek the most appropriate ways to use each person, providing the necessary training and support.

6. The best in any field know that they must continue to grow personally and professionally. In our busy personal and professional lives, it is easy to let this discipline slip. (Once, when asked what I'd read lately, I couldn't come up with anything other than "the Lands' End Catalogue"!) Read a new book in our field and one outside it. Attend a workshop at least every other year.

7. Be willing to consider changing or modifying a viewpoint, remembering the adage: "Don't die at 40 and be buried at 70."

8. Continually examine priorities. Another adage: "The difference between genius and stupidity is that genius knows its limits." Make a list of all the things necessary to keep the choir(s) running. Circle those things that another person could do (a parent, a secretary, another staff member, an adult or youth choir member, etc.). Especially if the director is a volunteer, write down names of people who might serve as a support system for various tasks. Rank the remaining items (ostensibly those which are best done by the director) in order of time spent on them each week. Recheck this to see what is getting insufficient time. Aim to get crucial things the director alone must do nearer to the top of the list, things like score study and lesson planning, people contact and worship planning.

Teaching Techniques:

9. Do not think of an unauditioned choir as 'just a group of ordinary kids.' That attitude tends to allow standards to slip.

10. Teach creative and critical thinking skills alongside text, pitch, rhythm and form. Doing so puts learning and artistry into the same realm. Develop an approach which both respects and nurtures the inherent inventiveness of the human soul. This deepens the relationship between singers and conductor and attests to the ongoing creation of God through our work as earthen vessels.

Endnotes

[1] Ruth Krehbiel Jacobs, "All or Not at All," *Choristers Guild LETTERS* 11 (April 1960): 165.

[2] Wallace M. Alston, Jr., *Guides to the Reformed Tradition: The Church* (Atlanta: John Knox Press, 1984), 136-7.

[3] John Shelby Spong, *Rescuing the Bible from Fundamentalism: A Bishop Rethinks the Meaning of Scripture* (San Francisco: Harper, 1991), 25.

[4] John Shelby Spong, 249.

[5] From a conversation with Michael E. Kemp, Director of Music Ministries, Abington Presbyterian Church, Abington, PA.

[6] I am indebted to Eric D. Johnson, psychotherapist, for insight into this technique.

[7] Eric D. Johnson, from a conversation.

Chapter 3

THE ORGANIZATION

"Haphazard work is dangerous....Nothing should be left to chance...Unless your purpose and proposed methods are firmly fixed, your surveys and publicity will lack point. Action without purpose or plan is futile." (p. 15)

Whether a particular church's music program consists of a single children's choir or numerous groups pre-school through adult, successful children's choirs have a well-thought-out structure within which the actual music making takes place. In terms of administration, this structure may consist of the director (in consultation with other members of the staff) or, in larger programs, the director, a secretary, numerous parent volunteers, choir officers and librarians and a music committee (which might be a sub-committee of another group, i.e., The Worship, Music and Arts Committee). As in any enterprise, the more efficiently the various mechanisms work, the better the overall product will be. As a guide, the following positions will be needed for each choir. They may be filled by one person or by several, depending upon many factors:

1. Director—The person who will actually teach and conduct the choir and be in touch with parents about the child's progress.
2. Administrator and /or secretary—The person who will meet and plan with the rest of the staff, communicate with other directors, inform parents of calendar details, etc., and cover office particulars (such as the typing and duplicating of communications, the ordering of music, reserving space in the sanctuary for a special rehearsal, etc.).
3. Choir parent—This may be a mom or dad, grandparent or another interested adult or older student. S/he is present at each rehearsal and on Sunday mornings when the choir sings. The job includes taking attendance, phoning, helping plan and carry out the activities of the group, etc. (A more specific list of duties of choir parents is found in Appendix 1A "Organizational Aids.")

How Many Choirs?

In a very small church, or a situation in which the support is not yet adequate for a substantial program, a single children's choir may be formed by treating all or part of the church school as a choir. A music period is held during the church school time, and the children sing periodically in worship or for a special program, usually at Christmas and Easter. Although clearly a substitute for a *bona fide* children's choir, this plan allows the congregation to "think what would happen if...," and perhaps catch a glimpse of the benefits of a real choir program.

Another way to begin is to organize an "official" choir of children in the elementary grades. Remember that the wider the age span, the more difficult it will be to keep the attention of the oldest and the youngest choristers. The ideal is no more than a three year age span, but in small churches, or churches just beginning a children's choir program, it is often necessary to increase the number of grades included. Here are some ways to deal with the problems inherent in a single multi-age choir.

If the group is quite small (eight children or fewer) the director will probably be able to individualize instruction and devise ways of reaching each singer within a wider age span and experience level. If the group numbers 8-16 or so, a "sandwich" approach to rehearsal schedule should be considered, for example:

1st half hour: younger children meet

2nd half hour: older children join the younger ones

3rd half hour: younger children dismiss, older children remain.

This format enables the teacher to work at appropriate levels with the children yet allows the full choir to rehearse together on shared music for Sunday mornings.

Experience levels are often, but not always, closely related to age. The groups in the schedule above could be arranged with musical competency as an equal factor rather than solely by age, remembering the importance of such criteria as peer relations, reading ability, size of voice and attention span.[1]

The best way to build a program is to "grow it up." That is, begin with pre-schoolers and children in the earliest elementary years. These groups serve as preparatory groups for the traditional "junior choir." In addition to helping young children learn the language of worship, such a training program develops competency in at least three musical areas: tone quality, ear training, and acquiring a taste for fine repertoire. As important, this preparatory program establishes the "choir pattern" or habit with young children and their families. Positive experiences at this early age can be the single most valuable recruitment aid for continuing choir membership through the high school years.

As the children in the program grow older, so does the need for adding another choir. An upper elementary choir is then begun in order to accommodate children who have outgrown the younger choirs. At this age (approximately grades 4—6) children often make better progress grouped by gender for rehearsals, with the intent of joining together for Sunday worship responsibilities. For both this age and the junior high or middle school age, this format allows both boys and girls to pursue vocal excellence without having to contend with the dynamics that the presence of the opposite sex can create. If the age groups are as small as two year groupings (i.e. grades 2 and 3, grades 4 and 5) this is less of an issue. Especially in the middle school or junior high, however, tracking the vocal development of both boys and girls in this period of major physical growth is far simpler when divided by gender.

Especially in small churches or in churches building a program, the Youth Choir might include, for reasons of numbers, both junior and senior high school students. But if the size of the group grows beyond a certain point, and that point will be self-evident when reached, the better course of action, both musically and socially, is to split into two separate age groups.

The Auditioned Children's Choir In the Church

A few congregations have experimented with the concept of auditioned choirs within the regular unauditioned choral program of the congregation. In essence, the Anglican Church has historically done this, using the system of groupings not only by age but by competency. A description of such a choir's conception and development in a mainline Protestant church and how it has helped to build the overall music ministry is given in Appendix 2A.

Community-based Choirs Begun In the Church

Another way to form an auditioned choir is as a community based choir whose membership core is made of those involved in an excellent children's choir program in a church. Membership is opened to all qualified children in the area and funding sources become community based as well.

For a church with a commitment to musical excellence as well as to outreach beyond the church walls, the development of a community based choir *targeting an inner-city population* is a challenge well worth the effort. Several churches can join together to sponsor such a program which will require not only musical and teaching leadership of high calibre, but also a battalion of volunteer staff to make the program go. By nature, this project involves far more than musicians: the clergy and church officers, the finance committee, outreach committee, director of religious education, etc., can all claim a part of the inner-city choir's success or failure. For those who tend to cast aspersions on church musicians' motives, or who feel that too much is spent on program and not enough on local mission, this aspect of the music ministry may help to bridge that discord. For more information on beginning and maintaining such a choir, see Appendix 2B.

Recruitment

"Boys and girls like to feel that they are doing something worth while. (sic) You gain their allegiance by expecting the best they have to give.... Membership then becomes an honor." (p. 22)

"Boys and girls, like adults, like to feel important. They like to be a part of an organization that is considered unusual or successful. They like to belong to a group in which they can take pride. Children should never be invited into the choir with the assurance that it will be easy work. On the contrary, tell them that being in the choir is far from easy, that the choir learns music that most other children would be afraid to attempt, that the choir has a reputation for absolute quiet during the service, and would not dare accept anyone who is not strong enough to live up to such a standard, that the only thing that keeps members away from rehearsals is sickness, that the choir has a big job and can use only those who are able to do a big job well. Then it is time to say, 'You look to me like a boy who would be able to do it. How about it; do you think you could live up to such standards?' Nineteen out of twenty children will square their shoulders and decide that they will show what they can do." (p. 22)

Mrs. Jacob's enthusiastic challenge has proven itself time and time again in successful children's choirs all over the country. Clearly, the easiest recruitment occurs in situations where an established program is a popular choice among the children in the community. Success breeds success. If the teaching is uniformly excellent and the organization efficient, then the program tends to require less active recruiting. But recruitment should never stop. Picture the current elementary choir(s) as the future high school choir. Even if there are plenty of singers at the present time, add four years, when some of those fourth through sixth graders may have moved away or dropped out for various reasons.

Always think of the choir program as an opportunity some young person wants to be a part of. If we don't actively recruit at all age levels, the choirs can become what may appear to be unwelcome "cliques," especially as the children approach middle school. Children and youth who attend a school other than the one that most of the choristers attend may need special attention to stay involved.

The key to recruitment in any field is to connect with people in a personal way. Placing choir program brochures throughout the building or in the pews is merely informative—it is hardly ever inspiring or motivating. And if the written word is the only means of recruitment, this may say something about the degree to which the director is invested in the choir and about how s/he relates to people.

Programming is not the ultimate goal. Finally, the Christian faith is relational, therefore, engaging, personal contact is much more likely to be successful. Follow a handout or a letter with a phone call to each child in the church school, each youth in the fellowship group. Especially with youth, go after the leaders, the others will follow. If a leader says, "I can't sing!," do not argue. Rather try something like the following: "Don't worry. I can teach you to do that. I need you now to help draw in the rest of the group. Have you ever noticed how kids are always around you? I have. Whenever you move to the other side of the room, they follow you there as well. My bet is that they will follow you right into the rehearsal room! Seriously, this choir can be a great thing for this church. Will you help me build it?" Very few young people will turn down a sincerely given compliment and request for help from a competent, engaging adult leader.

Talk with current members about friends who may be without a church home. Let it be known in the neighborhood that your church has a choir program. This may be all a family needs to become involved in the life of the church. A personal contact may take place on the phone, by visiting a church school class, scout troop, a chance encounter in the hallway on Sundays. It might be initiated by a choir member or by a member of the congregation, or by a staff member. A timely follow up with the parent is important, even for teenagers. Every parent wants to know that his or her child will be loved and cared for. This is just as true for youth as it is for preschoolers.

An early means of recruitment can happen at infant baptism. The music ministry can acknowledge this event with the presentation of a tape of hymns of the faith, perhaps sung by choristers of the church. With the tape comes a letter to the parents which recognizes the importance of their child's welcome into the covenant relationship and provides information about the music ministry's part in that relationship. This action says a great deal to that family about the church's awareness of and concern for their child. Additionally, ideas regarding music activities for parents and child to experience together at home might be sent, noting landmarks for parents to look for in their child's musical growth.

Publicizing choir activities is another means of recruitment: bulletin boards, church newsletter, local newspaper, etc. Enlist a volunteer to be the choir photographer and/or historian. If there is a choir component taught as a part of vacation church school or in a "summer arts week" at the church, be sure that the church community and possibly the community at large is aware of it.

Summer activities are prime occasions for recruitment, especially for families who have moved into the area recently and are looking for ways to feel at home. A pool and pizza party just before the choir season begins is a great way to start the year for returning choristers and to welcome new members.

Motivation

Once enrolled, motivation, or, to use Ruth Jacobs' term, "morale" must be established. Careful rehearsal pacing, a ready smile, firm control of the group, goals to set and meet, a service award system, are all ways to keep the choristers' attention and make them want to come back for more each week.

> *"Regularity of attendance is absolutely essential to success. The child will be regular only so long as he is interested. The surest intimation of an unsuccessful choir is frequent absences and plausible excuses. The leader who has any less than a 90% attendance average had better begin to cross-examine himself and his methods." (p. 39)*

Be aware of gimmicks or the quick fix. Each activity and goal must have musical and theological integrity or it will ultimately backfire. For example, a number of directors have learned that promising the choir a "musical" each year becomes a trap. There may be extenuating circumstances which would prevent such an undertaking in any given year. And even though there are many musicals on the market, very few are worthy of the choir's time, so the teacher who has promised a yearly musical is forced into the unacceptable and awkward position of having to work with an inferior product or of reneging on an expectation. What then are tried and true methods of motivation?

> *"Establishing morale is largely a matter of planning things and doing things, of arousing interest and holding interest, of creating standards and maintaining standards; and the degree of morale determines the degree of efficiency and effectiveness." (p. 26)*

A Service Award System

In the first volume of the Choristers Guild LETTERS (October, 1949), Ruth Jacobs presented the concept of awards for the children's choir. "Reward good work. Create some system of rewards. Use some visible evidence of recognition." Choristers Guild subsequently developed a pin, available to any choir that subscribed to the Guild, for use as a choir award. There was some initial controversy over the use of the term "awards" from the membership of the Guild. Jacobs responded:

> *"There is much pro and con discussion of awards. The Choristers pin is really not an award. It is an insignia representing consistent effort, and loyalty to a high purpose, and makes the wearer a member of international, interdenominational fellowship." (p. 2)*

Since children and youth do not any longer routinely wear pins, other means of service awards have been sought. While the form has changed slightly (a pendant for a pin), the spirit has not. One such program is outlined in Appendix 1A, Organizational Aids.

Additional Projects

Over the years, creative choir directors and parents have developed special events which build motivation and help produce a quality product. Here are a few ideas:

- *Summer Arts Week*—A team of planners engages specialists in a variety of areas: liturgical dance, signing, visual arts, puppetry, Bible study and, of course, choral work, to name some possibilities. There is often a theme. Presentation of the results of their efforts at the end of the week is a fine publicity device as well as a way of honoring the work of the choristers.
- *Vacation Church School*—Instead of songs being sung only as an activity of the curriculum in the classroom itself, plan an official music class which the choir director either teaches or supervises. This is a good way to involve, with the director's guidance, talented senior high choristers who might consider music teaching as a career. (Beware of the music repertoire included with VCS curriculum. Typically, the quality is uneven. A well written, Biblically based musical may be a more worthy project.)
- *Lock-ins and retreats*—A "lock-in" is usually held at the church building itself and is not for the faint-hearted. The experience of sharing floor space with a group of young people on an overnight, however, is certain to help them see the director as a real person! Rehearsal, games, food and fellowship all precede some amount of sleep, followed by breakfast and dismissal the next morning. A retreat is held away from the church building, often at a rural site, and over a weekend.
- *Camps and conferences* usually take place in the summer and consist of choir rehearsals intermingled with fellowship, worship, study time and recreation. This type of week might take place at a local camp with one or several choirs or churches involved. The formula of fellowship, worship, study and recreation happen, on a much larger scale, at the denominational conferences held throughout the country each summer, where choristers from many congregations come together. A similar but non-denominational conference is held each year by Choristers Guild.
- *Musicianship classes*—May be held regularly throughout the year or during the summer. These might be required for choristers involved in an auditioned choir.
- *Regional choir festivals*—Local chapters of professional organizations, such as the American Guild of Organists or the Choristers Guild, sponsor children's choir festivals annually or semi-annually, usually in the spring. Such an event can do much, especially for smaller choirs, to heighten expectations as to what is possible musically. Experiencing worship in another setting, the use of banners, fanfares, etc., and working with a guest conductor, are all potentially wonderful experiences for youngsters.
- *Choir exchanges*—Choirs from two or more churches agree to sing at one another's church. This usually involves a joint rehearsal, perhaps on Saturday, with the host choir providing housing for the visitors if necessary. The next time, the location is reversed.
- *Tours*—Especially for senior highs, this may be the highlight of their time in the program. Tours may be brief weekend events or a week's duration or longer. Tours might incorporate a theme based on a current event which the choir members study and then develop in a variety of ways (visual, spoken, danced, sung, etc.). The theological guidance of clergy and expertise of other staff is important. The tour might be a work-week, where a service

oriented project is combined with a performance or two. Another way to undertake a tour is to combine performing with a study trip to another country such as Israel, Russia, etc. Background readings would be assigned in the summer with classes, led by clergy and/or lay leaders, held in the months immediately prior to the trip. For a church choir which has been together for many years, this event will no doubt be unforgettable.

• *The Young Artists' Recital*—This annual event includes any student, college age or younger, who wishes to play an instrument or sing. Ensembles are welcome as well as solo performances. The audience is made up largely of parents (who each bring a refreshment of some sort for a simple reception afterwards) and members of the congregation are invited to attend.

The Boys

With few exceptions, adult choirs reflect all too closely what we see in children's choirs—more women than men, more girls than boys. It is an interesting question as to which begets which: do fewer young boys sing in choirs because they see fewer males singing with adult choirs? Or, do we have fewer tenors and basses because fewer men grew up with choral training? In the entire field of music performance and study, this phenomenon is limited solely to the area of choral singing. In the area of musicology as well as in instrumental ensembles, there are at least as many males as females. Aspiring professional singers seem to be women and men in equal numbers.

Irrespective of the cause, the problem is real. Singing is an intensely personal activity. Assessment of the sound of one's instrument, the voice, has to be more keenly and specially felt than assessment of one's competency at an externally played instrument. The male voice often struggles to gain control after the voice changes in ways not so obvious in women. This fact of nature alone may well account for fewer tenors and basses in our choirs.

The image of choir singing as sissy is still strong in some communities but in those towns where singing is valued as a skill and gift, no thought is given to such a false and silly standard. It is interesting that the number of famous male rock singers is significantly higher than that of women, and there are relatively few "sissy" accusations there.

The best approach is, once again, to address the issue actively. If little boys begin choir before stereotyping sets in (and in some places parents may have to be educated as to the value of the choir for their son) *and* if we have done our job well, we have made a major step because now the boy *likes* to sing and knows that doing so makes him feel good. He has also become aware that the church is grateful for his gift of time and service. He has friends in the group, activities he wants to be a part of since they challenge his mind and capture his imagination. He knows he is counted on to be his best in choir.

Talking to the entire group about singing as the very physical act that it is will also go a long way towards dispelling myths of its being sissy. Singing is an *athletic event.* If there is an appealing professional or semi-professional male singer in your community, ask him to come in and give a voice class for the entire male population of your program! Even the youngest ones will enjoy singing a song or two with the older boys and men. (Hint: try to hold this event at the usual rehearsal time of the age group you want most to be positively affected.)

As the voice matures and comes into the peak of its treble power, all possibilities for lavishing praise on this wonderful instrument should be explored. Boys with these "fully ripe" voices (usually between the ages of 11—13) should visit younger choirs, sing for them and talk about what they remember about being in choir as a younger boy (the age of their audience). And as the voice begins its trip downward, frequent, individual monitoring of the journey is important, not only for vocal reasons, but to remind the young man that this is normal, that you will guide him through it, and that he has a great adventure ahead of him with a completely new instrument with which to serve his church through his choir.

Keeping the Youth

Lamentably, in churches all over the country, the children's choir program comes to a halt after elementary school. The reasons given generally center around the theme, "We just can't keep the kids once they get into the upper grades." And yet, strong youth choirs are evident in numerous programs across the country. Let's look at some of the reasons why.

In a successful youth choir:

- The young people have literally grown up in the choir program. Many of them have seen their siblings do so. Choir participation is simply a part of the family's life.
- The boys have had a good experience in the choir as little ones. They enjoy how it feels to sing and how the choral experience effects them "on the inside," as one young tenor told his director. They are not perceived as sissy because singing is treated as the athletic event that it is and the director has interpreted this message to any potential detractors. They are challenged with high standards and want to prove that they can do it. The message given them is that this is a desirable activity to be a part of. This critical point bears repeating: these patterns and attitudes are "grown up" over a period of years, not weeks, or even months, and begin when the children are in early grade school or even younger.

- The successful youth choir will recognize the parallel importance of fellowship, choral experience and worship leadership. A common theory about teenage choirs has historically existed: if the boys are there, the girls will come too. This is a bit simplistic and more than a little chauvinistic. In a successful youth choir, the girls come because they love to sing and want to be a part of something important. It also happens that they like to be with their friends of both genders, in any setting.

- The youth are given *frequent* worship responsibilities. Although the music may not be difficult each time, young people need the challenge of being treated as young adults. If their schedule of worship responsibilities in high school is the same as when they were in the third grade, the tendency may be to take their choir commitment lightly.

- The youth choir is supported by an active fellowship program which meets just after rehearsal. Choir and fellowship events are carefully coordinated so as not to compete but complement the other. Give and take occurs on the part of both the choir director and the fellowship leadership.

- The members elect officers to plan and oversee choir events. This may well be done in coordination with the fellowship group which, ideally, contains the same people. (Young people are well intentioned, but often need prodding. The director must evaluate with the youth how much responsibility they wish to have, helping them to be realistic about their commitment of time and energy. The director will be wise to have a parent or other adult on board as well, to help in a myriad of ways—organizing robes, music folders, etc.).

- Staff leadership is convinced that sound investment opportunities for the future leadership of the church exist among the current youth. Programs for youth are supported financially and philosophically.

- College age alumni are welcomed back into the choir when they are home from school.

- The director is aware of the events in the young people's lives *outside* the church and is sensitive them. This may manifest itself in many ways—from attending a high school track meet to suggesting that a "stressed out" teen take a few weeks off from choir rehearsals, "just until the pressure lets up a bit."

- The director relates naturally to young people and has been around long enough to "grow the children up," either teaching them as little ones, or being part of a well coordinated youth and children's choir team. Even a well established program can suffer growing pains when there is a change in staffing. Set backs are usually temporary, however, if staff leadership (musician, clergy, music committee, etc.) are committed to the concept of a youth choir.

- The church leadership acknowledges the fact that the quantity of people and level of talent in choir continually moves in cycles, just as it does for the rest of the congregation. The senior high choir may have a "heyday" for several years, then not be as strong for a while. This is a natural sequence of events. The trick is to not despair. Keep what is happening in perspective. Continue to recruit and motivate the younger children. ("Have I told you that our

senior high choir sang almost as well as you do when they were your age?")
Those children are the future youth choir. Churches that have success with
teenage choirs never shut the program down for lack of singers. They may
be incorporated into a young women's or men's ensemble, even the adult
choir, but only *for a while*, until the youth choir can once again stand on its
own. It never looses sight of the youth choir's critical place in combatting
nominal church membership.

Some closing thoughts on motivation from Ruth Krehbiel Jacobs:
*"At the very heart of the whole question of choir morale, however, is the
director's personal interest in each child—not an academic, but a warm
human interest. At least once a year, the leader should have a personal
interview with each child, commend his fine qualities, discuss his weaknesses, and ask his advice on the policies of the choir.*

*"But the greatest morale builder of all is united effort for some unselfish
project. Membership in a good children's choir offers plenty of opportunity to receive, but to fulfill its obligation as a Christian organization it is
essential that there be opportunity for giving as well." (p. 25)*

None of the projects or good intentions suggested here, however, can motivate
choristers to remain enthusiastic about the choir program for very long if the weekly
practices are boring or unpleasant. Rehearsal activities and goals which challenge the
mind, the artistry, the commitment of the individual chorister as well as that of the
group build the *esprit de corps* of the choir. In short, the most essential motivator of
all is the rehearsal itself. On this we shall focus in the next chapter.

Endnotes

[1]   The Royal School of Church Music is noted for its scheme of grouping
      children by ability level. As they reach a level of competency, they move
      on to the next challenge. Further information is given in the Bibliography.

[2]   Ruth Krehbiel Jacobs, "This and That," *Choristers Guild LETTERS,* 5 (May
      1954): 76, as quoted by Larry K. Ball, in his dissertation, *Choristers Guild
      1949-1980.*

Chapter 4

THE REHEARSAL

"The backbone of the children's choir is a stimulating, interesting rehearsal." (p. 39)

Children are motivated when their minds are challenged appropriately. Rehearsals which engage their imaginations and their developing abilities are rehearsals where fewer discipline problems will arise, where choristers come eagerly because they feel wanted and important. They will be drawn, unconsciously in the early years, perhaps consciously later on, to a place where their evolving aesthetic sense is nurtured. They will be drawn to a place where they can learn and question and grow in their faith.

The majority of church musicians have particular constraints on rehearsal time as well as a diversity of talent and experience among their unauditioned singers. In order to make significant progress, this basic premise is crucial: What we do in each rehearsal must be so effective and memorable, that where we are offering our choristers an opportunity to be is a journey they will be motivated to take.

"Just what is it that induces children to make everything else give way to choir rehearsals? There are various elements that influence the situation, but one of the most evident is the attitude of the director....Children enjoy working with a person whose understanding they sense. And they want as a leader one who commands their instinctive respect....His command over his group will come from his evident sincerity, and equally evident certainty of method. He will not make the mistake of trying to teach music; he will teach children. He will know that he must have them quiet if they are to follow him. Outsiders will probably say that he has magnetism, but he himself would say, 'Nothing can be accomplished without intensity.' He knows that what children are told does not count half as much as what they experience. He will keep working as long as things are coming. When they stop coming, he will go after them in another way. He will keep the children alert. [He will] reacquaint himself with the voice and learning capacity of each child...and each child will think it is because his particular voice is so important....He will be serious in rehearsal because he knows how quickly children take advantage of levity....He will know that sloppiness is the death of his work, and he will train the children to scorn carelessness and the practice of getting by." (pp. 39-40)

A Checklist For Directors of Volunteer Choirs

The suggestions which follow are compiled from experiences in participating, observing, and conducting volunteer choirs. They are techniques which, when used consistently by a skilled director, exact a high quality product even in severely limited situations. None of them will ever be a substitute for more rehearsal time. All of them will reflect a person who uses well the time available.

Rehearsal Organization

1. After preparing a rehearsal plan, spend time alone in the rehearsal space to think through pacing, placement of visual teaching aids, movement possibilities, seating changes, etc.
2. Provide at least one visually beautiful spot in the rehearsal space, no matter how hopeless it may appear. Make certain the ventilation is adequate.
3. Have chairs the right size (and shape) for the singers. Use the chairs sparingly, standing for readiness activities, warm-ups, and for much of the singing.
4. The younger the group, the more necessary is a space for *locomotor* activity, not just "on the spot" movement.
5. Develop an efficient way to distribute and hand in music, to take attendance, to find seats, etc. Avoid sharing music, for as Ruth Jacobs noted a half century ago, doing so *"provides too many opportunities for nudges."* (See Appendix 1A - Organizational Aids.)
6. Use choir parents or officers effectively. Be sure they know their jobs. Have a job description visible as a handy check list. This is especially important for substitutes. (See Appendix 1A - Organizational Aids.)
7. Prepare, in advance, any handouts to go home (choir parent or officer task?) with each chorister's name on a sheet. (If left behind, it will be clear who to contact.) Arrange handouts in seating order for ease in distribution at the end of rehearsal, or, place in each chorister's cubby.
8. Make audio cassettes of anthems for choristers who have pitch matching, reading or attention deficit problems. Work with these choristers individually using anthems before they are begun with the group. (Try an "early birds" class each week. Groups of three or four children arrive for choir 20 minutes early on a rotating basis, organized so that inexperienced singers come more frequently than the others.) Surround uncertain singers (and readers) by secure choristers in a consistently followed seating plan.
9. Have a strategy for handling possible behavior problems. Set boundaries and develop a decorum code—perhaps with their input. Be fair. Be consistent. Be firm.
10. Attempt insight with chronic discipline problems, i.e., is there something the singer is *not* saying that may need to be attended to in order to handle the problem? (Learning problems, strife at home, etc.)

During The Rehearsal

11. Begin promptly, *no matter how many are late*. Have an opening activity no one wants to miss. End promptly.
12. Give instructions simply, clearly and only once. Give the choir time to follow them. Train the singers to find the place in the score by page, system or line, measure and word. Do not give directions to an inattentive group.
13. Develop smooth transitions so that attention is kept from one activity to the next.
14. Don't wear an activity out. Leave it before interest starts to slip.
15. Try to keep everyone interested at all times. Find legitimate ways to use a second group while rehearsing with another. (Pulsing the beat, analyzing what they hear, etc.)

16. Look for occasions to involve the singers in decisions of tempi and dynamics. This increases their musicianship and level of artistry, as well as giving them a sense of "ownership" in the music making.
17. Use snatches from current anthems as vocalises.
18. Tie in a mini-literacy lesson whenever the opportunity presents itself. Have a consistent approach to teaching literacy skills and use it weekly.
19. Model and gently insist upon beautiful vowels and spinning consonants *as the pitches and rhythms are being taught* for they are no less a part of the music.
20. Breathe for the singers as the preparatory beat is given. It must *prepare* them to give the desired sound.
21. Keep the conducting gesture low and wide to aid the singers' breath. (For a fourth beat preparation, try a slight extension of the third beat rather than a typical upbeat as an aid to indicating a low and wide breath.)
22. The director's facial expressions, posture, diction, tone, should be ones we would want our choristers to emulate. If the choirs efforts are not pleasing, the admonition we so often give to our singers, "watch the director," may need to be applied to ourselves.
23. Efficient conductors keep their own singing with the choir to a minimum. Demonstrate the tone desired, help the melody along in the initial stages, but remember that by singing with them, we do not hear the choristers accurately. Singing along may cover up errors but it usually will not fix them. The same is true for over-reliance on the piano.

"Making so much noise ourselves, it is impossible for us to hear what the choir is doing...A director should use his ears much more than his mouth. Unless he hears, he cannot possibly teach." (p. 42)

24. Use the (well-tuned) piano only a little and insist that it be played sensitively. Never bang out a starting pitch or a melody. Stroke the key with the intention of *lifting the sound out*, not pounding it in. If there is an accompanist, explain in advance your rehearsal style and expectations.
25. Encourage the singers to try to find their own starting pitch relying on the sounds already established. Directors must work consciously at developing their own relative pitch sense as well as that of the choristers.
26. Efficient conductors have developed diagnostic abilities so that they can quickly decide what isn't working and what is causing the problem. Have tricks on instant recall to help solve intonation inaccuracies, vowel thinness, breathiness, missed rhythms and pitches, etc. Make a card file to organize by type, quick-fix techniques. This will help commit them to memory.
27. Good conductors listen! To the choristers, to themselves, to their accompanists. They have super ears, not only the cultivated and highly trained ear of the musician, but also the ability to hear with honesty what is truly occurring. Don't just "hear what you want to hear." (Try taping rehearsals.)
28. Be certain that repetitions are meaningful. Drill is deadly. Do it again, but in a different way, on nonsense syllables, for example, or with a different

tempo. Ask the choir, "What are we going to do differently this time?"

29. Effective conductors keep their own talking to a minimum and use body language effectively. Teach, don't talk! Never explain something which doesn't need explaining. Bring the group to attention by some positive device (perhaps clapping a rhythm to be echoed). Never yell for any reason.

30. As a rule, do not take rehearsal time for discussions with anyone except the choir. That much time is lost, and with it, the time it may take to get back the children's attention. No matter how pressing an interruption, that time should belong entirely to the children unless there is an out of the ordinary, clearly planned alternative. Be sure that the choir parents understand this.

31. Pace rehearsals intelligently in planning, but don't be afraid to change if need be when "going live." Efficient conductors cultivate and trust intuition and creative instinct.

32. Be aware that the time table for accomplishing a goal may be different for the director than for the choir. Sometimes we, as teachers, move on too soon, without giving the choir adequate time on a particular skill. Or, we stay on one thing too long, simply because our lesson plan isn't finished!

33. Consciously make eye contact with each singer at least once during the rehearsal.

34. Effective conductors cultivate in their rehearsal style at least one of the following: a sense of the dramatic, a sense of humor, a sense of purpose, a willingness to play. Effective conductors always acknowledge in some way, the budding artist within each chorister.

35. Gently insist on the choir's best. Look for ways to affirm the choristers—singly and corporately. If the outcome wasn't spectacular, praise the effort. If the effort was poor, express confidence in their ability and their desire to try harder the next time.

36. Rehearse in the worship space regularly, especially on the rehearsal prior to a Sunday for which the choir is scheduled to sing.

Setting Goals

In preparing weekly rehearsals, it is important to keep in mind not only short-term goals, but those for the long term, the program year and beyond. Each age group should have its own particular set of objectives. As an example, the following might be asked: What should the choir be able to sight sing in six months time? What about expansion of range and tessitura? How many hymns will be learned and how will they be studied?

There must be non-musical goals considered as well: lining up and entering the sanctuary with poise and reverence, then reading and following the worship bulletin, finding hymns quickly and quietly, standing and sitting together, etc. There are theological discussions to consider: the start of each season of the liturgical year, invitations to the pastor to talk with the choristers about the text of an anthem and how it fits with the scripture lessons for the day, etc. If these important goals are not set and regularly monitored, then the old adage is likely to become true: If you don't know where you are going, you will probably end up somewhere else.

Even seasoned teachers would do well to keep some form of checklist of long-term and short-term goals. The checklist could be a form, photocopied in enough quantity for each choir's weekly rehearsal, which includes information such as on the one that appears in the Appendix. These may be collated in a binder for a complete record of the year's activities for each choir. This is a great help in preparing the lesson plan for the following week, especially if time can be taken soon after each rehearsal to make annotations about what actually transpired. (See Appendix 1B - Teaching Tools.)

Dealing With Distractions

Distractions for any age group steal valuable rehearsal time. The most well thought out lesson plan is not exempt from the possibility of children talking out of turn, choir parents coming into the rehearsal to ask a question, the director's uncertainty about what to do next, and "technical difficulties." All of these could break the concentration of both the conductor and the choir.

If at all possible, pauses in rehearsal must have a reason—not knowing what to do next is not a valid reason to pause! If relying on a lesson plan, memorize it, or somehow code the rehearsal resources so that there is no lag from one activity to another. Stopping rehearsal to read a lesson plan is an invitation to the children to become distracted. If all has failed and a break in teaching is unavoidable (i.e., the remote control on the CD player is malfunctioning and the director has to turn away from the choir in order to deal with the sound system or abandon the recorded example in the lesson) the best way to go is to "punt." Literally *play* with the situation: perhaps have the children count how many seconds it will take to get it working; call in that electronic gadgetry whiz "Mrs. Sonic" (the erstwhile choir mom) to work on it while rehearsal continues. In other words, if a pause is unavoidable, let it give the choir a humorous or relaxing break before resuming work. The key is to stay in control as though the break had been planned that way all along.

Rehearsal Planning: A Closer Look

"This subject of rehearsal methods is a big one, and one impossible to confine within a formula. No two rehearsals are alike, nor should they be."
(p. 44)

"What is learned with interest is absorbed readily and retained more firmly." (p. 34)

The next section explores characteristics of and rehearsal activities appropriate to various ages of children and youth. Many of the concepts basic to successful choral teaching of any age will be covered in the discussions of the two youngest age groups below. The reader should refer to them as the basis for activities designed for older choristers. Genuine learning, and therefore, good teaching is sequential. Skills build upon themselves.

Even as we encourage the inclusion of preschool and primary age choirs in the music ministry, it is also prudent to caution against embracing, without question, the philosophy, "the earlier the better." Just as there are advantages, there are clearly disadvantages in trying to shove too much into children too soon. In some sections of the country in particular, the pressure on parents can be enormous to insure a child's future at "Ivy League University" or "Elite College" by promoting endless activities while still in pre-school.

Educators can disagree over how much a child processes and at what age, but we must never find ourselves in the position of catering to current trends at the expense of good teaching. The goal is to infuse the young child with a sense of joy in music and in service, always remembering that true learning happens in the right order, at the right point in an *individual* child's development—and that this takes time.

The Pre-School Choir

Auditory Skills

Children are busy *auditory* learners. Especially before age seven they have listened, unconsciously, to the sounds of the mother tongue, then imitated what they have learned. As the child grows, auditory assimilation widens to include listening in a conscious way as well. Classes with young musicians therefore, should include listening experiences of two types: *unconscious assimilation* and *cognitive listening activities.*

Unconscious assimilation is a critical part of the development of proper singing tone. While more will be said about vocal development in Chapter 5, it should be pointed out in this context that consistent hearing of a light, focused singing model will make a deep impression on the youngest singers. Demonstrate the sound, or bring in older choristers to do so. Play tape recordings of good singing tone. *Get that sound into their ears! Comparing* other types of vocal sounds (speaking, shouting, whispering, murmuring, etc.) with the singing tone will help children assimilate the same information in a conscious, or *cognitive*, way.

Many cognitive listening experiences will involve other modes of learning, such as movement or sight. Games incorporating other perceptions with listening may become favorite activities. Adapt the activity to the age and experience level of the particular group:

1. Children use locomotor or on the spot movements to differentiate types of sounds given by the teacher. For example, a wood block might be represented by marching; a triangle by gliding, etc.
2. Children are shown two or more untuned percussion instruments. Experiment with them to establish the timbre of each, then listen, this time without looking, as the teacher plays one or more instrument. The children then identify the instruments used, in the order played.
3. Assign and identify particular melodies to represent locomotor activities.[1] Different children may be assigned to each melody played from the keyboard or xylophone (walk, gallop, and jump are good places to begin) and the class sits on the floor while the assigned child executes the particular movement each time his/her melody is played. After a while, the entire group may join in when the melody is played with an accompaniment, dropping out when the accompaniment stops, etc.[2]

It is this same process of listening, evaluating, then connecting (to the larynx and articulators) that children will eventually follow, either consciously or unconsciously, in order to sing a melody tunefully.

Especially at the pre-school age, children's ears are sensitive to quality, volume, sound, even nuance, for they must master all of these things in order to learn language. Therefore it makes a great deal of sense to do much of our teaching of songs to these youngest choristers by rote, using the finest models available to insure accuracy and tone quality. They will take pleasure again and again in hearing, then echoing, melodies appropriate to their age. (See Chapter 5 for more specific information on building tone.)

Melodic Literacy Skills

Even as we focus on the remarkable auditory powers of the pre-schooler, the wise director will incorporate readiness activities for the eventual teaching of traditional notation. These will aid in the learning of individual songs and put us a step ahead as our chorister's reading skills develop. The following readiness activities teach melody essentially by rote, but begin to bring the ear consciously to a more refined level of musicianship as well as connect it to the eye, via written symbols.

1. As the song is "lined out," *gesture the shape* of the melody with the hand, while the children echo vocally and with their own hands. Then *draw the shape* of the melody using at first a connected line, then individual dashes placed appropriately higher or lower to indicate pitch. The dashes may also be made longer or shorter to indicate duration.

2. Continue the echo process, asking if anyone can *remember* the first sound of each phrase (this time without giving the starting pitch). As pitch memory improves, continue to ask for the starting pitch of a song or phrase, lengthening the time between ending and beginning it again by injecting another brief activity, such as clapping together the rhythm of the phrase in question.

3. Teacher plays and children sing simple three or four note songs on a xylophone with unused bars removed. This links up two vital *visual* components with the ear and larynx. These will be used later in reading actual notation:

    —higher/lower/stay-the-same
    —relative interval size.

As the photograph indicates, by early elementary school, many children will be able to echo play these melodic fragments on the tuned percussion instruments as well as sing them. Take care not to introduce the tuned percussion too soon. During pre-school, the most important choral work will be between the voice and the ear, children listening to the teacher model, *then the teacher listening to the children echo.* The teacher/conductor should not sing with the children, unless the express point is to sing a song together.

4. Hand signals[3] can begin at pre-school and continue throughout elementary school. Introduce them slowly, and use them consistently, or they will have little value.

5. We can also help our choristers become good listeners in general. This is a survival skill which is necessary in every phase of their lives. It has to do with paying attention and recall. Encouragement of these skills in our rehearsals may occur in many little ways: "Who can remember the hymn number after only one announcement?" "Anyone can sing the second word. Can you be on time for the first one?" Consistent reinforcement and gentle insistence on accuracy will pay off greatly as the children learn for themselves to listen keenly. My own experiences with upper elementary and middle school children who have not had early musical training shows a significant deficiency in their ability to judge minute differences in pitch or subtle melodic and rhythmic changes. Indeed, even the ability to follow a sequence of instructions is at risk. To begin exposure to such keen listening at upper elementary age is not particularly productive. It appears that the brain's timetable for mastering this skill occurs at an earlier age.

Rhythmic Skills

From the activities already described it is apparent that both auditory and visual learning during the pre-school and early elementary years is critical to the success of children's choral development. It does not take place apart from movement and manipulation. Rhythmic development is no different. Movement is one of the primary ways children develop their rhythmic sense. The following comments and suggestions are based on the premises found in *Orff-Schulwerk Music and Movement for Children.*[4] Many current trends in music education for young children have borrowed heavily from the *Schulwerk,* surely a sign of its success and popularity.

In their play, children learn speech chants or "playground games" that are metric and that often have movement patterns.[5] Additionally, our nursery rhyme tradition is a vast resource for introducing children to the shapes and lengths of phrases. These activities involve ordinary developmental skills that occur naturally in most children: rhythmic speech accompanied by body percussion or sound gestures, i.e., clapping, jumping, patting, swaying, etc. This is the best way to begin assimilation of rhythmic skills. The primary goal at this age should be internalization of rhythm and the ability to keep a pulse, echo a phrase, then make up a phrase of one's own. The introduction of notated rhythmic values can occur during these early years *but not apart from or before regular experiences with rhythmic internalization.* As Ruth Jacobs said, *"Rhythm is more in the feet than in the head." (p. 31)*

Pre-school children can begin to connect *rhythm they feel and repeat* to *rhythm presented visually.* (This will be discussed more fully in the information about early elementary children.) A logical place to begin work in rhythmic development is with language. By using speech pieces rather than songs for some of their repertoire, children are able to remove for the moment the added challenge of melody and thereby concentrate more fully on other musical tasks.

There are many sacred speech pieces in print as well as other chants.[6] Original material can and should be developed by the director or in cooperation with the children themselves. Use published examples as models to get started and guide the children to the wonders of composition. The Psalms and the Gospels are rich resources. Take care that the children use a speech quality which is very close to singing tone, not harsh or monotone, and help them pay attention to dynamics and inflection. By early elementary school, the children should be able to combine a spoken ostinato[7] with a chant, thereby introducing the concept of maintaining separate parts, the mastery of which is so crucial to part singing. With the melodic element removed, this is accessible to many in this age group.

Rhythmic development may also be explored via body percussion (clapping, patting, etc.) and percussion instruments, notably the *Orff-Schulwerk* Instrumentarium: xylophones, glockenspiels, metallophones in various ranges, timpani, recorders, and a multitude of untuned percussion. The instruments are at once lovely to hear and fun to use. Take care however that the use of ostinati played on the instrumentarium not be undertaken until a steady beat can be maintained. (Many Orff specialists recommend waiting until the middle elementary grades before using the barred instruments.) And in a choral ensemble, the instruments should never be used at the expense of time given to vocal development.

In summary, remember: 1) pre-schoolers (and early elementary children) thrive on repetition because it allows them to practice a skill; 2) as with students of all ages, the more senses employed when learning a skill, whether consciously or unconsciously, the better it is mastered.

The Early Elementary Choir Ages 7—9
Much of the material covered in the previous section will remain pertinent for this age group. Building on the still strong rote skills of children in early elementary school, the director can now take advantage of the brain's significant developmental growth spurt that happens during this time, enabling the child to decode written information.[8]

Rhythmic Literacy
In the previous section, rhythm was addressed via its auditory and movement qualities. With beginning readers, it is time to focus intentionally, though not exclusively, on *symbols for rhythmic duration*. The easiest way is to continue to address the young child's need for movement and manipulation. (The activities described in the paragraph below work well for pre-schoolers too but transferring this data to the written page will not be appropriate until elementary school.)

Using a set of "rhythm blocks" (see Appendix IB for complete instructions on making such a set) children can readily see that two eighths equal one quarter note, four quarters equal one whole note, etc. Introduce the concept using syllables for note values (ta = quarter, ti = eighth, timitimi = four sixteenths, ta-ah = half, etc.). Using the whole note block as a four beat measure, lead the children to discover that it takes a quarter note four "steps" to arrive at the end of the measure, but the eighth note must take eight. What happens if they travel to the end together? The quarter gets there first. What can the shorter block do in order to arrive at the same time? Yes, it can "run" exactly twice as fast as the quarter. Why twice as fast? Because it is exactly twice as small. Once the relative values are established, begin to build simple rhythms beginning with patterns such as:

Add sixteenth and half notes next. The concept of relative values is easily transferred to any combination. Dotted values are understood as the note shown plus half of its value. "The dot is worth half of what it is sitting next to."

Children will enjoy playing games with these each week, blocks on a narrow table, the director sitting behind (silently reading backwards, i.e., the opposite side of the block from what the children see, and pointing to the blocks from right to left) while the children clap and say the names of the blocks. Encourage the choir to clap, positioning one hand flat like a drum, the fingers of the other hand serving as the drumstick. This is to distinguish our work from "stadium" or "audience" clapping in which the full lower arm moves.[9] This must be practiced and gently insisted upon or it will not be done and the group clapping will be unmusical.

Games can include teacher setting up a rhythm on top of the whole note block, then with great seriousness, clapping the pattern alone, but *incorrectly*. When the children note the error (which they will do instantly and with disbelief, at least until they learn the "game") the director feigns incredulousness and asks for help in *correcting the blocks* to sound like the pattern actually clapped. Children take turns coming forward to do so. Children will play this indefinitely, enjoying enormously their director playing the fool. In time, begin the transfer from the blocks to the board or overhead projector and to connections on the written page.

Pitch Problems

The noted American hymn specialist, composer and arranger Alice Parker has said, "Singing is a birthright—a primary gift of God." Although talent varies, each person can learn to sing in tune. Many pre-schoolers do so without any help at all, but as every director has experienced, there are older children who do not sing accurately without help. For years, some directors "solved the problem" by telling the "mono-tone" child to "just mouth the words." Most adults who knew that verdict as a child gave up on their birthright as singers, accepting the "expertise" of their music teacher as fact. (It would never occur to a child to question the director's lack of knowledge or ability to correct the problem.)

It is up to us to find ways to deal with pitch problems and truly solve them. It can be done. Here is how.

The chief culprit is nothing more than inexperience. The obvious antidote is to get children singing in guided situations, frequently. Often the child with pitch problems has not discovered the singing voice as different from the speaking voice. This is very common in the pre-school years and in elementary students who have not had prior vocal training. Our task is to help the child experience, again and again and yet again, *where the singing voice lies*, using sirens, yawn-sigh, bird calls of any variety, whatever activities one can think of to *exercise* the vocal cords so that they are *retrained* to work naturally in the singing range.[10]

As with anything, prevention of problems is best and in the case of inexperience, parents can be given a vital role in creating accurate singers. They should provide:

- Exposure to many sounds from an early age.
- Encouragement of early attempts at singing.
- Frequent, guided experiences in using the singing voice.[11]

Additionally, encourage parents to use their ears and eyes.

- Listen for danger signs: excessive, chronic huskiness.
- What is the sound of the child's "playground" voice?
- Discourage "belting" or shouting when singing.
- Look for danger signs: excessive high chest breathing when speaking or singing; tight neck and/or jaw muscles when speaking or singing.

The points above address a second major cause of pitch problems: faulty vocal production. Sometimes a child cannot match pitch because s/he cannot reach it. Most often, the pitch is higher than is comfortable but it can also be too low. The antidote for this is as for inexperience. The exception would be if the vocal cords sound damaged, either temporarily, as with a cold or allergies, or chronically, which may indicate nodes or polyps. In this case, singing may aggravate the condition and a physician's opinion should be sought.

No matter how good the prevention, inevitably some children will come to you in various stages of pitch insecurity. The steps to tuneful singing are the same for every person, whether or not the process is a conscious one. For those with actual *perceptual problems*[12] the following suggestions used consistently and frequently will work in both individual and group situations and are useful for less severe pitch problems as well:

- Exercise the voice using inflected nonsense sounds; sirens; speech pieces. Have the children place a hand on top of their head. "Send the sound out here."
- Involve the whole body through activities which improve breath, posture, attitude, energy level. Sometimes pitch is inaccurate because of underproducing, or undersinging it, day dreaming, poor concept of tone, too much information coming at once.
- Create visuals and manipulative aids to help the child "hear" and "feel" the pitch.[13]
- Find a range of notes that work better than the rest and begin there.
- Match the child's pitch before asking the child to match yours. Try singing his/her pitch first in echo and then simultaneously. The sensation of each is very different. Usually, an accurate echo is achieved before successful unison. Often children who sing above or below the pitch do so simply to hear themselves within the group. If there is relative ease in making an accurate echo but the child is inaccurate when singing with the choir, the problem is only inexperience and will work itself out with consistent gentle reminders.
- Use large gestures to indicate variations in pitch while the voice follows, i.e.: "yoo-hoo-yoo" on "sol-mi-sol," guiding hands, or using traditional hand signals to show the two pitches. (Patterns for the child to echo should *return to the original pitch* so that s/he is given every chance to begin

accurately. That is to say, the tonal memory may be so immature that the child will begin on the last pitch heard, thereby assuring inaccuracy if that last pitch is not the same as the starting one.

- Find more ways to involve the person's "normal" perceptions such as vision, and motor skills.
- Record songs the choir will be using and give them on cassette tape to all children with pitch problems. They will benefit by having time to listen and process as best they can before the rest of the choir begins work with the song, and by listening to the songs during the weeks it is being taught. *Give this tape also to children who are slow readers or who have attention deficit problems.* They may not have pitch matching trouble per se, but are likely to wander initially on unfamiliar songs because they must concentrate so hard on reading or on staying focused.

Above all, be patient and do not become discouraged! As the cartoon character in *Pogo* says, "This situation is full of insurmountable opportunity!"

Teaching a Melody

Often by second grade and usually by third, children are ready and eager to begin to decipher the mysteries of the printed score, especially if care has been taken to introduce the elements in a sequenced, logical, and creative way. Here are logical next steps.

1. In advance of rehearsal, draw the melody phrase by phrase on pieces of large staff paper (or an outline of the melody, depending upon the choir's overall readiness) one phrase per page of staff paper. Similarly, the text is printed phrase by phrase on colored tag board taking care that the words will line up to the correct notes when the two pieces of the puzzle are put together by the children. As the choir hears the words sung to the various phrase fragments, they assign each of the text phrases to one of the melody phrases. Children will enjoy the challenge of trying to arrange in order the entire song using tag board and giant staff paper.

2. Use an overhead projector to focus the group's attention on detail. Photocopy a page from the anthem presented in the "puzzle" above and reproduce it on an overhead transparency. (There are transparencies designed for photocopiers.) The group looks together at the information they have already learned, seeing how it looks on the printed page.

3. Next, hand out octavos to the children, reviewing what has already been learned and checking to see that the choristers have all made the transition to the individual score.

In this three-step sequence, the children have:

1. had a guided group effort in identifying and validating visually what the ear and voice had already experienced by rote;

2. looked together at a single score with the director aiding the focus by pointing out particular information;

3. had the opportunity to view the information in the traditional way.

Had any of the steps been left out, the result might well have been confusion rather than satisfaction.

Continue consistent use of hand signals. Couple them with pitches read from a visual aid such as a solfege ladder, the director pointing as the children signal and sing. Combine vocal warm ups with fragments from melodies to be taught, using signals to train the ear and voice to respond to the information gathered by the eye, first from the ladder and/or overhead projector, then from the individual score. (See Appendix 1B for instructions on how to make a solfege ladder.)

In the presentation of any melody, remember that the way in which a song is first presented may in large measure determine how well received the song may be by the choir. Keep variety and fun in the approach, coupled with standard tools with which the children become old friends, such as hand signals, a ladder and overhead projector. The irresistible combination of the *known* (the music reading aids like those above) with the *unknown* (the new music to be learned) is a mystery that children, especially those in the early elementary grades, will enjoy solving.

Beginning to Sing in Parts

Although part singing will not begin in earnest until the upper elementary grades, early exploration of this skill should begin now. Start with a brief ostinato pattern, sung on two or three pitches, to accompany the melody, as in the following example:

Watch - ing o - ver me,

All night, all day, An - gels watch - ing o - ver
me, my Lord;— All night, all day,
An - gels watch - ing o - ver me.

Note that the ostinato is a fragment of the melody, but does not occur simultaneously with the melody. Expand the length and difficulty of the ostinato as skills increase. Adding a second or third ostinato can make a simple melody seem quite elaborate. This technique will work with any pentatonic song.[14] The vocal ostinati can be supported by Orff-Instruments, played by the children themselves.

The second step in learning to sing in parts is to employ the ancient practice of *quodlibet*, or two separate melodies which fit together. Again, any pentatonic songs (in the same meter and key and of the same duration) will work. For example:

The compositions of the late Natalie Sleeth use this technique extensively.

The third step is to use simple canons.[15]   Combining vocal or instrumental ostinati can be a simple and effective way to accompany the canon if desired.

Improvisation

An opportunity which is often overlooked or placed lower on the priority list is that of improvisation. As children seek to master basic music skills, they enjoy using them to make up little compositions of their own, and, in the process, become better musicians. The material which follows may be used with any age level, simplifying or raising the level of challenge as needed for the particular group. Regular improvisation experiences are both fun and memorable. They build group and individual confidence. Children in early elementary grades especially delight in this type of experimentation.

Set ground rules as needed to avoid chaos and to encourage participation. Several "low-risk" activities are suggested here and may serve as a starting point for further adventures in improvisation.

Rhythmic Improvisation

1.   Give many examples of simple patterns to imitate. Begin with two-beat phrases using ♩= c. 60. The children echo the director. Children may take turns as leaders, copying examples heard or making up their own. Increase over time to four-beat phrases, then eight. (Expand to meters beyond common time as skills increase.)

2.   Move from echo to a "question/answer" format. A pattern is assigned to the choristers to use as a common "answer" for each "question." The director begins the "question"—a different pattern of the same beat length as the assigned answer. Move from 2 beats, to four, etc. as above. Children may take turns making up the "question."

3.   Children work in groups of two (teacher directed, one set of partners at a time) one child asking the question, the other giving the answer. The pattern selected by either child may be a predetermined example given to the group, or one of the child's own, depending upon the teacher's goals. Again, phrase length builds from two to four to eight. Work may also be in compound time, increasing from two beats (of two dotted quarters) to four and to eight. Try this next with multiple partners simultaneously, the director keeping the common beat on two different sounds, one for the first partner and the other for the second.

4.   Assign children a single body percussion[16] part (or an untuned instrument) and a finger cue from the conductor. (The index finger of the right hand

might mean snappers, two fingers the clappers. On the left hand, one finger could refer to stampers and two fingers to those responsible for patschen. The entire right hand might indicate both of the 'right hand' groups, etc.) Instruct them to watch the director and to make up whatever pattern or patterns they wish but *only when you are indicating their particular finger cue* and *only within your beat*. As confidence increases, encourage 1) frequent changing or alternation of the rhythmic pattern chosen, and 2) cuing several groups at one time so that an extended composition is created: the framework conceived by the director, the particulars, cradled in a low-risk environment, by the children.

5.   In all of the above, use body percussion first (attending to technique details and such artistic considerations as volume and articulation) then add unpitched percussion. Eventually dispense with the finger cues and simply conduct, using face and hands to bring in the various groups.

Melodic Improvisation

1.   Give many examples of simple patterns to imitate.

   a.   As in #1 under rhythmic improvisation (above) begin singing two, then three note scales for the choristers to echo.[17] Increase the length of the patterns.

   b.   Transfer melodies to pitched percussion instruments.

   c.   Following #2 in the rhythmic improvisation section above, move onto question/answer, this time in melodic form, first with the voice then on tuned instruments. (Some children have an easier, less threatening time making their first solo efforts on an instrument rather than singing. They should be encouraged to do both.)

      d.   Over time, increase the scale to full pentatonic, first in "authentic" form (no pitches lower than do) then adding examples in plagal form. (Pitches go both above and below do.) Use the voice and the pitched percussion.

2.   Using pitched percussion, the director establishes a bourdon (do and sol) and pairs of children use the question/answer technique described above, either using voices or an instrument. Students may eventually take turns at the bourdon. Vocal and/or instrumental ostinati may be added as well.

Movement Improvisation

1.   a.   The children are given many examples of *on-the-spot* body percussion patterns. They practice improvising rhythm patterns simultaneously to a given and continuous beat.

      b.   The second element is an assigned *locomotor* activity (i.e. gallop).

      c.   The children alternate between the locomotor movement ('b' above) and the improvised on-the-spot body percussion ('a' above) as determined by specified instrumental cues provided by the director. (For example, gallop pattern played on a drum is alternated with a steady beat played on another instrument. This signals the beginning of the improvised body percussion section.)   Later, children may provide the accompaniment.

2.   After ample experience in exploring locomotor activities, children identify combinations (such as four walks and three jumps) as directed by the teacher on unpitched percussion or the piano. They may suggest and/or play combinations.

3.   Each child invents an individual locomotor ostinato, finding his/her own pattern as the rest of the group experiments simultaneously. The director observes these and chooses one to accompany. Upon hearing this accompaniment, the children decide (silently, on their own) if the sound matches their pattern. If not, they sit down and observe the movement of the child whose pattern is being played. Further investigation of the pattern is possible by joining it, varying it, making a form out of it, etc.

The Upper Elementary Choir Ages 10—12

Vocal Work

By this age, children have substantially greater technical command of their voice. Coupled with increased cognitive skills, they are capable of keeping track of independent parts. The problem of the inexperienced singer is now limited to those who join the program as an older child, for those who have had training since preschool have usually caught on. In Chapters 5, 6, and 7 much more will be said about tone, however, a warm-up is given here in anticipation of a study plan for an anthem to be used by this age group.

Vocal warm-up designed for attention to:

- rhythmic inhalation
- controlled exhalation
- effect of correct breathing on tone
- accurate consonant placement

Place the visual aid (fig. A) in full view of the choir. As the director counts and points, the choir takes a singer's breath on the circled number and exhales properly on the others. To get started the director says in rhythm (fig. B), "Ready, set breathe now." The staves (fig. C—F) are not intended for use with the choir, but rather, are directions for the conductor. At each sequence, simply say to the choir, in tempo: *"staccato 's'"..., "sustained 's'"..., "finish with a 'k'"..., "staccato 'teh too'"..., "sustained 'teh to'"..., etc.* Each sequence should be repeated at least once before proceeding to the next. These verbal cues, combined with the single visual aid, enable the singers to focus their attention on rhythmic inhalation, controlled exhalation, and watching the director. Once the idea is familiar, conduct the eight beats (using a divided four pattern) rather than pointing to the numbers.

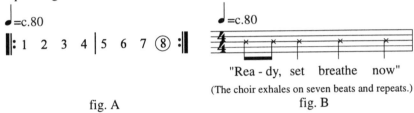

fig. A

"Rea - dy, set breathe now"
(The choir exhales on seven beats and repeats.)

fig. B

fig. C Unvoiced, sustainable consonants, i.e., "s" or "ch"

• pulsed, breath on the 8th beat

• sustained, for seven beats, breath on the 8th

• with another consonant, such as 'k' on the 8th beat

fig. D Single pitch, alternating open and closed vowels

teh too teh too   teh too teh

• first, pulsed

teh oo eh oo   eh oo eh

• then, sustained

teh oo eh oo eh oo eh k

• then, with consonant on 8th beat

fig. E Descending five tone scale, alternating vowels

mee meh mah moh moo oo oo

• first, pulsed

mee eh ah oh oo

• then, sustained

mee eh ah oh oo k

• then, with consonant on 8th beat

fig. F Down/up five tone scale

• first, pulsed: (Avoid "h's" on the second half of each beat.)

mee - ee meh - eh mah - ah moh - oh moo

mee__ meh__ may__ moh__ moo

• then, sustained

mee__ meh__ may__ moh__ moo k

• then, with consonance on 8th beat

Monitor each chorister's breathing at all phases, checking for diaphragmatic/ intercostal action on the inhalation, (not shoulder breathing) and for the chest remaining high, abdominal muscles active on the exhalation.

A Study Plan and Approach for Teaching an Anthem

"Children of the Covenant" [18]

Before beginning:

Be sure the choir is ready. Although a unison piece, this anthem requires a considerable repertory of choral skills as background, and enough preparation time to develop the nuance necessary to sing it well. In general, a group singing "Children of the Covenant" should:

1. feel comfortable using the upper range of their voices for more than an occasional "high" note. The sections in each verse beginning "But trusting" require a free floating sound (or the piece will be a detriment rather than an aid to worship!)
2. be advanced enough to readily grasp the subtle rhythmic changes in each verse. (Compare ms. 10-11 and 23-24 to ms. 37-38 for example.)

Choirs which include children grade three and younger would do well to save this one for older children.

Text and Mood

The words of this anthem begin in ancient Israel, visit pioneer America, and then move to the present day. In each of these periods, the accompaniment is intended to evoke a mood descriptive of that time, even as the melody stays the same for the three verses. To effectively interpret the piece, the children must understand that they are telling a story. (Note that there is no rhyme scheme, an unusual feature in children's choral literature.)

Teaching Ideas:

1. Read a brief portion of any story book narrative to the choir, first in an obviously dull, non-dramatic way. Ask for their comments. Follow this by reading the same passage with careful (but not overdone) inflection. Ask for their comments.
2. Sing measures 3-8 to the choir with strict attention to beats and bar lines, making your presentation very marcato and regimented. Again, elicit their comments. Encourage them to discover with you how word phrases may be shaped by thinking full thoughts (rather than word by word, as a beginning reader might do) and by gently stressing specific words, in particular, the initial and final consonants. The process of looking (with the choir) at the text in a poetic way will heighten their sensitivity towards the artistic shaping of the melody.
3. Consider playing an example of a great *lieder* singer such as Dutch soprano Elly Ameling. (This anthem is patterned after a strophic *lied*.) What techniques does the lieder singer use to convey the poetry of the song in an interesting and artistic way?

Melodic Considerations and Theological Focus

Each verse of the anthem begins in Dorian mode, the lowered third degree and raised sixth giving it its characteristic flavor. Help the children discover that the mood (and the mode) changes at the 'trusting in God section' on each verse, ending in a joyous (major diatonic) and reassuring refrain: "Children of the Covenant, Pilgrims of the Promise of God." Be sure to interpret what that covenant, that promise, is. Encourage discussion of God's constancy and God's presence in the lives of their forebears, for us today and for their children tomorrow.

Teaching Ideas:

4.   Invite a minister to come to rehearsal and talk with the choir about the ideas above. (In making your plans, mention the age group of the choir. Share the text with him/her in advance as well as suggesting a time length for the discussion.) Or, check out the church school curriculum for resources. Make full use of this wonderful text to assure them that the promise is for each of them too. We remember what we sing!

5.   The children will not find the modal melody difficult to hear, but be prepared to help them with intonation. A good warm up is vital. A full, low breath on the inhalation, controlled by an active "support system" on the exhalation will prevent most flatting problems.

6.   Approach the Dorian section of the melody with a vocalise accompanied by an Orff-Schulwerk instrument, handbells or organ playing an ostinato:

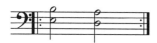

Once established, begin a series of brief Dorian melodic fragments loosely taken from the song. Sing them on a neutral syllable for the choir to echo. (Note: The tone used to model must be pure and simple (no excessive vibrato) and *impeccably in tune!* If a suitable singer cannot be found, use a wind instrument—recorder, flute, organ.)

Here are examples:

Literacy Skill Development

Choral literature can be the starting point for developing so many skills. Particularly in our limited rehearsal time, it is crucial to use it for furthering music reading ability.

Teaching Ideas:

7. The interval of the perfect fifth is a common motive in this anthem. Help the children identify it not only on the lines used in the piece (E to B) but on other pitches. Try an overhead projector and a transparency with an empty staff drawn with spaces the width of pennies. Use coins to mark the lines and spaces in question. Work at singing intervals accurately then transpose them to other places on the staff. Chants may be useful in the case of teaching the sight and sound of the intervals, for example:

Per - fect   fifth   looks   like   this:

Line   skip - a - line, Line   Space   skip - a - space, Space

8. To contrast the work with the relatively wide interval of the perfect fifth, use the descending step-wise passages found at each refrain. (See ms. 15-16, 28-29, and 42-43)
9. For rhythmic skill building, contrast the even eighth notes in the first scale with the dotted eighth and sixteenth of the next.

Miscellaneous Technical Trouble Shooting

Some possibly troublesome words:

"Children"—keep the 'l' forward and very brief in duration. It should be treated as the (brief and clean) beginning of the second syllable, not the end of the first.

Teaching idea:

10. Sing the word as above, but substitute the letter "n" for the "l," forming "chin-dren." Notice that the "n" sound is made by the entire tongue covering the top teeth. Now peel away only the smallest amount of the back of the tongue from the teeth to form the "l." This automatically places the sound forward and guards against flatting. Try this substitution exercise for any word using the letter "l," particularly in the middle of the word, i.e.; "pilgrims," "wilderness," etc. In all cases, the vowels on either side of the "l" get the longer duration. Do not let the consonant stop the air flow.

    "knowing"—Omit the sound of the "w;" sing "no-ing" rather than "no-wing."

    "them"—The vowel is "eh," not "uh" or "im." (Think about the accent common to your area.)

CGA-495

CHORISTERS GUILD

Commissioned by the Singing Children of the churches of Tyler, Texas

Children of the Covenant

Unison voices and organ

Sw. Strings 8'
Ch. Flute 8'
Ped. 16', 8', Ch. to Ped.

Eric D. Johnson

Sue Ellen Page

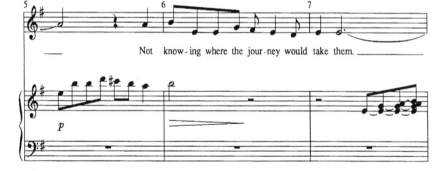

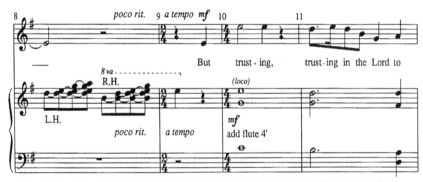

Sound effects, synthesized and/or acoustic, may be used judiciously throughout the piece, taking care not to obscure the voices or the organ accompaniment.

Published by CHORISTERS GUILD   2834 West Kingsley Road   Garland, Texas 75041
Distributed by THE LORENZ CORPORATION   501 East Third Street   Dayton, Ohio 45401

lead them on;   by don-key,   a - cross the vast   des - ert   they came:

Chil - dren of the Cov - e -nant,   Pil - grims of the Prom-ise   of   God.

2. Chil-dren of the Fron - tier,   Liv - ing in the wil-der-ness, not

know-ing where the jour-ney would take them;   But   trust-ing,   trust-ing in the Lord to

CGA-495

lead them on; by ox-cart, in search of a home-land they came:

Chil-dren of the Cov-e-nant, Pil-grims of the Prom-ise of God.

3. Chil-dren of the U-ni-verse, ex-plor-ing the wil-der-ness,___ Not

know-ing where the jour-ney will take us; But trust-ing in the Lord to lead us on; by

*Piano should roll chords from the bottom.

"trusting"—Two areas for attention. First, the initial consonant blend—*tr*—must be moved through quickly, with a flipped "r" sound, sustaining a bright "uh" vowel the full duration of the note value. Secondly, treat "st" as the crisp, initial sound of the second syllable.

"Lord"—omit the "r"

"covenant" = "cuh-veh-nehnt"

"promise" = "prah-mihs"

"God" = "gawhd"

"us" = "ahs"

Begin to cultivate beautiful vowels *as the notes are taught.*
Teaching Ideas:
  11. These two images work well and are described in detail in Chapter 5:
    a. Keep a ROUND SOUND on every word.
    b. Sing with a PEAR SHAPED TONE.

Organ registration

General suggestions are given in the score, and organ is preferred to piano. Possibilities also exist for exciting use of synthesized accompaniment, especially on the final verse. A sound effect evoking space and motion would be particularly effective in the last five measures, remembering that with children's voices any accompaniment should be sparse rather than cluttered.

The Middle School Choir Ages 11—14

Maintaining Is Gaining

  Working with the ages of 11—14 can be at once gratifying and terrifying. Every conceivable physical size and emotional maturity level are placed in one group. In many ways it is simpler to train these singers in two smaller sections grouped by gender, rehearsing separately but coming together in worship. This is especially true if the grade span is three or four years rather than two.

  Children who reach adolescence with positive experiences in the younger choirs will hopefully bring with them the good posture and vocal production habits practiced for so long. These tools will help them through the voice change which undoubtedly will at least begin for both boys and girls during this period. However, pressures of the peer group to appear bored or detached can wreck havoc on posture, and therefore on tone quality. Remember that their popular vocal idols are most likely singing with jaws tight and jutted up, brows furrowed, neck muscles bulging and chests sunken. Never tell junior highs that this production is *wrong*, only make the point that it is *different* from that which is used for choral singing, and leave it at that.

  And speaking of sunken chests, remember too that junior high girls can be sensitive about their new anatomy, the presence of it or the lack thereof. Either way, girls may not be comfortable with the words "keep your chest high," especially if boys are in the room. Instead, point to the top of the chest (on a parallel with the shoulders) and say "stay tall." Keep the choristers vocally on track by reminding them how well they sing when using optimal support and energy. Couple this with consistent modeling both vocally and in conducting gesture. This is the age group which, without attention, will be most at risk for undersinging. Getting physical, i.e., lifting heavy objects while singing, smacking the hands together, etc., will jump-start the support system and the resulting adult-like tone production will surprise, and please, the choristers.

A basic axiom of early adolescent singers: they want to sound wonderful, even if they act like they do not. The director's job is to 'seduce' them into singing well. Direct hits are often scored in oblique ways with junior highs.

No matter how many choristers are involved and no matter the way in which they are grouped (by gender, or all together), the following points are important for successful rehearsals with middle school or junior high singers. Note that many of these elements will be a continuation of the tradition, the style and the procedures established in the earlier grades.

1. Decide on a seating chart that groups the boys together by range immediately in front of the director. If a mixed gender group, the girls sit to one side (or on both of sides of the boys, depending upon the size of the choir.) Each chorister has an assigned seat, and his/her own music, pencil and folder. (See Chapter 6 for information on range and repertoire.)

2. The director must have a working knowledge of the changing voice and give clear cut, reassuring and direct information about it to the students—often.[19]

3. Arrange to hear choristers individually or in small groups at least three times each year.

4. Make frequent comments which validate the present and point to the future: "You all sing so well. Have I told you what a fine high school choir you will make? I can hardly wait!" Corny, but they get the message and are inwardly pleased.

5. Decide on THE RULES. Fewer are usually better than more, but the need to get them established is imperative.

6. Such traditions as lining up outside the rehearsal room door, done for years and years in the younger grades may be waived for junior highs as a sort of "privilege." But customs must be resumed if the privilege is taken advantage of, i.e., coming into the rehearsal space in a disorderly manner.

7. Allow these young, eager critical thinkers time to discuss significant theological issues raised in anthem texts. Remain in control: decide in advance how long you'll let dialogue continue; ask the choristers to raise hands in order to speak; remind them that the entire group listens to each speaker's ideas.

8. This age group particularly enjoys events away from the regular rehearsal/ worship site. Exchanges and collaborations with other middle school choirs should occur each year, or perhaps in alternation with a service-oriented project.

9. Phone call follow ups are especially important at this age in the case of absences or behavior problems. Out of respect for the young person, try to deal directly with him/her on issues which need resolution, but do not hesitate to go to the parents if this has failed, or as a means of follow up.

Parents of this age group need to be informed of their child's general progress, successes and any problems, just as in the younger years.

10. Choosing section leaders can be a way to honor the attitudes, talents and seniority of model choristers. Their job is to listen within their section to "their singers," model tone and demonstrate as needed, keep track of any missed notes, etc. Exceptional choristers who are not exceptional musicians can be honored too, by serving as librarians, role takers, robe monitors, phone chain starters, etc.

Formal Reasoning Meets the Adolescent Aesthete

The single, major focus for middle school students is their physical growth and their emotions. This often manifests itself in strongly held opinions about a variety of issues: from ethical questions to fashion, from theology to rock stars. Some students will be extremely vocal, while others quietly form their own thoughts and assess those of others, especially their peers. Capitalize on and celebrate this unique point in life. Most assuredly, it will never again be repeated in quite the same way!

Here is a group activity which junior highs enjoy. To do it, the choristers need to be familiar with and know how to use the various indexes common in hymnals. Instructions should be given to the entire group, then divide into smaller groups, with at least one pianist (a student or an advisor) in each group.

1. Select, in advance, hymn texts which are not familiar.[20] Reproduce them in some way for the choir.
2. After dividing up, each small group refers to the metrical indication given for the text or texts they choose, or figures it out if not given.
3. Using the metrical index in the back of the hymnal, the group looks up tunes in that meter, finds them in the hymnal and sings through all or some of the them depending upon the number of choices. The idea is to try them out with the new text and make aesthetic decisions about their appropriateness for that particular text. (Put a time limit on this segment.)
4. As a group, they decide on the best (and worst?) "marriage" of tune for their text, and, prepare to defend their point of view.
5. The final assignment is to sing their choices for the full group.

When used on a retreat, the results of this search could be incorporated into a closing vesper service.

A simpler way to proceed with the above activity would be to use familiar texts with a familiar tune other than the one it is usually sung to. For example, a group of junior highs married the text *Amazing Grace* with the tune *Antioch* (commonly sung as *Joy To the World*). With great hilarity they sang, but after some discussion decided that the joyful tune actually provided them with a new way of thinking about those profound words, "was blind but now I see."

It is "the job" of this age group to question and to turn away from traditional adult standards. Many of these young people are extremely argumentative, just for the sake of being argumentative! Many are having strained relationships with their parents. Most of them are worried about how their peers, of both sexes, perceive and accept them. Junior highs need to feel successful as young adults and will shudder at the thought of doing anything "babyish," even though they need T.L.C. as much as they ever did. Adolescent bravado is a common masquerade for the insecurities they all feel.

It is tempting sometimes to simply be a "pal." Some aspects of this style will work well, but the truly effective director of middle schoolers will remember to serve them as an adult. Try to enlist the aid of "twenty-something" supporters to help out with dinners, trips, and other activities, in addition to, and sometimes in place of, parents. Work closely with other junior high program leaders to co-ordinate events both in terms of schedule and content.

The Senior High School Choir

The Maturing Voice

In the early years of high school, both boys and girls will be placed in sections depending more upon range considerations than timbre of voice. By the junior year, placement will begin to be more like it is with adults, assessing the weight and quality of the voice, the most comfortable range, etc., in order to place the young singer in the *probable* correct section.

Statistically, there are fewer alto and tenor voices to begin with. Some girls, new to the choir, will insist they are altos. This is because the have not yet found their singing voices, and therefore, "can't sing high." Work with these young women on yawn-sigh and siren for this technique works as well with this age as with little children learning to find the singing voice. Additionally, place some of the sopranos in the alto section on a rotating basis. Working with the lower range in this way can help build the upper and middle voice. And, of course, learning to sing an inner part is an important aspect of choral training.

Do not place girls on the tenor part, at least not permanently. For a phrase or two, there will be no problem, especially if the part is not too low. If there are no tenors among the boys, choose SAB music.

With teen voices especially, the conductor must remember that the voice can tire readily, especially if posture is poor, or the young people are exhausted, as is often the case. Take care not to demand loud volume or high tessitura too early in the rehearsal or too often.

Non-vocal Considerations

Although somewhat self-absorbed over worries of acceptance by peers, many senior high students will have moved beyond the awkwardness of the middle school years into articulate young adults. They are a good deal more pressured than their younger counterparts, especially as they enter the junior year and face decisions about college and/or a job. They are capable of thinking on many levels. Generally there is less need to prove independent thought than when they were a few years younger. For this reason, rehearsals and projects which respect and encourage these qualities of evolving maturity are effective with senior highs.

Following is a service of worship conceived, written and lead by a group of senior high school students in consultation with the choir director and the youth minister. All but three of the senior highs involved in this particular group are members of the choir (and several of the choir members do not participate in the fellowship group). It was important to plan the service so that choir members could both sing *and* participate in such other ways as preaching or reading scripture. All of the components of the worship service could be handled by the young people, with attentive and sensitive adult guidance, depending upon the skills available in the particular group of senior highs. The possibility of incorporating a student pianist or organist, a student conductor, audio supervisor, as well as student ushers, greeters, readers and even preachers should not be overlooked.

As they plan, the senior highs may need to be reminded that worship is not an appropriate forum for getting on a "soap box," or for any agenda other than worshipping God. Worship leaders strive to become vessels through which the spirit can move—using scripture to *proclaim* the good news, *explicate* it through speech, song and other art forms, so that those who experience it will be moved to *apply* the good news to their lives.

Weeks of meticulous preparation go into a successful "Youth Sunday" service, taking up not only part of the weekly choir rehearsal but some of the fellowship time and/or church school class as well. If student conductors are used, weekly rehearsals and private coaching sessions must be planned, just as student preachers will have private sessions with the pastor. Such an endeavor is well worth the effort, and components of the resulting "product" might be considered the basis for a choir tour. *(Further discussion on planning worship in general may be found in Chapter 8. Appendix 5 contains suggestions for seven other worship services involving children and youth choirs.)*

ORDER OF WORSHIP

Fourth Sunday of Easter

Prelude and Silent Meditation
Concerto #1   J.S. Bach
(student violinist)

Introit   Cantate Domino[21]   Rupert Lang
> *Praise the Lord! Sing to the Lord a new song; His praise in the assembly of the faithful. Let Israel be glad in its maker; let the children of Zion rejoice in their King.* (Ps. 147: 1-2)
(Middle School and High School Choirs)
(tenors/basses double alto line down one octave)

Call to Worship   (Student leader)
> Leader: Praise the Lord! How good it is to sing praises to our God:
> People: The Lord builds up Jerusalem; and gathers the outcasts of Israel.
> Leader: The Lord heals the brokenhearted, and binds up their wounds.
> People: Sing to the Lord with thanksgiving. Praise the Lord!

Hymn   Sing Praise to God Who Reigns Above   MIT FREUDEN ZART

Prayer of Confession   (Student leader)
> Dear Lord we turn to you, our refuge and strength, for you are our very present help in time of trouble. We have beheld and admired your works, yet we have failed to be good stewards of all that you have entrusted to us. How often you have broken the bows and shattered the spears of war, yet we have not learned to walk the way of peace. You are always with us, yet we act as if our ways are hidden from you. Forgive us, we pray, and help us to be still and know that you are God; through Jesus Christ our Lord. Amen.

Choral Response   O Still Small Voice of Calm   Irish Melody: Turtle Dove
arr. Austin Lovelace

*Dear God, Creator of us all,[22] forgive our foolish ways. Reclothe us in
our rightful mind, in purer lives Thy service find, in deeper reverence,
praise. Breathe through the heats of our desire Thy coolness and Thy
balm; Let sense be dumb, let flesh retire; speak through the earthquake,
wind and fire, O still small voice of calm.* (text: John Greenleaf
Whittier, alt.)

(Senior High Choir)

Promise of the Gospel
Congregational Response   GLORIA PATRI

Sacrament of Baptism   (The child of a couple who serve as senior
high advisers)

Concerns of the Church   (Two student leaders)

Prayer for Illumination   (Student leader)
May the seed of your Word find good soil in us, O God. Let not your
truth be choked by competing concerns or swept away by floods of indif-
ference. We want to hear your Word and live it in such a way that those
who seek and hope in you will be led by our life and witness; through
Jesus Christ our Lord. Amen.

Old Testament Lesson Psalm 46   (Read by student)

Anthem   Serenity   Charles Ives
*O Sabbath rest of Galilee, O calm of hills above, where Jesus knelt to
share with thee the silence of Eternity, interpreted by love. Drop thy still
dews of quietness till all our strivings cease. Take from our souls the
strain and stress and let our ordered lives confess the beauty of thy
peace.* (text: John Greenleaf Whittier)

(Small ensemble of girls)

Gospel Lesson   Luke 12:22-31; 35-37 (p. 517, NRSV)
(Read by student)

Sermon   Three (six to eight) minute homilies written and preached by students

Hymn   If Thou But Trust in God to Guide Thee   NEUMARK

Offering
Offertory   Trio Sonata Op. 3, No. 2   Archangelo Corelli

Adagio

Allegro

(Played by student flutist, violinist, cellist, and pianist)

Doxology   LASST UNS ERFREUEN
   Praise God from whom all blessings flow,
   Praise God all creatures here below, Alleluia, Alleluia.
   Praise God above ye heavenly host,
   Praise Father, Son and Holy Ghost.
   Alleluia, Alleluia, Alleluia, Alleluia, Alleluia.

Affirmation of Faith   Apostles' Creed
                                                             Student leader

The Prayers   (Two student leaders)

   Leader: The Lord be with you.
   People: And with your spirit.
   Leader: Let us pray. O Lord, show Thy mercy upon us,
   People: And grant us Thy salvation.
   Leader: O God, make clean our hearts within us,
   People: And take not Thy holy Spirit from us.
   Leader: *The prayers, concluding with the Lord's Prayer.*

Hymn   A Mighty Fortress is Our God   EIN FESTE BURG

Benediction   Lead by Minister for Youth
Choral Response   Keep Your Lamps[23]   Spiritual, arr. André Thomas
   Keep your lamps trimmed and burning, the time is drawing nigh. Chil-
   dren don't get weary, the time is drawing nigh. Christian journey soon
   be over, the time is drawing nigh.
   (Senior High Choir, student conductor, student liturgical dancer, accompanied by
                              conga drums)

Postlude   Toccata   Leon Boellmann
   (Played by the church organist so that the youth could gather to greet people.)

Endnotes

[1]   These melodies might be used:

Walk

Gallop

March

Skip

Giant-step

(Note that skipping is a more advanced locomotor skill than gallop, even though the rhythm is the same. Many children do not master skipping until early elementary school as it requires a more sophisticated switching of the brain's hemispheres than does the gallop. Likewise, giant-step requires an ability to balance which may be beyond pre-schoolers.)

[2]   Numerous ideas for this type of activity may be found in Elsa Findlay's book on Dalcroze Eurhythmics entitled *Rhythm and Movement*. See bibliography.

[3]   See Appendix 1 for a chart of the hand signals, developed by John Curwin and popularized by Kodály music educators.

[4]   Many resources exist which are based on German composer Carl Orff's *Schulwerk* (his "opus for the school"). For further information, the reader is directed to the bibliography.

[5]   The case is often made that games of this type are more likely to be played by girls than by boys, and, that this may partly be the reason that so often girls are ahead of boys in their rhythmic development. It is also interesting to speculate how much if any of this oral and physical tradition will be neglected in the age of TV, video and computer games.

[6]   One of the first and still among the best collections of rhythmic speech chants for use in the church is by the late Betty Ann Ramseth, *That I May Speak*, published by Augsburg.

[7]   An ostinato is a pattern which repeats. Ostinati may be rhythmic or pitched (or even visual—a striped shirt, a pattern in the wall paper). Point out that ostinati we hear may also be written down in music notation, traditional or non-traditional.

[8]   Dr. Dee Joy Coulter's article *The Brain's Timetable for Musical Growth*, printed in Orff ReEchoes, Book II, published by the American Orff-Schulwerk Association, 1985, is most enlightening and highly recommended.

[9]   The distinction serves two purposes: 1) using the smaller muscles and more limited range of motion is more akin to the action of playing tuned and untuned percussion instruments, for which this can be practice; 2) this way of clapping is simply more musical, pulling the sound out of the hand, not pounding it in.

[10]   Children in kindergarten and older, will eagerly welcome a sports analogy of training the proper muscles to be used for the athletic event known as singing. An oversimplified but accurate explanation follows: The voice box contains two sets of muscles both of which can produce sound by rubbing against each other. One set is short and thick, the other set, long and thin. We use the short muscles (called *external thyroarytenoid*) when we speak and yell but since they cannot move quickly, they cannot make high sounds. But those amazing long muscles (the *vocalis*, or, *internal thyroarytenoid)* can make both low and high pitches. It is these which are best used for singing. To demonstrate, try an exercise which contrasts the two sets of muscles; making a fist of each hand, push downward at sides of legs while voicing a low and staccato "huh" for each push, then contrast that gesture and sound

with one which has open hands above heads, voicing a legato and high "whoo." Demonstrate a gesture pattern using both the low and high positions (perhaps in a familiar rhythm such as "ta ta ti-ti ta") but without the voice. Ask the children to both gesture and voice what was shown. The children can then take turns leading a pattern for the group to interpret.

[11] I am grateful to Helen Kemp for insight into this and many other areas.

[12] Defined for our purposes as "auditory" and "kinesthetic" perception. Faulty auditory perception has nothing to do with hearing impairment. It is a missing link between how a sound is heard and how it gets processed in the brain. Likewise, faulty kinesthetic perception (or muscle sense) in the larynx will make it difficult for the chorister to sing a specific pitch, even though the ear may perceive it accurately and the vocal tract is capable of making the sounds. The problem comes in producing it consciously, on demand. If *faulty production* has been ruled out, people who still cannot match pitch probably have to some degree, *faulty perception* in one or both of these modes.

[13] Try using a hose (1½"—2" diameter). One end goes from the child's ear and the other alternates between the director's voice (held about 1" from the mouth) and the chorister's. This focuses attention on the pitch and enables the child to hear his/her own voice *with* the others—a necessary step to singing in unison.

[14] Pentatonic melodies are those which omit the semi-tones fa and ti. The tonal center may be on any of the remaining pitches. In Western music these are usually do and la: Do Re Mi So La (Do) and La Do Re Mi Sol (La).

[15] Two fine collections have been compiled by Helen and John Kemp and are listed in the bibliography.

[16] Body percussion, or sound gestures, are the terms used in Orff-Schulwerk to designate the use of on-the-spot action with hands, legs and feet. This particular activity uses snapping (done at ear level), clapping (chest level), patschen (patting thighs), and stamping. Untuned percussion should be assigned to each gesture, trying to match timbre: resonant metalics (triangle, finger cymbals) for snapping, woods (claves, woodblock, sticks) for clapping, shakers (maracas, tambourines) for patschen, and skins (drums) for stamping.

[17] Some directors begin with sol—mi and add la next. I prefer to begin with do, re, mi on a starting pitch of G.

[18] *Children of the Covenant*, text by Eric D. Johnson, music by Sue Ellen Page. Choristers Guild CGA-495. This lesson plan first appeared in the Choristers Guild LETTERS and is used here by permission.

[19] Two excellent resources on the changing voice are listed in the bibliography. See Cooksey, J.M., and Gackle, M.L.

[20] Although many of his texts are well known, two fine resources in this regard are: *The Hymns and Ballads of Fred Pratt Green*, and, *Later Hymns and Ballads of Fred Pratt Green*, Hope Publishing Company, Carol Stream, Illinois. 1982 and 1989.

[21] All choral repertoire used in the service is listed with publisher and octavo numbers in the Appendices under Exemplary Anthems.

[22] Another inclusive alteration is "embracing humankind."

[23] As the song ended, the dancer lead the choir, still singing, down the aisles and out to the steps of the church. There they formed two lines and greeted the congregation.

Chapter 5

DEVELOPING
A BEAUTIFUL SOUND:
Part 1 Tone Production

*"A children's choir reflects the director's conception, or lack of concep-
tion, of tone. If the director knows what kind of tone he wants to hear, and
knows how to deal with children, there is no excuse for uninteresting, much
less offensive tone." (p. 20)*

*"Whatever the degree of difficulty, the music must be worth the effort,
worthy of a place in the library of a child's memory." (p. 53)*

*"If we expect the children to follow our conducting, we should in all
courtesy make our conducting correspond somewhat to the vocal practices we are trying to instill." (p. 44)*

There are three parts to the question of how to develop beautiful singing in the
children's choir: *tone production, repertoire choices* and *conducting technique*. The
director will need to work at all three disciplines in order to bring about the choir's
maximum potential. The next three chapters address each area singly, while recogniz-
ing that these areas are vitally connected, so much so that a completely separate
discussion of each is not possible.

*"Good tone cannot be achieved unless we know what we mean by good
tone. Good group tone is never an accident; it is the result of careful
cultivation." (p. 29)*

In 1948 when Ruth Krehbiel Jacobs wrote *The Successful Children's Choir*, she
opened her chapter *Vocal Training for the Children's Choir* with these lamentable
words: "Sources of information on the vocal training of children are limited indeed."
Due in large measure to Mrs. Jacobs' efforts, this is, happily, no longer the case. The
bibliography of the current volume attests to the many resources available to the
children's choir director today. These resources are not only in print, but in audio and
video form as well. Furthermore, the growth of the children's choir movement in the
church and in schools and communities throughout the world, the recordings and
concert tours undertaken by those fine choirs, give every teacher with any interest the
opportunity to hear, and compare, choral tone. No doubt Mrs. Jacobs would be pleased
to observe that finding and developing the child's true singing voice is no longer an
underground movement.

But there is still a long way to go. Although steadily improving, many college
teacher training programs are ineffective in teaching *how* one actually goes about

developing fine singing tone in children. The result is a large percentage of public school music teachers and choir directors who may have a concept, but lack the skills to develop it with their choristers.

Pop and music from various cultural traditions may contribute to a misguided conception of choral tone among the general population.[1] Factoring outside pressures into their own inability to get a full, soaring sound, a director may resort to having the children use a shouting tone when criticized with the words, "but we can't hear them."

Any attempt at complete discussion of tone must contain not only information for the eye, but also for the ear. And, as Ruth Jacobs pointed out, unless the director has an internal concept of desired tone, the result will never be satisfactory, no matter how fine the literature taught or how skilled the conductor may be. Therefore, the reader unsure of the sound of fine choral tone, is encouraged to listen critically to concerts and recordings of exemplary children's choirs, those grouped by gender as well as choirs made up of both boys and girls.

"There are two characteristics of good choral tone generally conspicuous by their absence in children's choirs. The first is vitality. Spineless singing interests no one. We have been told so often not to push children's voices that we have fallen into the opposite evil of making their singing devitalized....It takes energy to do things worth while, and it takes energy to produce interesting tone....Virility alone, however, will not produce good tone. Yelling is extremely virile, but far from pleasant. Coupled with virile projection of tone, there must be a uniform conception of tone." (p. 29)

Recreational Singing vs. Choral Singing

We must instill in the children (at least as much by example as with words) the idea that the tone used for *recreational singing* is different than that used for *choral singing*. Often, we must help the congregation to understand and accept this difference. In places where "Sing LOUDER!!" has been the rule, the process of change to the true singing voice may be lengthy. It is best to begin a children's choir in the first place with the sound distinctive to *choral* singing.

When we are gathered around a campfire singing *Kumbaya* or riding on a bus belting out *100 Bottles of Beer on the Wall*, we are involved in informal music gatherings with no performance goal in mind. We enjoy ourselves, we relax, we often have conversations while others sing. This is recreational singing, a rich tradition in every culture the world over. There is absolutely nothing wrong with it, unless it is confused with choral singing. When it is, it takes its form in one of two ways: the "spineless" tone or "yelling" described in the quote above.

Belting and Undersinging

The most egregious misuse of vocal tone is that of "belting," essentially, shouting or yelling the notes. While this may be appropriate on the Broadway stage or in popular music, it is not stylistically or acoustically suited to most choral singing. The possible exception is certain songs from cultural backgrounds which would originally have been sung in this style. This use of belting in the choral setting must be done with great care and only on occasion with experienced voices, since permanent damage in the form of vocal nodes can result if used excessively. Allowing the belting to continue higher than third space C is risky business in any case.

Belting is a common reason for chronically flat choral singing. And, since the belt cannot be carried very high, a child who has not discovered the true singing voice may simply stop singing once the notes reach an area higher than the shouting range, insisting "I can't sing that high." Using this faulty production, they are, of course, correct.

A less egregious, often unnoted, and very common misuse of vocal tone is that of undersinging, or singing "off the core." "Spineless" singing is how Ruth Jacobs defined it. In the many children's choirs which sing this way, there is certainly no trace of shouting or belting, but there is also not enough energy and support given to the exhalation of the air. The inhalation may have been taken correctly, but *the air is used inefficiently once the exhalation begins.* This style of singing can also result in intonation problems, both flat and sharp, since there is little connection of the tone to its support system.

Unconscious Assimilation of Choral Tone

In many ways the remedies for these two very different sounds are virtually identical. The single, most effective means by which a child will develop a beautiful singing tone is to hear, especially at an early age, frequent examples of it and then be given guided experiences in imitating the example. As discussed previously, the ears of children in the pre-school years are particularly primed for learning the nuance of language; thus, the capacity will never be greater for hearing, retaining and eventually repeating the subtleties of well produced vocal tone. It follows then that one of the best things we can do for the tone of our children's choirs is to get the desired sound "into the ears" of our youngest children. These children may not yet even be choristers!

More than likely, the typical, daily auditory environment is not one which is concerned with the child's proper vocal technique. The opposite production is more likely to be what children will hear on audio and video recordings, on television and from nursery school teachers and day care providers. We need a powerful antidote!

Find ways for both the young children as well as their parents to have regular exposure to the true singing voice. This will instill in them, unconsciously, the sound of beautiful choral singing. Consider using the baptism tapes discussed in the chapter on recruitment.

Posture for Choral Tone

A second common remedy for both types of faulty production is that of correcting posture errors. In a day before television and video games, Ruth Jacobs noted that

> *"Children are frequently permitted to stand and sit in spineless attitudes that are the deadly foe of tone production. The director who trains his children to carry themselves correctly will have given them valuable training even if they never produced a note of music. The first essential of health as well as of singing is proper posture; so find means of making your choir posture-conscious and posture-proud." (p. 27)*

In the pre-school and primary years, when children are so eager to please, the model of the director simply standing and conducting with good posture may be enough. Verbal suggestions such as imagining a balloon attached to the crown of the head (not the forehead!), or walking like kings and queens may be a way to create a memorable experience for the child while striving for good posture habits.

"You must have a definite idea of what you mean by good posture. To tell them to keep the chest up or the stomach in is not enough. Good posture is the proper coordination of the whole body." (p. 28)

In the case of older choristers, try this posture check:

1. Place the feet so that the heels are about six inches apart. One foot may naturally be slightly in front of the other. The toes should be in a normal stance, not straight ahead, nor turned excessively out. (Once the feet are in position, the head and eyes should face directly forward and not look down to check what the body is doing. This would throw off the posture you are trying to achieve.)

2. Lean slowly forward on the balls of the feet and then slowly backwards toward the heels, stopping each time before balance is lost. Now, find the mid-point between the heels and the balls of the feet and settle there.

3. Line up the hips directly over the ankles. (Remember not to look down.) This action automatically causes the knees to flex ("soften the knees" as the aerobic coaches say) to prevent locking them. Locked knees cause a curve in the small of the back.

4. Proceed upward in this mental check, lining up the shoulders directly over the hips.

5. Now to the head. Help the choir to discover that the spine does not stop at the base of the head, but rather reaches up to the point where a rod would be, if it were placed in one ear, through the head, and out the other ear. The long spine, which starts at the coccyx bone and travels all the way up through the neck and into the head, should feel very long.[2]

6. Ask the choir to move the chin slowly toward the chest, noting that the neck vertebrae are now separated. Slowly return the head to its forward position while keeping the sensation of the separated vertebrae.

7. Go through the same check in a seated position, back away from the chair, both feet flat on the floor as though standing.

A posture check can be done within one minute near the beginning of each weekly rehearsal. It provides a clear and consistent reminder of what is necessary before good singing can happen. Especially while the concept of the "singer's posture" is being taught, posture checks should be practiced regularly.

Connecting the subject of posture to sports is a visceral experience for the children. "What would happen if you stood like this (slumped and lazy) while up to bat? Or when going to kick the soccer ball or swing at the hockey puck? What do you look like when you shoot a basket or prepare for a dive?" Have the children demonstrate proper posture for each of these actions and any they suggest, then follow with a little pep talk that gets right to the point: "Singing is an athletic event too. You are all team mates. How well you hold your body determines how well you get the job done. If even one person has poor posture, the whole team is weakened. It is as simple as that!"

Another strong connection for pre-school and early elementary age children is thinking of the body as a musical instrument. Ask the children to demonstrate proper posture for holding a violin, for example. What if the violin was held over the head instead of under the chin? Or the trumpet under the chin instead of at the mouth? The pep talk continues: "If the instrument isn't held properly, it just can't do the job well. It is no different for singing. Your body is your instrument and you must hold it properly to allow it to do its job well."

Breathing for Choral Tone

"The second habit to establish (after posture) is correct breathing."
(p. 28)

The singer's breath is felt low and very wide around the rib cage. Again, in the case of younger choristers, more is "caught than taught" and the less said technically, the better. If the teacher conducts with an inviting, open, and supportive gesture, and models singing tone with good breathing technique, all alert singers, especially the youngest ones, will respond. For older choristers and for any who have poor breathing technique, try the following exercise as suggested by Ruth Jacobs:

1. *Standing tall, with hands on lower ribs (not hips, or waist) inhale slowly through nose and mouth, the lower ribs expanding. Exhale slowly. Make the exercises rhythmic; four counts for inhalation and four for exhalation.*
2. *Again slowly inhaling and expanding, let the breath out all at once, but without allowing the chest to fall.*
3. *Inhale and expand slowly; exhale slowly on a light "oo."*

Four precautions must be carefully observed in all breathing exercises.

1. *Easy, coordinated posture must be maintained.*
2. *Inhalation should never be noisy.*
3. *The chest must not sink on exhalation.*
4. *With each inhalation there should be an expansion of the lower ribs."*
(pp. 28-29)

This establishes of course, diaphragmatic breathing. The diaphragm, in its relaxed position, is a dome-shaped muscle which lies horizontally at the floor of the rib cage. It divides the trunk into two parts: the lungs and heart above, and everything else beneath it. When the lungs fill, the diaphragm flattens into its taut position to allow more room for the air taken in. Because the diaphragm is attached at its circumference to the lowest ribs, the intercostal muscles (muscles between the ribs) expand as well. Since the diaphragm always flattens during inhalation, the body organs beneath it expand outward, making the lower abdomen appear fuller. This is why singers are well advised to eat lightly before a concert. "The body simply cannot be full of food and full of air at the same time." [3]

At the exhalation, the muscles of the abdominal wall take over, contracting to push the air up and out. The vocal cords vibrate as the air passes through the larynx, past the pharynx and out of the body through the mouth. It is this link up, or the lack thereof, of the air with the support system of the abdominal muscles which determines whether or not the tone will be full of energy or "spineless."

If singers have difficulty with breathing, it is more likely that it is with the exhalation than with the inhalation. Getting the air into the body using diaphragmatic and intercostal inhalation is relatively simple to achieve. Connecting the tone to a supported column of air is the job of the exhalation, and may require more practice. (Note the exercise found on pages 49-50.)

A technique used for decades in private voice studios involves the student, lying down, with a large book balanced on the lower abdomen. The singer relaxes as though going to sleep. Once relaxed, note that the book rises on the inhalation and lowers as the air is exhaled. The next step is to achieve this in a loosely set rhythm, the inhalation taking less time than the exhalation. Begin to focus the action even more, consciously using the abdominal muscles. Work toward: exhalation on counts 1, 2, 3, 4, 5, 6, 7 and inhalation on beat 8. (Beat = 72-80).

The next step is to sing "doo" on the seven beat exhalation, first lying down, then repeating the whole process standing up. (Start the pitch at mid-range, perhaps G#.) This exercise is enjoyed by children. Divide the choir into groups of two or three with the task of monitoring each other. Hymnals are the perfect size books.

In all beautiful tone production, active support is the key. Lifting a heavy object or clapping the hands together vigorously and rhythmically while singing are both tried and true paths to connect support system to the tone.

Never assume that once correct breathing is achieved, it is a permanent skill. The singers' breathing technique must be monitored carefully, particularly over the first months of each choir season, until it becomes unconscious. Make regular checks of the choristers, lest bad habits develop unknowingly. A good way to monitor the singers is to use a vocal warm up which visually confirms the proper use of inhalation and exhalation. Singers stand as described earlier. Using unvoiced consonants, the proper abdominal support is noted by the slight response of the hand placed on the abdomen to reflect its action as the consonants are produced.

t,   k,   p

fig. 1

Similarly, use the consonant blend "ch" or "sh" in the same way, but also sustaining it on a single breath, finishing with "k." Remind the singers to keep the chest high and the jaw loose. Have them touch their fingers to the tip of the sternum, the inverted V shape where the two sides of the rib cage join, to note how it feels when relaxed and when taut. A cough, lifting a heavy object or hearty laughter will cause it to tighten. It must be in this firm state when singing, for this is part of the system of support the muscles of the abdominal wall provide for the breath.

Vowels for Choral Tone

Pure, spinning tone produced by young people with good posture and adequate breath support is no doubt the first hallmark cited by fans of fine children's choirs. A very close second is *vowel uniformity*. In countries such as England, where cathedral choirs are a centuries old tradition, or in Iceland, where the Icelandic language is spoken with virtually no regional accents, the question of uniform vowels is hardly if ever an issue. In places like North America, where accents are many and varied even among specific regions, uniform vowel color is far more difficult to achieve.

Too often opportunities for sublime beauty are lost because of the director's careless attention to how vowels are shaped and matched. Poor vowel color and sloppy handling of diphthongs and triphthongs[4] has become a sort of 'trademark' of the amateur choir, in which *pronunciation for recreational singing is carried over into choral singing.* This may occur even when the tone quality is quite good. There are many popular recordings for children done this way, using a light singing tone, but with inattention to vowel color and inattention to supported sound. These recordings may do more damage to the concept of fine choral singing than belting ever did, since "recreational vowels" are less blatant in their transgression.

Some choirs, particularly in the United States, in an effort to sound edified, mispronounce difficult vowels, falling back on [a] (ah). This artificially over-corrects such problem vowels as [ae] for example, in the word "glad." Pronouncing "glad" as "glahd" only substitutes one problem for another. In the same vein, some American choirs routinely sing with a British accent as a means of managing problem vowels. This again is an unnecessarily artificial tactic. Here are some techniques to help American children sing their language beautifully, without the wide, flat, nasal or "squished" vowel sounds so often found in the United States, and, without faking an accent not their own.

The Pear Shaped Tone

Vowels for choral singing, in order to be fully resonant, all need to have the space of [a] (as in "hot") and the focus of [u] (as in "shoe"). These two vowels are on opposite ends of the vowel spectrum, [a] being open and [u] being closed. Go through the various vowels[5] saying each three ways:

1.   Artificially pharyngeal, using only space [a] and no forward focus.
2.   Artificially forward focus [u], with insufficient space in the mouth.
3.   The correct balance between space in the mouth [a] and forward focus [u].

The famous "pear shaped tone" concept is not difficult to achieve with children. It has everything to do with vowel shape as well as maximizing space for tonal resonance. Draw a pear lying on its side. Imagine the pear in your mouth, fat-end first (fig.2). Model for the children a phrase from an anthem, singing it first with the "pear shape," then with the pear "squished." Ask them to repeat it. Try hanging a drawing of a pear from the music stand. When approaching a hazardous vowel, simply point to the drawing—no need to discuss it further. The image of a hot light bulb works equally well.

fig. 2

North and South, Not East and West

A classic example among the arsenal of "tricks" for children's choir directors originated by Helen Kemp is that of a rubber band held by the director in front of the mouth. When stretched north and south, rather than east and west, vowels "stand up" in the mouth without resorting to overdone, artificial pronunciations. Choirs should sing vowels in both ways so as to sensitize the ear and train the proper shape of the mouth.

The Fishmouth

Another technique for uniform vowels is developed from Frauke Haaseman's famous work with Group Vocal Techniques. Remind the choristers to sing with a "ROUND SOUND," using a slightly pursed "fishmouth."

fig. 3

Sprechstimme

20th century music has developed a technique termed "sprechstimme." It refers to a quality which is sung, yet is almost speech. Borrow this technique to train vowel uniformity. The choir "speak/sings" the text, not on exact pitches, but in rhythm using the rules of choral diction. i.e., tall vowels, quick consonants, omission of final "r's," etc.

Singing Only on Vowels

Singing phrases on the vowels [a] and/or [u] without consonants is a time-honored method of opening up the voice. Similarly, sing the phrase on the vowels (only) of the text; i.e., "Praise to the Lord the Almighty, the King of Creation" is sung:

[e] [u] [ə] [ɔ] [i] [a] [ai] [i] [ə] [i] [a] [i] [e]   [a]

Remind the singers to "put space above the sound." Show a gesture with the hand well above the head to re-inforce this concept visually.

Intonation

Tuneful singing is the product of good breath support and resonant tone quality, but vowels also play a major role in determining the choir's intonation. Any given pitch can actually change depending upon vowel color, especially if voice timbres are different. Therefore, non-uniform vowels fight each other and can cause tuning problems. The key to good intonation is "corporate listening"— listening not only by the conductor, but by every singer.

In the youngest choirs, intonation problems take the form of actual pitch-matching problems. From these earliest experiences, each chorister must be taught to *"listen louder than you sing."*[6] This is because human beings are essentially an egocentric species. We simply want to hear ourselves.

When a child does not match pitch, it is often because in unison singing, one cannot hear one's own voice while singing within the group. As one six year old said woefully, "My voice got lost!" She had echoed a phrase accurately when singing it alone, but unsuccessfully when singing with the other children. She "remedied" the situation by pitching the phrase lower than the rest of the choir, which solved the problem nicely, at least from the inexperienced child's point of view![7]

Youth and adults are generally much more sophisticated in their handling of the "my voice gets lost" feeling. The basic issue is the same however: we want to hear ourselves. In the case of upper elementary, youth and adult choirs, singers may unwittingly "duke it out" in an attempt for their own voice to be heard, one soprano (tenor, bass, or alto) battling another soprano (tenor, bass, or alto) for timbre territory. As one of them increases volume just a little bit, the other pumps it up a notch, which causes the first to "see your volume and raise you two" so to speak. The end result of course is a section that has poor blend, poor tone and is out of tune. There are several well known choral conductors (and no doubt hundreds of their protegees) who manage this problem by seating singers with similar timbres together. The strongest opposing timbres are likely to have different vowel colorations and are therefore seated as far apart within their section as possible. This makes it easier for the director to encourage a brighter vowel here, a darker vowel there, until finally, they blend. But no effort on the conductor's part will pay off unless each member of the choir is trained to "listen louder than they sing." Only then will they learn to savor the joy of feeling one's voice blend into the quantity and quality of sound unique to the choral experience.

Consonants

"Health, help, helm, held, all become uniformly hell with the omission of the last sound." (p. 35)

Assume for the moment that consistent work with posture, breathing and vowels has resulted in the "open throat" and "relaxed jaw and tongue" so necessary for good tone. The most soaring melody has been practiced on vowels and even the highest notes stayed open and free. Alas, it can't be sung consonant-free on Sunday morning! Every singer and conductor has lamented the problems which consonants can cause. They seem to get in the way of beautiful tone. Volumes have been written on managing that necessary evil: consonants.

LoRean Hodapp Powell trained four decades of young singers at Westminster Choir College. "Hodie" had a way of approaching consonants which made them a part of the line of the phrase, rather than interrupters of it. She told us again and again to "spin the consonants out," to love their sounds, to maximize their potential as aids to an artistic performance. Using this approach to consonants can help immensely in the training of children's voices. Let us examine how this can be done.

As in teaching concepts of breathing, posture and tone, the benefits of consonant awareness with singers at the early elementary grades are several. In particular, the youthful muscles of the articulators (tongue, lips) combined with the receptive ears of children enable them to quickly hear, adjust and produce the necessary "gymnastic" moves required to sing consonants clearly and easily. It is important to remember that singing is done on the vowels, but that the consonants make the sense. Think of consonants as an aid to lifting out the vowel. *Consonants help the vowels do their job.*

Knowledge and awareness of the basic groups of consonants is necessary for good diction to take place. Learning about them can also be fun for the children. Try this game with any choir, adapting the amount of material covered to the age group involved.

Have some or all of these consonants posted:

B D F G (hard, as in "good") H J K L M N P R S T V W Z ch

Note that not all of the consonants are listed. The ones omitted are those which actually use the sound of other consonants, i.e. the letter "c" is pronounced either as "k" or "s."

Go through the consonants asking the children to say the *sound* of the letter (not the name of it). They should say it precisely, and only when you point to it. (Insist upon this since it helps control potential chaos and it trains good choral attacks.) Help the choristers discover whether or not the consonant uses the "vibrator" (they should place their hands on the larynx) and thus is a *voiced* consonant (B D G J L M N R V W Z) or if it is *unvoiced* (F H K P S T ch). Is it *sustainable*? (F H L M N R S V Z) Or is the sound finished as soon as it is produced (*unsustainable*)? (B D G J K P T W ch) Help them see *partners* between voiced and unvoiced consonants: B/P, D/T, G/K, J/ch, V/F, Z/S. Which ones have *no partner*? (H L M N R W)

Now, make a group composition using consonants as the sounds (sometimes called "vocables"). Encourage the choir to use compositional principles such as imitation, variation and contrast; form (such as ABA or rondo); and to use dynamic markings and other illustrative musical terms, i.e. ritardando, rubato, fermata. Try repeat signs, first and second endings, etc. The compositions might also be done individually. Here is an example:

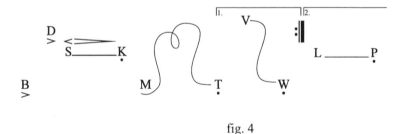

fig. 4

One of the happiest results of conscientious work with consonants is the way rhythmic precision is enhanced. The forward motion of the phrase is virtually guaranteed when consonants are articulated cleanly, quickly and thoughtfully.

Other Considerations in Developing Choral Tone
Relaxed Jaw and Flat Tongue

Many singers substitute tight jaw and tongue for what should be abdominal support. Often the position of the jaw is too narrow, that is to say, not enough space is given between the upper and lower molars and the tongue is bunched up, creating tension in the lips as well. Even on bright vowels such as [i], the jaw must remain lowered and the tongue relaxed as much as possible. Often the jaw is open wide enough, but is locked and tight. This happens sometimes as a result of our own instructions: Helen Kemp has pointed out that the traditional "three fingers width between the front teeth" can *set* the jaw with tension. The better suggestion is to focus on the molars, which are nearer the jaw. Have the children think of the bolt going through Frankenstein's jaw. Now loosen the bolt. What happens to the jaw? The tongue should parallel the jaw as much as possible.

Another way to explore jaw relaxation is to place the fingers at the corner of each jaw, then drop the jaw down and back until it seems to disappear into the neck. From this position, inhale, then "sigh" on the exhalation. Use the air efficiently (connecting abdominal support to the tone) while feeling the sensation of (the early stages of) a yawn. Combine this with a consonant which activates the abdominal wall such as ch or k:

ch   ch   chah (sigh)   OR   k   k   kah (sigh)

fig. 5

In the case of the tongue, practice tightening it then letting it relax, noting the sensation of each. No matter the vowel or consonant, the tongue must be more relaxed than tense and the lips in a slightly rounded neutral position.

The Yawn-sigh

William Vennard, in his ground breaking book *Singing: The Mechanism and the Technic*, coined the term "yawn-sigh." Used by studio teachers and conductors the world over, this time-honored warm-up reminds the singer to open the space while exhaling on a controlled breath. The sensation is that of the beginning of a yawn, and causes the jaw to drop, the tongue and lips to relax, and the *larynx to lower*, all desirable for beautiful tone. See also the exercise in fig. 5 above.

The Lowered Larynx

Margaret Harshaw, of the voice faculty at Indiana University, uses the following exercise to help the singer become aware of larynx position: place the hand on the larynx and swallow, noting that the larynx rises. The reverse will happen when beginning to yawn, the larynx lowers. She points out that during the course of a normal day, swallowing is likely to happen with much greater frequency than yawning, therefore, the larynx is unconsciously trained to rise more easily than to drop. A raised larynx is in an unhealthy position for singing. Singers can learn to use and control the sensation of the yawn and should practice it faithfully so that it can be recalled on demand.

Two More Warm-ups for Building Tone

1. Hum, molars apart. Hum a "sigh" up, down and around the full extension of the voice, singers working concurrently on whatever part of the range they particularly need to warm-up, breathing as individually needed. (The resulting sound effect is not unlike an orchestra warm-up.)

2. Sing the following, rising by half steps. (When articulating the L's, keep the front of the tongue on the gum bump just above the front teeth and the sides of the tongue touching the teeth, except for the back molars.) Correct any mispronunciation of the vowels, for example, the second syllable is "leh" not "laye":

ah - leh-loo - (ee)yah
[a] [ɛ] [u]   [i a]

Al - le - lu - ia,   Al - le - lu - ia.   *Continue up by half steps.*

Reinforce the Concept of Tone

To focus attention on developing vocal technique and pride in the current level of accomplishment, try the following exercise, adjusting the specific ages mentioned here to the age group of the particular choir: "Sing that phrase the way you would have when you were (four) years old... Now, sing it the way you would have when you were (ten...) Try it now, thinking of your own age... What will it sound like when you are twenty?!"

With the newly lowered male voice, reinforcing the concept of tone production will take on an additional dimension as the young man learns to identify the new sensations associated with becoming a baritone or tenor. In his work with boys this age, Michael Kemp has them place a hand on their chest as they sing. "Think of your voice box as being here." (He indicates the upper chest.) "Now sing 'ah.' Don't let your voice box get any higher than your hand."[8] Use resistance devices: "lifting" a piano, pushing against a wall, etc. The boys must learn to trust the new feeling in using their new, true singing voice, not the under produced "wimpy" sound so often heard in untrained voices. Women can approximate this technique in a limited way by singing in full "chest" voice on middle C and lower, but the best models will, of course, be male.

We move now to the area of repertoire, the second of three areas necessary for developing a beautiful sound with young choirs.

Endnotes

¹ Traditions from some cultures, notably African-American and Hispanic, use an historically established tone quality which is sometimes "borrowed" by Anglo congregations. When using this quality for the purpose of musical integrity towards the particular repertoire being sung, this may be considered appropriate. The focus of this discussion is on situations where this particular tone quality is substituted for more traditional tone due to the conductor's lack of training.

² A visual way to reinforce this concept is to take a piece of rope (¼" to ½" in diameter) cut the length of the spine. Wad up the rope so that it is crinkly. Now, holding one end in each hand, pull the hands apart vertically, until the rope is fully extended. An example of the fully lengthened spine is the goal. As the rope is drawn tautly, maximize the singing stance and ask the children to mirror this as well.

³ William Vennard, *Singing: The Mechanism and the Technic,* Revised Edition, (NY: Carl Fischer, Inc., 1967), 29

⁴ The problem of *diphthongs and triphthongs* is simple and will best be taught by example, with little explanation: sing on the sustained vowel as long as possible, placing the vanishing vowel just as the syllable ends, giving no more time to it than it takes to produce it. For example: in the phrase "right now", both words are diphthongs. The word "right" involves the vowels [a] (ah) and [i] (ee) and the word "now" involves the vowels [a] and [u] (oo as in "soon"). In both words, as in the case of most diphthongs, the first vowel is the sustained vowel. In words beginning with the letter "w", the vanishing vowel comes first and is always the vowel [u]. Go quickly through it to the sustained vowel, for example "with" = [u] to [I]. (Exceptions to this include some words beginning with "wh" as in "who".)

⁵ The vowels below are all of those sung in English, not including diphthongs and triphthongs which are combinations of these vowels. They are arranged from [a] the most neutral of all, to the highest tongue and widest lip position [i], sometimes called "bright vowels", then from [a] to the lowest tongue and most rounded lip position [u], sometimes called "dark vowels". Finally two more neutral sounds are given.

International Phonetic Alphabet (IPA) Sign		Keyword
neutral	[a]	father
to highest tongue,	[ae]	sat
widest lip position	[ε]	set
	[e]	say (without dipthong)
	[I]	sit
	[i]	see
neutral	[a]	father
to lowest tongue,	[ɔ]	saw
rounded lip position	[o]	open (without dipthong)
	[U]	foot
	[u]	soon

The schwa [ə] is the neutral, unstressed sound, as in sofa. The same sound has a different IPA character [ɜ] when used in stressed syllables, as in sir.

6   A phrase learned from Helen Kemp at a Choristers Guild Seminar in 1966.

7   For a more complete discussion of pitch problems, refer to Chapter 4, pages 42—43.

8   Here is an example. If the teacher is a man, demonstrate vocally. If a woman, play it on the piano, in combination with using "chest" voice.

(Up by 1/2 steps, gradually closing the [a] towards [U] ('foot').

Ah

Chapter 6

DEVELOPING A BEAUTIFUL SOUND: Part 2 Repertoire

"The building of a fine library of music is a continuous process. It is a process not only of acquiring but also of discarding, for choirs, like people, often outgrow earlier tastes." (p. 51)

When choosing repertoire, conductors of choirs in churches, schools and communities all evaluate such common criteria as range, tessitura, style, pedagogical opportunities, etc. Church musicians however, have another area to consider which is primary in its importance: it is the anthem's function in worship. We will deal at length with this important factor in Chapter 8, *The Choir in Worship*. It is mentioned at this point because this is a consideration that should affect all other decisions regarding repertoire. For now, let us examine those criteria which are universal to all directors who use the selection of repertoire as a means to building a beautiful sound.

Range, Tessitura and Intervalic Considerations

Choice of music has *everything* to do with vocal development. It is the primary means through which vocal goals are achieved. In every age group[1], the singing range and melodic challenges should be constantly expanding. The notes with which choristers come to us should not be the only ones they have when they finish a choir year! The accuracy of the ear should improve over the course of the year as well. Therefore, it is advisable to assess repertoire choices in an overall way, looking at the entire year, i.e., pieces chosen for the end of the choir year should reflect anticipated growth in the vocal tract as well as in choral technique.

Range ability of a given choir has to do both with age—the physiology of the body and vocal tract—and with choral experience. For the purpose of this section, recommendations are given by age group, using the premise that the majority of those choristers who begin as pre-schoolers will stay in the program and become experienced young singers by upper elementary school. It is therefore assumed that the reader will apply to a *beginning* group of upper elementary children, at least in part, the observations described here for a younger age choir. The first of the notated intervals in each group indicates the suggested span of usable notes in a particular *song*. The second interval indicates *tessitura*, the range in which most of the song should lay.

Pre-school

Children six years old and younger without vocal guidance will likely sing songs most easily in a range of about a fourth beginning on middle C or D. Begin to work

within this range but right away move an ocatave higher to
about C or D. This will become the natural placement of the
voice as the longer "head tone" muscles (or cords) of the larynx
gain control in equal measure to the shorter "speaking" muscles.
To begin with, melodies which move stepwise or in intervals of
a fourth or less are best, using the compass F to D. Bypass chromatic melodies. Avoid
pieces which begin on an ascending "sol-do," since it is likely that the (lower) first note
will be in the speaking range. For inexperienced singers, this could 'trap' them,
resulting in the entire song being belted. Many songs begin this way, so beware, until
a secure singing tone has been established.

Early Elementary

For children between six and eight years old, the singing range is larger,
depending a great deal on experience, from about middle C to the G an octave above.
Warm-ups can be taken as high and low as possible, but songs
should focus on the most usable (plus a bit of the nearly usable)
part of the voice. Intervals as wide as sixths, even an occasional
octave are workable, but continue to avoid chromatics. As with
pre-schoolers, be careful with phrases beginning below F,
making sure that the singing voice is being used and not the
speaking or yelling voice.

Upper Elementary

By upper elementary school (ages 10—12) children who have been singing for
several years should have no difficulty with a two octave range of A—A. It is, however,
wise with any age choir to choose anthems which are set in the
median range of the suggested compass, with only an occa-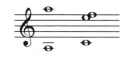
sional trip up or down to the outside notes. These children will
have a greatly increased control of their voices and for this
reason can handle octave leaps and chromatics more easily than
younger children.

In all of these age groups, sequence the choice of songs *so that the range expands
upward rather than downward*. This keeps the emphasis on the light, but supported
"flute-like" quality so sought after in children's choirs. Expanding upwards builds the
voice and discourages the heavy "belting" production so often used to obtain volume
at the sake of beautiful tone.

"Altos" in the Children's Choir

People who specialize in work with children's voices generally agree on the
matter of "altos": unless caused by damage to the vocal cords from chronic sinus drip,
nodes or polyps which render the upper range painful to use or unpleasant to hear, *there
are no true altos among elementary children*. Children are trebles. Some of these
trebles may have a naturally low speaking voice and can sing in the lower range easily.
This does not mean they are altos! It simply means that they are children who can (and
should) be encouraged to sing both high and low notes.

One boy with whom I have worked for many years has from his pre-school days,
spoken and sung naturally in quite a low range. There was never any huskiness in the
voice (which might indicate unhealthy vocal cords) nor was he suffering from "macho

syndrome," the need that some boys have to try to be pre-adolescent baritones. His upper notes were, however, somewhat difficult to control until age ten. Since he has an excellent ear, it might have been tempting to assume he was an "alto" and never work to build the rest of the voice.

Fortunately, that was not the approach taken and he now has, at age thirteen, a confident, "fully ripe" three octave range. What a shame it would have been to limit him to a traditional alto part throughout his childhood based on his limited range in pre-school and early elementary school and his good ear! Had that been the case, he might not have developed the powerful and beautiful upper extension he now has at the peak of his treble years. His control of a wide treble range will aid him as he begins the inevitable transition to "baritone land."[2]

Middle School

By middle school (ages 11—14), even with experienced singers who practice good technique, a few of the girls may feel more comfortable in the lower register, while many more will "bottom out" below middle D. This has more to do with their adolescent voice changes than with any assured prediction of the mature voice settling at alto or soprano. Meanwhile, the boys in this age group are all over the map. Some, like the thirteen year-old seventh grader mentioned above, will be able to sing any treble or tenor part, but others will be well into their voice change. This is no doubt the most challenging group for which to choose repertoire.

Many songs written specifically for middle school singers are in three parts, each with a very narrow range. Many have a part, ostensibly designed for the changing boy voice, which generally encompasses G—G. Interestingly, this is the section of the voice which is often "missing" in this age boy. Many can sing higher than G and lower than G, but the notes in between are extremely undependable and weak. Generally these G to G parts work well only for those boys who are still trebles but don't any longer want to "sing high," for social reasons, even though their best sounding notes may be in the upper range.

There are several ways to approach the placement of these young men. The first is to foster such a tradition and love of singing that every boy will want to sing wherever his voice sounds best, be that smack dab in the middle of the Treble I section or with the baritones. The second approach is to group the treble boys into a pseudo "tenor" section (using the approximate range G—G) and form a baritone section for those whose voices have truly lowered. In this approach, only girls sing treble.

At the beginning of the year, either of the above formats may have a non-existent baritone section, or, far worse, be populated by one lone member. By mid-spring, other voices will probably have begun the migration downward, but until then, this young man may do well to attend the senior high choir rehearsal as well as that of his own age group, if his social adjustment doesn't preclude such an idea. This is where a Youth Choir encompassing both junior and senior high school singers can be a real help.

No matter the format, sectional rehearsals are especially important in order to monitor individual vocal growth at this critical period of development. This is the church's future high school choir and the prime source for adult choir singers in just five to seven years!

In terms of actual selection of repertoire, the director must first decide how to group the singers available in this particular choir, *this particular year*. Theoretically, the assortment of potential voice types is the same for all middle school choirs, but since the voice types vary so much *numerically* within each individual choir, there are few foolproof repertoire choices. No matter the total number of singers, the number of changed voices, or the approach to handling unchanged boy voices, the following suggestions for choosing repertoire for this age group are generally helpful:

1.   Look for music which challenges the vocal ability of the girls and those boys who remain in the treble section: wide range, long phrases, soaring melody and interesting harmony lines. On the other hand, choosing songs which require long phrases in the upper range for new baritones is asking for trouble.

2.   Beware of part music limited in range to less than an octave, particularly for girls singing alto. Alto parts for girls (and unchanged boy voices) should travel *frequently* above third space B. When used exclusively, music which does not provide this extension for the "altos" in fact breeds a uniquely lackluster sound, common to this section, which usually carries through to the adult choir as well.

3.   Be ready to suggest individual note or phrase changes to accommodate singers whose range cannot handle what is on the printed page. Singers should have pencils ready to notate these customized editions. (Presenting a "doctored" copy via overhead transparency assists less skilled music readers in making these notations in their own score quickly and accurately.)

4.   Music which has an instrumental obligato playable by one or more of the choir's instrumentalists can be very beautiful and rewarding for the choristers involved. Likewise, consider using an instrument to support (double) a vocal part.

5.   For young baritones, the range C—A is nearly always safe. Above this, many boys will need to sing *falsetto* and many are able to do so depending upon where they are in their voice change.

6.   Open discussion of what is occurring is necessary to healthy choral growth. Reassure everyone that the cracks and gurgles they experience are all normal and, if they stick with it, that is if they *sing through the voice change* with guidance, their vocal development will be far easier on the other side of it.

7.   Continue to practice good vocal technique, be flexible in terms of part assignments and remind the singers that in time, the problem areas will become less so and the correct long term voice part more evident.

Senior High School

Many churches combine senior highs with junior highs to form a single youth choir. If that is the case, the comments in the section above (Middle School) remain accurate, but particular care must be taken to challenge, both vocally and musically, those senior high singers who are more advanced. In churches where children have come up through a graded program, a separate senior high choir is probably more desirable. It can and should be part of the social and spiritual pinnacle of a young person's childhood experiences in his/her church.

With this type of group, any accessible SATB literature is eagerly sung, especially music of the Renaissance, early Baroque and Classical periods, as well as 20th century music of various genres. High school students who have been brought up on fine choral literature as children will insist upon the best and will resist a steady diet of watered down, pop-like "youth anthems" so typical of church choirs. This goal may be lofty but it can be attained. Chapter 8 discusses this point from a theological perspective.

Watch out for tenor lines in which the tessitura lingers around or above middle E. Young tenors may actually be baritones "on the way down," and even in the case of true tenors (a rarer species than baritone) constant singing in the upper range will produce tension. With all singers, especially teenagers, guard against the high chin-low chest posture they observe from their popular music stars. If there is an overflow of sopranos, challenge them to sing the tenor line for a brief period when it "rides high" for the boys (leaving the altos on their own part). This is a good way to build the developing female voice.

This chapter has limited itself to those aspects of repertoire selection concerned with building tone. Chapter 8 contains other major considerations for the selection of repertoire particularly for choirs in the church. We move next to a third area of achieving a beautiful sound with the children's choir, that of conducting.

Endnotes

[1]   Here as elsewhere, overlapping ages are given for various grade levels. This reflects the wide range of ages in any single grade level in schools. Some parents choose to push ahead children with fall birthdays, some hold them back; other children are retained a grade level for developmental reasons. The choir director needs to be sensitive to this reality and not assume for example, that all second graders are seven years old. In general, grade in school, not age, should be the determining factor in choir placement, social and developmental factors taking precedence over vocal development.

[2]   A termed used by Harvey K. Smith, director of the Phoenix Boys Choir, for the changed boy voice. Young men seem to enjoy this expression and respond well to its use as a sign of their future as singers.

Chapter 7

DEVELOPING
A BEAUTIFUL SOUND:
Part 3 Conducting

*"No number is ready for performance until it satisfies the ears of the
director and the choir on each of the following points: breathing, rhythmic
flow, tone, diction. If these four factors are well established, the number
can be molded by sensitive conducting into a 'thing of beauty and a joy
forever.'" (p. 43)*

The Children's Choir Director: Conductor or Cheerleader?

In Chapter 2, the story was relayed of the gentleman who wondered why a person
with obvious conducting skills bothered to work with "kiddie choirs." His own lack
of knowledge not withstanding, there is, unfortunately, a long tradition of children's
choir directors who have caricatured this "standard": wrists and elbows flapping away,
heads pecking out a beat. While this may be an extreme description, there are in fact
many choir directors who may be fine teachers, even vocally secure, but who scarcely
know more about a four beat pattern than "floor-wall-wall-ceiling." Rebounds, attacks
and releases are unclear and feeble, or, on the other extreme, excessively vociferous.
In both cases, the directors usually sing along with the choir and would possibly argue
that if they did not, the choir would not be heard at all.

If repertoire is *skillfully chosen* and *well taught* with a *healthy singing technique*,
the director is three-quarters of the way to achieving optimum choral tone. But unless
the conducting is also of high quality, the tone, indeed every other aspect of the choral
experience, will never be what it might. Fortunately, more and more children's choir
directors are taking themselves seriously as conductors, realizing that people of all
ages and stages respond to clear, efficient, intentional gestures.

Acquiring an Image of Conducting

Just as a director needs a clear concept of vocal tone, so does s/he need an image
of what good conducting looks and feels like. Conducting, like voice, should be
studied.

Many colleges offer courses and short-term seminars in conducting during the
academic year as well as in summer session. Denominational and professional
conferences usually offer conducting workshops and seminars. Do not always opt for
the sessions specifically geared to children's choir directors. Much can be learned in
adult choir/conducting sessions which can and should be applied to work with children
and youth. On the evaluation and suggestion forms traditionally given out at these

conferences to aid in planning future events, request conducting seminars scheduled at a time which does not conflict with observing and attending children's choir sessions.

Whenever the opportunity presents itself, study other conductors. This could include the maestro of a major orchestra, live or on television, or the choir director down the street. The best conductors know that there is always more to see and observe. No good models around? One can learn at least as much from the negative habits of others as from scrutinizing the finest technique.

Ask questions of your observations. "How did he get that incredibly beautiful tone when his hand position resembled a claw? Was it the shape of his arms? The expression on his face? His rapport with the children? The concept and established tradition of tone within this choir?" Or, "How is so much happening when the conductor seems to be doing so little? What rehearsal techniques might have been employed to *train into* each singer such artistic nuance?" Alert observation of other conductors has always been and will continue to be one of the best teachers.

It is important for directors of volunteer choirs to remember that sometimes the finest choral groups have conductors whose gestures are not good models of choral technique. They obviously have many other finely developed skills or they would not be involved with these fine choirs. These ensembles do have, however, extraordinary singers who will sing well despite the gestures in front of them. Most of us do not have that luxury and must therefore use all of the forces at our command to help our choirs to sing well.

Excellent instructional videos on conducting technique are commercially available through such organizations as the musicians' groups of the various denominations, Choristers Guild, and the American Choral Director's Association. Owning these may be more reasonably done through a local chapter of a professional organization, rather than through individual purchase. These chapters often have video tape lending libraries. The national office of these organizations may have a rental program.

As one concept presented on the tape is mastered, watch the video again and again for something new to be gleaned which the mind was previously not ready to process. Take notes on the tape, then study a particular anthem looking for ways to incorporate the new or modified techniques.

Professionally produced instructional tapes are not the only means of using video technology in order to become a better conductor. In planning an assessment and possible overhaul of conducting skills, a great teacher can be found in the form of one's own video camera.

Tape the conducting from the front and side, *and also from the rear.* (This is, after all, the perspective from which the congregation or other audience is most likely to observe the director.) Then watch the video tape critically, noting such basic elements as attack, release, size of gesture, wrist and elbow position and upper arm and shoulder movement (check the latter especially from behind). Note the overall posture of the conductor and any torso, leg or knee motion. Observe facial expression and movement. Then, for every movement and gesture, ask the question: *was there a purpose behind it?*

Watch the video again, *listening* this time as much as watching. Did the choir respond the way the conductor wanted them to? What was happening in the gesture when the choir successfully reflected the conductor's intent? What was happening when the response was not what the conductor intended? Try to diagnose what got in the way or what was lacking. Did facial expression agree with gesture or were there mixed messages? Did preparations for attacks, the shaping of phrases, dynamic changes, etc. come early enough? Too early?

Habit vs. Intentionality

Certainly a goal for all conductors is to have our carefully practiced technique on "automatic pilot" so to speak—*habitual*. Unfortunately, poor technique becomes habitual as well. Let's look at one area, particular common to children's choir directors. Many conductors mouth the words as they conduct. While not as glaring an error as singing with the choir, at least two possible problems present themselves as an outgrowth of this habit. Mouthing the words, routinely and constantly, indicates that: 1) the director is thinking more like a singer than a conductor; and 2) the conductor does not completely trust the choristers to do their job.

In the matter of the first point, a singer needs ample preparation and suggestion for so many things in order to sing well. If the conductor sings or even "mouths" along, those preparations and suggestions (if they are given at all) may occur a split second too late for optimal use. Mouthing results in the conductor being less able to anticipate and control matters of phrasing and dynamic changes, entrances and releases. The problem increases in repertoire with two or more parts where, for example the second treble part might have eighth notes at the end of a phrase while the first treble part has a quarter note. If the director is mouthing the upper part, it is likely that no indication will be given for the choir to listen to and phrase with the lower part. Therefore, the release of that phrase and the attack of the next will be shoddy.

In the matter of the second point, consider what mouthing (especially singing with) the choir potentially says to the singers. In what is intended as an effort to help or in some way communicate an *esprit de corps*, the director who does the singers' job *with* them may, in fact, be suggesting a lack of confidence in the choristers' ability to do their part of the choral work on their own. That perception, real or not, may translate into an actual lack of self confidence on the part of the singers, individually and collectively. How bold are any of us when we are unsure as to whether or not we are doing a job well? Might we not begin to depend upon that secure voice or on "lip-reading"? And to note a very practical matter: what if the director sings or mouths incorrectly? This issue is no doubt more of concern in volunteer choirs. Professional or highly skilled singers are generally confident, be they children, youth or adults. But the question remains valid. Is it *habit* or is it *intentional*? What others means of facial expression might be open to the conductor if mouthing was monitored? How much more precise might cues and gesture be if the conductor was freed of particular words to think of the overall concept of sound? How much more sensitive would the choristers be to the conductor's facial cues if mouthing was reserved for a particular purpose, such as to indicate a taller vowel or final consonant?

Time after time, this issue of *trusting the choir as a means of building its confidence* has proven its validity. When the singers know that they will not be bailed out vocally, that *their* job is to produce the tone, the vowels, the diction, the phrasing, the accurate response to the conductor's conceptualization of the overall interpretation of the music, then both choir and conductor are freed to do their respective jobs better.

This is as true for the pre-schoolers as it is for the senior high choir. Although difficult for many directors, these concepts may be particularly trying for conductors who are trained primarily as singers. One's own vocal skills are available to help the sound and the security of a section. After all, they are just children! But these young singers are also our future youth and adult choirs. This is their training ground. Building confident, independent singers now will better serve them and the choral art in the future.

"But the words are right there on the music stand. I could prevent a possible memory problem!" There will, of course, be emergency occasions when a conductor can and should help vocally in order to avoid or recover from an obvious problem. The point here is to examine the reasons behind *constant and habitual* use of the conductors' singing and/or mouthing and to suggest that better choral conducting technique is available when mouthing is saved for times when it is truly needed and *intentionally* used.

If we accept the premise that mouthing and singing with the choir are to be avoided, what then shall we substitute to get the desired result? A good beginning will be: 1) Efficient gesture, 2) Well-tuned ears, 3) Well-trained eyes, and 4) A voice class as a part of each rehearsal.

1. *Efficient gesture*

   Every choral gesture must have a function. For a gesture to be valid, it must do one of the following, or it is likely extraneous and probably gets in the way. Each gesture then should either:
   • keep track of the beat, and/or
   • shape phrases while indicating dynamics, articulation, energy, and/or
   • suggest vocal production and style, and/or
   • start or stop the sound.

   Within each of these points are a multitude of nuance. The shape of the fingers and path of the hand, the span of the gesture, the contour of the release, the energy of the attack all suggest at least as much as verbal descriptions of the desired effect.

2. *Well-tuned ears*

   In Chapter 5, we elaborated upon the necessity for the conductor to have a clear concept of tone. The conductor's ears become highly sensitive to pitch and timbre. The singer's ears need to do the same. The issue of *listening* and *blending* voices is a long-term goal and begins as soon as a chorister first sets foot inside the rehearsal space. For the very inexperienced, listening may be as basic as trying to match the same pitch. For youth and adults, listening may be as sophisticated as blending vibratos and matching vowels. There are suggestions for "ear-cleaning" given throughout Chapter 4—The Rehearsal. They are intended to aid the choristers as they each take responsibility for their own part in sensitive choral music making.

   The piano has a key role to play too. Monitor the accompanist who, in an effort to be helpful, often gives the pitch three and four times while the conductor is speaking, or getting ready to begin, or while the choir is coming to order. This is probably unconscious on the accompanist's part, but a widespread practice. *Intentionality* is again the issue. If a conductor and accompanist want a subtle "calling to awareness" as a rehearsal transpires, then this technique is valid. It only becomes a crutch if done habitually.

Ask a group to listen to and observe what another group has sung. Do *they* have suggestions for achieving the desired tone? What approach would they take? Does anyone have an image in mind that could help achieve the sound we are after? Encourage active listening of the entire choir *to* the entire performing ensemble, not just to themselves or their section. For example, help them get really excited about the beauty of "the accompaniment in measure 52," or the importance of "the inner voices in measures 7—15." Our goals must include sensitizing each singer to the possibilities of the exquisite beauty in choral music, and their active part in accomplishing it.

3. *Well-trained eyes*

   a. *choral "shorthand"*

      Beginning with grade 2, children can begin to understand that written-in symbols on the printed score can remind them of things the director has said to avoid or to do. Using an overhead projector, mark the transparency as desired with a simple code, not just circling a note. For example, an arrow up means "think higher on this note," a wavy line means "slow down just a little bit here." Circle a secure pitch and connect it with an arrow to the same pitch several beats later, if the second one is somehow troublesome.

      By grade 4, most children will be able to make simple, well practiced marks in their own scores, perhaps copying them from a transparency at first. Tell the children that you will be going through their folders to examine their music and to check for a sharpened pencil. Offer rewards or commendations to those whose music is well marked. Intentional guidance in marking music during grade school should produce habitual score markers in youth and adult choirs since the singers will already be convinced of the value of choral shorthand and its routine use.

   b. *watching the director*

      Be sure that the choristers fully understand the technique of watching the director. This is a skill which must be practiced, not just required. As an exercise, ask the choir to stare at your nose (eyes, chin, etc.) then without taking their gaze off of you, gradually move their score into a position where they can see it peripherally. It is now at an optimum place for a quick glance downward (moving only the eyes) to "grab" information before looking back up at the conductor. Practice gathering information from the score for a count of two, then using that "data" while looking at the conductor, going as far as possible before more information is needed. Repeat. Often.

      The conductor should monitor his/her own "watching" technique. If more time is spent looking at the music than looking at the choir, the words "watch me" do not carry much meaning. This is, of course more difficult to do in situations where the director is also the accompanist. If there is no choice but to accompany one's own choir in rehearsal, deliberately get away from the keyboard and work with the voices alone at least 50% of the time. Try to have someone else accompany when the choir sings at worship services or other performances.

4. *A voice class as a part of each rehearsal*
    The weekly choir rehearsal may well be the only place where the majority of choral singers get their vocal instruction. This must not be taken lightly. The instruction given in the choir rehearsal must be consistent with what would be taught were the choristers each studying privately in a competent voice teacher's studio. As a singer, I can tell within moments whether or not the conductor in front of me understands the voice. S/he doesn't have to be a singer by trade, but must have sung enough to appreciate what the singer's art is about and know how various voice types work.

Vocal demonstrations by the conductor will be important, whether or not the individual considers him/herself a singer. One must learn to use one's own voice effectively, to the best potential it can be brought. (This might include private voice study.) Conductors of children's choirs must especially be aware that the director's voice quality—both singing and speaking—will have an effect on the tone of the group, whether that sound is an adequate model or not. If the voice is not the model the children should emulate, find a reasonable substitute while setting to work on improvement of one's own instrument. (A reasonable substitute to model tone might be a teenage girl, a light soprano from the adult choir, or a treble chorister of either gender who has the quality of sound sought for the full choir. A "live" singer is best, but taped will do.)

No matter the quality of the director's voice, s/he *can* sing with careful attention to posture, vowels and consonants, artistic phrasing and dynamics, and to the basic rules of producing good tone: correct breath intake, supported exhalation, lowered jaw, loose tongue and neutral lips, raised soft pallet.

Score Study

The study of a piece of music, whatever the level of difficulty, serves two purposes: 1) to aid the director in preparing to *conduct* the piece; and 2) to aid the director in preparing to *teach* the piece. An implicit goal in this preparation is to "free" the director from the mechanics in order to *listen* to what the music is trying to say.

An assessment of a simple unison children's choir anthem may not be much of a challenge to the experienced teacher/conductor, but it is always wise to spend a little time on even the easiest piece, looking at the score with an eye to the following:

*   **The framework.** How it is constructed? Is the form through-composed, ABA, etc.? How does the melodic/rhythmic material vary and what are the potential challenges therein? (Meter changes, rhythmic surprises, intervalic variations, etc.)
*   **The nuance.** Find subtle points in the piece that are opportunities for stretching the tempo or quieting the dynamic, etc. What is the interplay between the accompaniment and the voices?
*   **The vocal challenges.** There may be points where vowels, for example, will need extra preparation due to regional accents, or, to the pitch on which the vowel is placed. Opening the vowel [i] (towards [a]) on a high pitch, or brightening the vowel [a] (towards [i]) on a low note are two common considerations. The same question should be asked of intervals. Are there places where intonation is likely to suffer? Plan ways to troubleshoot the situation before it becomes a problem. Score study should enable the

conductor to design warm up exercises which prepare the ear and voice for work on the anthem.

- **The musicianship opportunities**. Look for elements in the piece that further the understanding of a concept recently explored in rehearsal (i.e., a theme built around the interval of a fourth). Find new concepts the choristers will experience in the singing of the anthem and which they are ready to learn about *theoretically*.

- **The theological opportunities**. What elements of the text will enhance the children's understanding of a faith concept with which they are already familiar? How will the text fit into the scripture lessons of the Sunday the anthem will be sung and how will the children become aware of their part in the explication of that text? Would a Bible story read as a means of introducing the anthem be useful? Perhaps inviting the minister to speak to the choir about the text in relation to the upcoming sermon would be effective.

The complexity of the anthem and the skill of the director as a conductor or a teacher will determine the amount of time spent in score preparation. There are many sources available which go into great technical detail about preparing a score before the choir begins to work on it. Color coded pencils, symbols, methods of keeping track of measures within sections, etc. are carefully explained in numerous conducting books and in articles in professional journals. The reader is encouraged to refer to the Conducting section of this book's bibliography for further information.

Chapters 5, 6 and 7 have dealt with the complex issue of developing beautiful choral sound: tone production, repertoire selection and conducting technique. A final suggestion as we close this three-part section. *All* conductors would do well to be choristers, at least from time to time, but better yet, on a regular basis. Putting oneself on the other side of the music stand is a good reminder of the essential messages needed by choral singers. The act of *singing* in a choir should provide a different experience than the act of *conducting* a choir. We all have, to some degree, the need to replenish the soul by joining one's voice in song. And, as we have discussed, this should not be done *while* conducting. Assuming the role of a chorister intensifies the director's three-part task as voice teacher, chooser of repertoire and conductor.

Chapter 8

THE CHOIR IN WORSHIP

In this chapter, the opening material is a compilation of Ruth Krehbiel Jacobs' writing from two sections of The Successful Children's Choir: "Training in Worship" (pp. 45-48) and "How to Use the Children's Choir" (pp. 19-21). Again, no attempt has been made to update the language for gender inclusivity.

Training In Worship

"Training children to express themselves through music is a worthy objective, but the church choir has a much greater obligation. Artistic singing in the church has a higher purpose: making real the experience of worship. To guide children in the discovery and experience of worship, we must ourselves know its power; not theoretically, but actually.

"What is worship? It is an experience of fellowship or communion with God in which there is a consciousness of His reality and love, which results in increased strength and devotion. Real worship is a vital experience. It deepens insight and lengthens vision. It is not to be achieved by mere artificial stimulus; it requires an inner spring of communion with God. And yet the spirit of worship may be cultivated and developed. We can learn to worship. In this training in worship the children's choir may have an important and very special part, for the choir, in its position of leadership in the worship service of the church, has a grave responsibility. Unless its director is capable of 'raising shrines within the lives of children,' the most polished service will be an empty shell and will only hasten the trend toward insincerity and artificiality.

"We should appreciate the subtle influence of beauty as an aid to worship. It is not necessary to build a cathedral of St. John the Divine to create in our children a sense of the majesty of God. The writer will never forget the experience of entering the nave of that cathedral for the first time after the scaffolding was removed, but just as impressive was the service of worship in a New England choir camp. The chapel was the haymow of an old barn. The benches were logs, the cross two straight branches from a tree; but the cross stood before a window that revealed the majesty of God in lake and sky and forest.

"Surroundings conducive to worship must not be canceled by the service itself. In it, too, there must be reverence and beauty. The distractions of latecomers and irrelevant business should not be allowed to intrude. Children often have a poor example set for them in the behavior of the adults who show little reverence for the sanctuary and for the service itself. The Friends discovered a tremendous worship value in the communal silence in which they wait for the spirit of God. The superficiality with which many of us are accustomed to enter upon a worship service promises little likelihood of a deep experience of communion with God. A well-trained children's choir can, by its quiet reverence, help to create a spirit of worship in the congregation.

"The presence of a children's choir in a service of worship is not a social event, but a ceremony. People come to the church to commune with God. This should be uppermost in the minds of the children. Just as in the arch there is the keystone that gives security to the whole structure, so the practice of the presence of God is the keystone of the children's choir. It is the one consideration that gives supreme purpose to all the rehearsal and discipline.

"It is not enough to *tell* the children repeatedly that they must be quiet and attentive through the whole service, although this may sometimes be necessary. Proper behavior must come as the result of a deepening experience and understanding of worship. Intelligent guidance is essential to such growth. Overemphasis upon the emotions can work havoc. True worship is not an artificially assumed attitude. It is rather a response to the sense of the presence of God.

"The sense of the presence of God is strengthened by a knowledge of great events of the Bible, of the strong men of all ages whose convictions gave them courage, of the influence of opportunities for courageous Christian action that lie before the children of today. The more the child's religious horizon expands, the more his spirit of worship will grow and his opportunity for leadership in the service of worship be appreciated. Worship is not an end in itself. It should be thought of as the nurture of a flower which will ripen into the fruit of Christ-like character.

"If the training of children in worship is ever to be truly fruitful, it must have a threefold result. It must establish a substantial and honest background for the practice of worship; it must create worship habits and attitudes; it must train for leadership in worship.

"Familiarity is an important element contributing to the value of material used in worship. A program of memorization of hymns, selected Scripture, and meaningful prayers should be an essential part of the choir's schedule. The first to be learned are those which are in regular use in the service. New hymns, Scripture passages, and prayers which are memorized should be used frequently.

"The worship education of the children is too important a task to be assumed by the director alone. It requires the assistance of an understanding and deeply spiritual minister who realizes the subtle influence of beauty and quiet, sincerity and reverence, and will spare no effort to establish these elements in the service of his church. This is the soil in which true worship grows. In such an atmosphere it is not difficult to create worship attitudes and habits. It will seem natural to bow the head in prayer, to refrain from whispering, to sing with devotion, to listen with attention, and to enter and leave the sanctuary quietly.

"The proper management of the necessary arrangements for the beginning of the service is a key to the success of the service itself. The children should come early enough to get into their robes without hurrying. If there is a procession, they should be in their places well before the minister joins them to lead in prayer. A simple prayer, made familiar by regular usage and said in unison or privately after the minister has finished, helps to prepare them for the service. Such a prayer need not be more than a sentence, for example:

'Our Father, grant that with steadfast minds and with loving hearts we may worship thee today;' or, 'O God, lead us in our worship today, that our lips may praise thee, and our thought and lives may glorify thee.'[1]

"To become leaders in the worship service, a sense of the dignity of this office and an understanding of the purpose of the various parts of the service are essential. The sensitive minister who believes that worship should have an impact on the lives of the congregation will welcome the opportunity to explain the service to the children. He can do much to impress upon them the essential unity of the parts and the responsibility of the choir for the whole.

"If the leadership of the choir is to be effective, it is imperative that each child should accept his individual responsibility. Each must learn the music as completely as if he were the only one singing. He must learn it, not because the director says so, but because he has his own sense of honesty. He must respect the vestment that is the badge of his office. He must be conscious of the congregation as fellow worshipers. He must be conscious of God, to Whom worship is addressed.

"To carry on such a profound program of education there are several imperatives: intelligent and devoted leaders, a planned approach, consistent regular training, recognition of the interest level of the children, and the application of knowledge to choir responsibility.

"Many children's choirs (*most* children's choirs probably would not be a gross exaggeration) are ineffective, and detract from, rather than enrich, the service. But the fault of poor performance lies at the door of the director. It is he who is responsible for the training, the appearance, and the deportment of the choir. No one of these phases can be ignored without serious detriment. It takes just one bright red hair-ribbon to rob the finest tone of its audience reaction. A congregation would be properly scandalized if members of the senior choir would wear Easter bonnets with their vestment, but conspicuous hair-ribbons seem to go quite unchallenged. Choir vestments are intended to submerge personalities, to blend them into a group personality. One conspicuous individual ruins the effect of the whole group.

"How often are vestments kept clean and attractive? Do we take time to adjust the length to the individuals, or do we permit a ragged row of uneven hem lines to straggle down the aisle? No detail of appearance dare be considered unimportant. A neatly robed choir sounds even better than a slovenly group of singers.

"Perhaps the greatest objection to the use of children's choirs is their deportment. It is not uncommon to see the chancel infested with a restless mass of giggling wrigglers. We see an orderly, reverent boy-choir in an Episcopal Church and marvel, never stopping to think that if boys can be trained to reverence in one church, there is no reason why it should be impossible in another. Children like to be entrusted with responsibility. If they know you are depending on them and do not intend to play policeman during the service, they will measure up, with very few exceptions. If those exceptions are conspicuous, they must be denied the right to sing in the next service, and the rest of the choir should know why they are not singing. When their behavior is exemplary, they should be given full credit. They should know that they have done a difficult thing well, and that you are proud of them. Let them feel that you consider them a very superior group. Pride in one performance will make the next much easier.

"Good deportment means not only quietness but alertness. At the signal to rise, all should be ready and rise as a unit. The manner of standing should be uniform. If books are held, they should be on a level plane. The rows should be straight, shoulder to shoulder. When the choir is seated again, there should not be any of the usual twisting and turning to get comfortably settled. The children can learn not to move until attention is diverted to some other portion of the service. Those who bungle it badly will hear soon enough from the other children."

Reflections on Ruth Jacobs' Words

As I read and reread the words above, several thoughts came to mind. The first was anticipation. I recognized those old-fashioned precepts of appearance, deportment and reverence from childhood, for it was her book that formed the basis of the children's choir movement in this country after World War II. These rules were so ingrained in us as choristers that as I read, I could actually anticipate what was written next. I remember liking this strictness and discipline as a child, glad to know clearly what was expected of me. I was charged with an important task and wanted to rise to the occasion.

The second thought was lament. Somehow we have continued to lose a general reverence for things spiritual. This may not be altogether bad since false piety never helped and probably has hurt the work of the church. But still, we can lament the fact that so many children today are not taught a sense of reverence about the room in which we meet to worship, or respect for the robe we wear to represent our role as worship leaders. Even taking care of music octavos and folders must be taught to children growing up in this disposable society. Furthermore, we often compete with the secular world's demands for time on Sunday morning. Families will sometimes send choristers to church long enough to sing the anthem, then tell the child to leave "worship" for another activity.

The third thought was one of hopefulness. Ruth Jacobs' ideas inspired me as a chorister. Her words encourage me now as a director to work ever more diligently with my young singers on these issues. I am convinced that helping to instill these important attitudes is worth the time and effort, not only for the choir program, but simply as a way of living. We will need to go about this task creatively and convincingly. As we have discussed, we live in an era where singing in a church choir is but one of many options for young people, where families often do not worship together regularly, where the popular culture of the secular world dictates form. Ruth Jacobs' wisdom serves as a clarion call to action.

Just as her forthright words lead us to think again about proper decorum, appearance, and reverence, they lead us as well to reflect anew upon the planning of worship and upon the kinds of resources appropriate for worship. There is ample biblical justification in both the Old and New Testaments for making music in the context of worship. Ruth Jacobs' philosophy supports the biblical mandate that those who offer it—composer, author, organist, instrumentalist, conductor, chorister or congregational singer— must do so by bringing their finest fruits to the altar out of a well defined sense of praise and thanksgiving for God's continual grace to us.

Worship Planning: Communication is the Key

The widespread practice of using anthems that appear to have no connection to the rest of the worship service is unfortunate testimony to the lack of communication between staff members. Lucky is the congregation in which the pastor recognizes music as an integral part of the liturgy and initiates worship planning with the church musician. In congregations that use the lectionary, worship planning is partially done, since the musician can look up the readings for any given Sunday and begin searching for appropriate texts and settings. In congregations where no lectionary is used, the pastor and musician must coordinate efforts so that anthems are not merely "stuck in." Of course, planning must begin early enough for music to be ordered and taught to the choir. This takes commitment and discipline on the part of both clergy and musician, and may be the main reason why this type of planning is so infrequently practiced. In this regard, pastor, musician, and hymnologist Erik Routley wrote,

> *"The responsibility for this rests squarely on the shoulders of the clergy. The idea that no sermon can have spiritual content if it is prepared earlier than Saturday night, and that any planning for worship on this scale diminishes the field of the Holy Spirit's action, is one that should be roundly denounced as egotistic presumptuousness on the part of preachers.... Surprise is precisely the domain of the Holy Spirit; solid, honest, and disciplined work is the domain of the preacher and it is time he learned it.... This has to be put quite uncompromisingly. Until the discipline of decent neighborliness is accepted by the clergy, until they are content with preaching from Scripture instead of preaching on topics...the choirmaster's job remains chaotic and religiously frustrated. It is not enough to encourage choirmasters to make the best of this situation. Making the best of it perpetuates it. No, they should rebel, and insist that the clergy do their work properly."[2]*

This censure from a preacher to other preachers is certainly a rallying point for those church musicians whose head of staff does not match Routley's description of "doing their work properly." This is not new information for those of us on this side of the music stand! Just *how* to go about "rebelling" and "insisting" is, of course, not a simple question.

One point *is* clear. At the heart of any significant and positive change between clergy and musician is *mutual respect*, even if personal style is very different. It is not within our province here to study in depth and propose solutions to this problem, only to say that in order to help rectify the situation, we must embark upon whatever may be in our particular domain to do. For example, in one situation, the musician discovered that she had often given voice to her frustration on the issue of worship planning, but never to the minister or the worship committee, only to those whom she knew felt as she did. Screwing up her courage, she put together a list of anthems with texts typed out and scripture references given, took it to the minister and explained that these were all songs that would be appropriate for her various choirs between fall and Christmas. In an accompanying note, she explained her frustration and concerns about anthem selection and worship planning. The care and time she took in this matter was evident and caused the minister to inquire further about her concerns. Slowly, the manner in which worship was prepared began to change. This situation worked because:

- there was mutual respect between the pastor and the musician; therefore,
- the musician took the initiative, and did so in a style that reflected concern for the act of corporate worship, rather than her own irritation.
- the pastor, because of the respect he held for the church musician, was willing to view her efforts as potentially significant, thus opening up the possibility for subsequent communication.

If we take seriously the premise that music and preaching must serve worship, then thoughtful, timely, coordinated planning is assumed. More voices must emerge, *from among the clergy themselves*, echoing Routley's admonition. (Hopefully among these voices will be seminary professors of every denomination.)

If one *is* lucky enough to obtain a list of sermon topics and the scriptures upon which they are based, working independently on anthem selection is probably insufficient for the task, whether the scriptures are from a lectionary or are selected by the pastor. Sitting together with Bibles, a concordance, hymnals, and possible anthem selections can be fruitful not only for the musician but for the pastor, who, while discussing the direction he or she plans to go, in fact clarifies that direction in preparation for the actual writing of the sermon.

There may be times when the musician takes the lead, as in the example above, giving texts to the pastor that the director would like to use with a particular choir. The minister might appreciate the inspiration! Particularly with children's choirs, there are musical goals to be set as well as constraints on the amount and type of repertoire the choir can successfully learn in a given amount of time. Generating anthem ideas can help us meet artistic and pedagogical objectives as well as plan worship faithfully.

On particular Sundays and seasons, anthem choices might appear to be obvious. Careful planning with clergy might be abandoned on those occasions. However, simply following the liturgical seasons in such periods as Advent and Lent, or on Christmas Sunday or Easter is not always entirely satisfactory. We may miss opportunities for remarkable liturgy. If the pastor will share with the musician the focus of the sermon, the musician can do a better job of selecting a text to coordinate with that focus. Additionally, communication can help the worship planners discern the optimum point in the worship service where a particular anthem might be placed. This can and should be flexible. Perhaps there is a text most appropriate as a response to the Old Testament Lesson. Use it there, and forgo the usual "anthem slot." Anthems of praise are actually prayers of praise and are often suitable as introits. Use them there if that is where they fit best. In general, any anthems used after the sermon should be a response to it. Anthem texts should routinely be printed in the worship bulletin, even if the acoustic of the sanctuary and the choir's diction are adequate. Assisting worshippers by means of a visual image better allows them to *hear*, rather than simply to listen.

Children can and should provide worship leadership in other roles than their place in the choir. The Call to Worship or a litany lead by a young person can be a significant event in the life of that child. The congregants too, may hear words with new ears when read with confident mastery by a lay reader who happens to be quite young. Many children and youth are excellent public speakers and need only a little coaching. The time spent with the child by a staff member in preparation for worship reminds the child of the importance of the task for which s/he has been chosen.

A quiet but discernible drama is important to the order of worship. Each of the musical components—hymns, anthems, instrumental pieces—are critical elements in the overall "flow" of the service. The successful selection, placement, and finally performance of an anthem or piece of instrumental music can testify to the spirit of cooperation of the staff as we seek to offer our best efforts on behalf of the corporate worship of the congregation.

A word might be said about the worshipper for whom music has little significance. Although these souls are probably in the minority, it behooves worship planners, especially musicians, to remember that such people do exist in our midst and that perhaps, as Erik Routley suggests, "they do us a great service by being there. They call a necessary halt to starry-eyed notions that music is a great unifier, or that through music everybody is assisted in worship."[3]

Clearly no argument will be made here to eliminate music from worship! But providing a quiet sanctuary in the fifteen minutes or so before the service formally begins is a necessary consideration. Contemplative congregants mentioned above and others who, on a particular Sunday might need an undisturbed environment in order to prepare for the act of worship, should not be subjected to the last minute rehearsing of the choirs or the activities of other worship preparations. On the other hand, the choristers must have ample time to prepare before a service in order to compose themselves for their leadership role in worship, and this may involve using the sanctuary. This potential conflict is an issue which must be carefully considered when planning the Sunday morning schedule.

Worship Resources

"The choirmaster can help to create an appreciation for fine hymns by his example and encouragement. If the response seems slow, he need not be too discouraged. Comparatively few people ever take time to enjoy the sunsets, but God continues to paint them as magnificently as if the whole world had stopped to admire." (p. 50)

Hymns are perhaps the most well known part of the musical heritage of the church. A chorister may sing an anthem only once, but a hymn will be sung again and again. Dietrich Bonhoeffer, the Lutheran pastor who participated in and was hung for his part in the German resistance movement during the second World War, discussed the power of hymns with his students at the underground seminary founded at Finkenwald:

"Why do Christians sing when they are together? The reason is, quite simply, because in singing together it is possible for them to speak and pray the same Word at the same time; in other words, because here they can unite in the Word. All devotion, all attention should be concentrated upon the Word in the hymn. The fact that we do not speak it but sing it only expresses the fact that our spoken words are inadequate to express what we want to say, that the burden of our song goes far beyond all human words. Yet we do not hum a melody; we sing words of praise to God, words of thanksgiving, confession, and prayer."[4]

Carefully chosen hymns can be both voice and faith builders. Many pastors spend hours in the selection of just the right hymn to reflect and enhance the sermon. Musicians can never have the kind of insight into hymn selection as the preacher who practices that craft with integrity. But the musician can work alongside the pastor on hymn selection in order to assure that the youngest members of the congregation are able to participate, at least in part, on one of the hymns in each worship service. A list of recommended hymns for young singers is given in Appendix 3, along with suggestions for enlisting the aid of adults in helping children learn this part of their heritage.

"It is next to impossible to define a good hymn. The qualifications we set up are inevitably colored by our personal preferences. But this we can say: a good hymn is good both in text and in music. A good hymn is not necessarily an old one, although a hymn which has weathered the acid test of time must have enduring values. With a heritage of such hymns as 'Now Thank We All Our God,' 'All Creatures of Our God and King,' 'All Glory, Laud, and Honor,' 'O Come, All Ye Faithful,' 'Now Let Every Tongue Adore Thee,' 'To God on High Be Thanks and Praise,' 'O Sacred Head Now Wounded,' 'The God of Abraham Praise,' there is no need for inferior hymns." (p. 50)

In the editor's introduction to *Rejoice in the Lord: A Hymn Companion to the Scriptures*, Erik Routley made an earnest attempt not only to "define a good hymn" but to define a good hymnal. He based his conclusions on John Wesley's 1780 hymnbook.

"...we are convinced that a believer, or a seeker, who reads through this book from one end to the other, using it as a companion to the Scriptures, will find that it is just that: theology for people who are not theological specialists, poetry for those who claim not to be literary, and a lyric illumination of the Christian way."[5]

Hymns as a Part of Choral Repertoire

Beyond congregational singing, however, the hymnal is a rich, but often overlooked source of repertoire for the choirs. Nearly every denomination has produced a new hymnal since 1978. Many have very fine hymnal companions. (Several of the best are listed in the bibliography.) There are many very fine 20th century hymns included in these newer hymnals along with some older but unfamiliar titles. An effective way to introduce these hymns for later use with the congregation is to present them first as anthems sung by the choirs, especially the choirs of children and youth. Congregations are likely to support the young people and to try things with them which they might otherwise be reluctant to attempt.

An example of a hymn used in this way is included on pages 105-110. It is a setting of a newer tune and text, probably unfamiliar to most congregations. Even though it is simple and very singable, those congregations that only like "the familiar," might well react negatively. Remember that "It's too hard" often means "I don't know it."[6] Given a sensitive introduction, the hymn "In Bethlehem a Babe Was Born" could become a favorite Christmas carol of even the most reluctant congregation.

Arranging hymns as anthems has at least three advantages: 1) the director can use the arrangement to fulfill a particular liturgical need, (i.e., supporting a particular sermon topic for which a suitable published anthem has not been found, or, as a means of introducing a new hymn to the congregation); 2) the arrangement will be tailor-made for the particular singers involved; 3) the cost of a set of octavos is saved.

In the case of hymns in which either or both the text and tune are under copyright, the publisher of the hymnal should be contacted and permission to do the arrangement secured. If there is no plan to market the arrangement outside of the use for which it was originally intended, there may be only a low, one time fee assessed. With public domain texts and tunes, there is no need to obtain permission to do an arrangement.

This selection is available in a separate octavo edition. Published by H.T. FitzSimons Company, catalog #F5029.

IN BETHLEHEM A BABE WAS BORN

for unison choir, or unison with SATB choir;
keyboard, flute or alto recorder, optional chimes or handbells,
finger cymbals, hand drum and triangle, and optional congregation

Words and Music by
Barbara Mays
Arr. by Sue Ellen Page

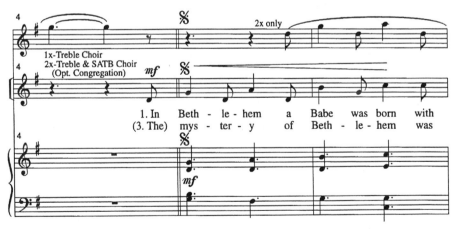

love e - nough for all,_____ While king - doms slept, the
long a - go_____ they say,_____ But mir - a - cle of

Lord came down to grace a man - ger stall; And with a
mir - a - cles, the Ba - by lives_____ to - day In each new

glo - rious light, an - gels ap - peared that
heart that hears love com - ing through the

*Each of these four chords may be
played or doubled by handbells or chimes.

* If sung by unison choir, sing melody with accompaniment.

Combining Choirs in Worship

Many church choir programs provide occasional opportunities for various age groups to sing together in worship, and sometimes in concert. Inviting the senior high choir to sing with the adult choir, for example, can be a boon for all concerned. The enthusiasm of the youth is infectious to the adults and the discipline of the adults keeps the youth on their toes. The youthful tone of the senior highs can "firm up" the sometimes sagging, adult tone. The experienced musicianship of the adults can give the younger singers the security they need. The same is true for having the senior high choir sing with a younger children's group. In addition to a satisfying anthem rendition, this can be an unspoken but very powerful program building tool for the younger children. As they see the older choristers, they both admire and desire to be like them someday.

Upper elementary children's choirs, especially when combined with treble junior high voices can do a masterful job on some of the solo repertoire from standard oratorios and cantatas. One of the highlights of our choir program has been the involvement of children in the annual Spring Music Festival. Children's choirs have sung chorale melodies, cantata duets and solos, and in fact, entire soprano lines. (On *Requiem* by John Rutter, the children sang soprano, along with two light, lyric women's voices, the rest of the adult sopranos singing with the altos. The sound was just right.)

There may be festival Sundays or other special services when combining choirs provides the opportunity for special interpretations of an anthem or a hymn. For example, for a Maundy Thursday service, the hymn "My Song is Love Unknown" (using the tune LOVE UNKNOWN) was to be used as an anthem by the adult choir. As the staff began to work with it, we realized that the use of the personal pronoun in each of the seven verses gave the text the feeling of a conversation: "This is what He meant to me!" "Did you hear what happened?" "I don't understand why." "What did *he* do? I am the one who does things wrong." So, following our instincts, we divided the verses the following way:

1. A group of children
2. Adult male soloist
3. SATB, a capella
4. Adult female soloist
5. Choir (ATB, sopranos, children and congregation on melody)
6. All, unison
7. The group of children

The organist's sensitive accompaniment carefully reflected the different voices used and the bulletin indicated the hymn number and on which verses the congregation was to join. This simple assignment of verses straight from the hymnal made an effective combined choir anthem and in the process, a not so familiar hymn has become part of our tradition.

Music Is the Servant of Worship

Despite differences in style preference among musicians, clergy and congregations, there is at least one truism: *the music we choose and how it is performed must serve worship, not the other way around.* That is to say, if the text or the tune sound unremarkable, or "common" as Ruth Jacobs' era would have said, if the song's merit is found only in its ability to make the congregation "feel good," if the text is fine but has nothing whatsoever to do with the lessons and sermon of the day, we must ask the question again, "Does this anthem serve worship?" The question must be asked about each possible offering, from the anthems for the youngest children's choir to the adult choir, to the music from vocal soloists, a handbell group, the organist and other instrumentalists.

In Chapter 6, repertoire considerations were confined to voice building factors. Now we will look more closely at other criteria used to determine which anthems should ultimately be chosen for use in worship.

Mediocrity vs. Finest Fruits
"Whatever the degree of difficulty, the music must be worth the
effort, worthy of a place in the library of a child's memory." (p. 53)

Unlike the day in which Ruth Jacobs wrote *The Successful Children's Choir* and certainly as a result of her having written it, publishers are now in the happy position of reviewing and publishing many manuscripts of sacred compositions for children's voices and young mixed voice choirs. Some of this material is very fine. Much of it is not; adequate perhaps, but not truly fine. Inferior music continues to be printed because it continues to be purchased and used. Unfortunately in the church, mediocrity is widely unidentified. It is accepted, even sanctioned, sometimes more so than in the secular realm. Using anthems that are mediocre, or merely adequate, works against the basic premise so critical for success with once-a-week volunteer, unauditioned choirs in the church: *What we do must be effective, challenging, memorable, and distinctive.* We must apply this philosophy to every musical *and theological* decision regarding anthem selection, for we are after all, Christian educators. Music is our tool.

What then do we look for? In addition to considering range and intervalic difficulty, choose only anthems in which the melody, the accompaniment, and any harmony parts are inspired and finely crafted. *"Fine music" is not necessarily difficult music.* At all levels of challenge, if the music sounds unremarkable, tiresomely trendy, or, if the song seems overly fond of itself, rethink the choice.

Similarly, select only those texts that are of the highest caliber, both in theological content and poetic construction. Words are a primary means by which we teach the Christian faith. As every jingle writer knows, we remember what we sing.

Often, a song or hymn will have a "fine" text, but the vehicle for conveying that text, the music, is unremarkable, taking its cue from worn-out, popular conventions. The reverse, of course, is also true. We can find many examples of each throughout hymnody and choral literature. Somehow, the standard for "great" is skewed to the degree that inferior music and texts are acceptable merely because they *sound familiar* and are *accessible.* To be sure, those two criteria are significant, but without combining the element of *inspired craftsmanship*, they fall short of the mark. When these songs are sung at national conferences and seminary graduations there is an assumed credibility about "greatness" as well as their potential use in local churches.

Should it matter? Yes. Congregations build patterns for acceptability based on frequency of use. *Form conveys value.* Just as the eye can be trained to identify solid oak from a veneer, or a quality hand-crafted quilt from less expensive imitations, so can the ear be trained to listen aesthetically. If church musicians become immune to the difference, resigned to, or, apathetic about repertoire choices, or if we are unable to articulate the crux of this issue to clergy and congregation, a great deal will be lost.

"A society that cultivates commonness, that is suspicious of genius, that has more esteem for the entrepreneur who caters to the tastes of the many than the visionary who challenges the spirits of the few—such a society is always in danger of defining worth in terms of immediate demand rather than eternal significance."[7]

Feel-good Religious Music and "Top 40" Anthems

American churches in the last decades of the 20th century have experienced, in general, a shift to a more subjective and interior religious focus, a direct reflection of the popular culture's emphasis on the here and now. The importance of "my personal relationship to God" has, in many settings, become the exclusive locus for theological thought. This inner-self fixation significantly affects worship style[8]. As discussed in Chapter 1, poor theology coupled with "sounds like" music is rampant and accepted as appropriate because of the celebrity status given it by television. Rather than being judged by any thoughtful, studied theological standard, the integrity of these worship styles is assumed and unquestioned simply because of their popularity. "How it makes me feel" seems to be imperative enough. This phenomenon may well leave a profound impact on our children and youth, the worship leaders of the next generations.

Texts which "talk down" to children or are "cute" have been widespread for years in sacred choral literature for treble voices. Particularly in the last two decades of the 20th century, however, anthems abound (in all voicings) in which the texts are so "relevant" to contemporary daily life that any other two syllable name inserted for "Jesus" would render it a place among "Top 40" hits on the nation's soft rock stations.

To its credit, much "Contemporary Christian Music" is finely crafted, has a memorable melody, interesting harmony, appropriate range, etc. Thus far, an anthem of this type would fit our criteria for repertoire selection. The question in this case, however, becomes not so much whether or not the song sounds as though anyone could have written it, but rather, can it be *distinguished* from the popular, sensual songs of the secular world? The aesthetics of the popular culture have come to define, in too many churches, the aesthetics for worship.

Sacred music which has its roots in "popular" culture tends to leave us comfortably where we are. Music from the "high" culture, on the other hand, asks our minds to take a step, maybe even a *leap* forward, to look at the world by getting ourselves out of the way in order to receive the new possibilities for growth. (High culture is not to be confused with "old." Every period in history has its fine artists, composers, architects, etc. and the present time is certainly no exception.) Somewhere in the middle of these extremes is "folk" culture. *Music from a folk culture* comes out of a community, *usually a religious one*, and reflects that community's beliefs and values[9]. At a lecture entitled "Leonard Bernstein: A Lodestar for the American Church Musician," Steven Pilkington pointed out that Bernstein distinguished between two types of sentimentality; one which is sweet and simple and "gets into our music from hymn singing, especially from Southern Baptist hymns" and another kind "that comes out of our popular songs, a sort of crooning pleasure, like taking a long, delicious, warm bath."[10]

"In actuality, the issue is not one of sentimentality but sensuality. Crooning usually speaks the language of romantic love....The essence of the problem as regards contemporary Christian music is that, stylistically, it

is the servant of eros not agape *[emphasis mine].... Yet, if contemporary liturgy is to be an experience which is characteristically American, I believe it must embrace the sentimentality which is simple, sweet, and forthright in character. And although it may be full of lyric and melodic invention it must not be weighted by the intoxicating stylings of another seductive language which ultimately and intimately addresses a very singular activity."[11]*

There are those who would argue, and this includes many clergy, that we must apply only the "vernacular"—the ordinary musical and poetic language—to repertoire choices for worship. But can we support a reasoning which essentially maintains that people cannot be taken beyond their current artistic and theological level of awareness? Would we presume to claim that new insight and therefore (even radical) change is impossible in other aspects of people's lives?

While there are notable exceptions, the aesthetic of popular culture has taken its toll. Several generations have grown up with little in the way of theological, musical, and artistic depth, despite earnest efforts on the part of many teachers, preachers and musicians. How can we be surprised at the unfamiliarity of some clergy, for example, with appropriate music for worship when what many of them grew up on was not of high calibre or lacked breadth of style? In many seminaries, very little, if any, training in music for worship has been taught. *Until young people have experienced excellence and diversity in their musical training, they will not know to demand it in their higher education, or in their churches and concert halls.*

"In the face of today's overwhelming musical ignorance, we, as church musicians, must be teaching and preaching the Gospel and another gospel which believes that musical literacy and musical appreciation are a means of birthing spiritual lives and sustaining Christian journeys. With Bernsteinian zeal and enthusiasm, we must teach and explore ways of making music which profoundly communicate to American hearts and minds the great and simple truths that carry the faith. I employ the word 'profoundly' with great gravity, for education is one of our only hopes in combatting the music of a cheesy charm which is catastrophically sweeping the American church, a music which seductively disfigures the realities of the Gospel."[12]

If people come to worship for a Word *apart* from the secular world so that they might return to it "rooted and grounded"[13] in the knowledge of God's grace in their daily lives, let us give them anthems (and sermons) which *engage the mind as they capture the imagination.* Let us not sell out to emotion-laden, mindless, and common entertainment, no matter how slick or well crafted it may be. Let us "never substitute superficiality for substance."[14]

Keep confidence in a piece of music which meets the criteria for fine repertoire but which does not have immediate appeal to everyone! Re-examine it, but do not succumb to dictates from the choir, the congregation, or the clergy. Work to convince those involved to think through these issues together. There are far greater implications on the lives of children and youth than the face value of teaching a little song. Be diligent in the search for quality and do not settle for less because it happens to be familiar, currently popular, easy to learn in a hurry, or handy. (See Appendix 3: *Exemplary Anthems for Children's Choirs in the Church.*)

Music can and should be a catalyst for combining and balancing worship forms that engage the heart as they challenge the mind. It bears repeating: Church musicians must find ways to insure that emotion-laden, mindless worship will not prevail. We will succeed only by confronting and influencing those who have not yet considered its many negative ramifications. We will also need to challenge ourselves, to look at our own affinity for the popular aesthetic and question the degree to which *we* have become immune to its seductions.

American Originals and Forgotten Gems

There are church music programs that would never use "contemporary Christian music" and yet, with equal aloofness, would not deign to use any music other than that which fits only the most narrow compass of "high" standards. There are for example, extraordinary anthems that do not have the esoteric elegance of English cathedral music but are profoundly moving in their simplicity. We would do well to remember that Jesus spoke in parables—simple, memorable stories which contained at their core the message of God's never-ending love. "If liturgy is the 'work of the people' we must speak to them, not beyond them, and we must certainly not create a time warp which smothers liturgy with the musical artifacts of a 'better time.'"[15]

Equally worthy to the traditional imported fare are many of the sacred compositions and arrangements by contemporary American composers. American churches can celebrate cultural diversity as reflected in our own religious poetry and music. This is often best manifested by the art of the people themselves, folk tunes and texts that have stood the test of time and are beloved in each generation. While there is a bounty of printed music of this genre available, American church musicians should also be arrangers and users of this vast treasure of raw material for worship, whether or not the publisher's desk is an intended destination. A well-known example of this genre includes *What Wondrous Love is This* in which both tune and text are from "folk" sources, and of which numerous arrangements have been made. Many of the tunes collected in *Christian Lyre (1830), Southern Harmony (1835), Kentucky Harmony (1816), Songs of Praise (1925),* and *The American Singing Book (1785)* are superb. When combined with sacred texts (which may also be from the folk culture), scripturally based poems, or metrical settings of psalms, these treasures become distinctive and accessible *American anthems.*

One particular segment of American music has taken a beating from erudite church musicians: written in the 19th century and known as "Gospel hymns," some would be tempted to throw out the entire genre. Indeed, a large number of 19th century hymns would fail most of the criteria thus far established for fine music and text. Acknowledging the difficulty of making value judgements where personal taste and sometimes powerful memories are obvious factors, there is still compelling and timeless merit in some of these old hymns. Their occasional, well thought-out use may be a powerful means of bridging the gap between the church musician and the members of the congregation who are reluctant to move beyond their favorite "old-time hymns."

As an example, *Softly and Tenderly Jesus is Calling* is rarely if ever sung in churches with highly developed music programs. And yet the simple character and integrity of both text and tune keep the song from being "out-of-date." These words, and their engaging melody, will always be relevant.[16]

SOFTLY AND TENDERLY

Words and Music by
Will L. Thompson
Arranged and adapted by Sue Ellen Page

A Look Towards the Future

If we are to build the congregation as the primary vehicle for a Christian impact on public life, the church must make its appeal, effectively, engagingly, winsomely, to people who must often become motivated to want what the church has to offer. Since no single style of music serves God better than another, be it cultured Anglican motets or gripping African-American spirituals, we would do well to include in our worship all types of well crafted, distinctively sacred music. Put together as a whole, we can hope that such variety will fortify and uplift the many diverse people in our congregations as we seek to glorify God.

It is prudent to remember, of course, that an arrogant, superior attitude—"I know more than you do about choosing church music"—will create antagonism among those to be converted, especially clergy. As we noted, without seminary training in church music, many pastors are inclined to judge what is "good" on the basis of personal preference, or that of the most vocal members of the congregation. They need the guidance and suggestions of a competent church musician. On the other hand, we must be willing to make careful compromises, remembering that there are anthems and hymns with fine texts, tunes, and craftsmanship to be found in every distinctive *worship* genre. Patience will be necessary in order for progress to be made. The old adage "Make haste slowly" will be effective in the long run.

"We must stop being angry with our congregations, choirs, and clergy for their lack of skill and taste in matters musical, and instead, we must joyfully and skillfully lead them on a great journey of learning which admittedly begins far from the finish line in these aesthetically parched days." [17]

It is important to acknowledge that part of our mission as choral conductors in the church is to train up literate singers who will populate the church and community choirs of the future. These young artists will insist upon a wide variety of superior choral music, and they will support the fine arts, historically the domain of the church. But this goal will not happen unless the children and youth we teach are involved with fine repertoire in far greater numbers than those who have been exposed only to, and are therefore content to settle for, choral "fluff." Growing bodies need carrots and broccoli, not just sweets. So, also, do growing musical tastes (of every age) require exposure and discipline.

Expanding Worshippers' Consciousness

It is an altogether hopeful sign that many denominations have adopted formal statements that support the premise we outlined earlier, that music must serve worship, not the other way around. These statements reiterate the context in which the church musician must consider all decisions concerning appropriate musical offerings. Here is one example:

1. "Christian worship ascribes all praise and honor, glory and power to the triune God....In worship the faithful offer themselves to God and are equipped for God's service in the world." [18]

2. "The Church has acknowledged that the lives of Christians and all they have belong to the Creator and are to be offered to God in worship. As sign and symbol of this self-offering, the people of God have presented their creations and material possessions to God. The richness of color, texture,

form, sound and motion has been brought into the act of worship."[19]

3.   People are called "to bring to worship material offerings which in their simplicity of form and function direct attention to what God has done and to the claim that God makes upon human life. The people of God have responded through creative expressions in architecture, furnishings, appointments, vestments, music, drama, language, and movement. When these artistic creations awaken us to God's presence, they are appropriate for worship. When they call attention to themselves, or are present for their beauty as an end in itself, they are idolatrous. Artistic expressions should evoke, edify, enhance, and expand worshippers' consciousness of the reality and grace of God."[20]

Can we ever be *certain* that our *"artistic expressions...evoke, edify, enhance, and expand worshippers' consciousness of the reality and grace of God?"* Probably not. But we can keep the statements like the one above in the front of our collective consciousness, and we can acknowledge that the world in which we live may have a subtle, yet profound, influence on our *own* perceptions and discernment. We can be on the alert for signals that may warn us when we are off-track.

This is *not* to say that there is nothing of value to be found in popular culture, only to remind ourselves that much of it, *intentionally,* is of little substance. We must make judicious choices, ask good questions, and not be afraid to challenge anything that claims intrinsic value simply because a lot of people like it.

Popular culture, by definition, survives on trends, on what is "in," on the *currently* popular. "New," "first," "exciting," "exclusive," are adjectives we hear and read daily. The common assumption is that a product or service is "better" when it is new, first, exciting, or exclusive. To what degree have we as members of this society who happen to work in the church, succumbed to this premise? Can we afford to settle for this standard as we strive to be the Church? Made in God's image, can we honor God through our worship with forms which convey nothing more than a subjective "I feel good?" Dare we, after presenting an anthem (or a sermon) which requires some effort on the part of the listener, acquiesce to those who respond with "I didn't get anything out of it?"

No. We come to worship to *give something to it.* In a culture that pampers us with immediacy, it is easy to forget how to wait, how to listen, how to open oneself, how to follow the admonition of Psalm 46:10a: *"Be still and know that I am God."*

The perceived need for immediacy is everywhere. We can talk on the phone from our cars (while an "easy listening" station soothes our frazzled nerves). We can buy our groceries, and nearly everything else, on credit (with *Muzak* in the background). We can "nuke" a meal in minutes while watching arrests and trials, wars and the workings of government on television *as they happen.* Immediacy is as important to the popular culture as timelessness is to high culture and to the folk cultures of our once tightly knit communities. Is it possible that the demand for immediacy has dulled our senses to those forms which *take time* to process? And, if so, what has this to say to us about the preparedness of worshippers each Sunday morning? What values are conveyed if we as worship leaders choose only those forms which immediately gratify the congregation? What do we teach our children if in worship services or choir rehearsals, we attempt to replicate the brief attention span formula so familiar on television?

Once again, this is not to claim that there is no value in any of the trappings of our secular world, only to remind ourselves that our first responsibility as Christians is to try to reflect, in all that we do—and this must include our worship forms—the God who made us, is for us and will not let us go. As Christians, we see that reflected most clearly in the life, death and resurrection of Jesus for whom "new," "first," "exciting" and "exclusive" had no significance whatsoever.

Not surprisingly, Ruth Krehbiel Jacobs had some things to say about expanding worshippers' consciousness of the reality and grace of God.

"The church should be the place where the spirit learns to kneel, a place set apart for communication beyond the human. It is well enough to teach our children to stand for the right, but it is when the spirit kneels that it gains the strength to stand.

"We speak glibly of the art of worship as if it were the process of fitting together a few prayers, readings, and choral responses. These may encourage worship, but they quite as frequently intrude between worship and worshipper. Worship is a sense of the presence of God, and the commitment of our will to God's will.

"But how is this 'sense of the presence of God' fostered and nourished? The burden of responsibility rests on us who direct most of the corporate expressions of worship. If our children graduate from the choir without a consciousness that the church is a place for experiences and thoughts that transcend those of school and club, if they have not learned to expect quiet of themselves when they enter the church, if their participation in the service does not reflect the sense of obligation to their own and the congregation's higher aspirations, then we have failed.

"Tending the worship attitudes of our children is like tending a rare plant. The seed must first be planted, and the soil kept in a condition that encourages growth. Once the seed has been planted, it requires patient care until it reaches full flower. When it does put forth a bud, fragrant with the richness of true worship, we may be humbly grateful for the privilege of having been the gardener."[21]

Church musicians who work with children and youth are uniquely positioned to address many of the challenges the church faces in its 21st century. Working as we do with the very young whose attitudes and tastes are still developing, we have the chance to establish worship patterns and forms which "deepen insight and lengthen vision," to use Ruth Jacobs' phrase. Furthermore, the opportunity to effect change is open to us: persuading unconvinced clergy to carefully plan worship with theologically proficient musicians; challenging the mind-set of those people so entrenched in the popular culture that "feel good" and "familiar" become the mainstay of religious experience; broadening the palette of the highly trained professional musician in order to include in worship those musical forms which may be unsophisticated but nonetheless sacred in their origins.

Achieving all of these goals may not come about in our lifetime. That is alright. If we believe that we are a part of the ongoing renovating work God is doing in this world, we must simply "keep the faith," reevaluate our own work and open ourselves to new challenges, as we prayerfully lead and are led by those with whom we are called to work.

> *Now thank we all our God, with heart and hands and voices.*
> *Who wondrous things hath done, in whom this world rejoices.*
> *Who, from our mother's arms*
> *hath blessed us on our way with countless gifts of love,*
> *and still is ours today.*[22]

Endnotes

1   A favorite prayer from my childhood in the church choir program was written by Ruth Jacobs:
    "God of all lovely sounds, grant us a share in Thy great harmony of earth and air. Make us Thy choristers that we may be worthy to offer music unto Thee."

2   Erik Routley, *Church Music and the Christian Faith* (Agape 1978), 116.

3   Routley, 133.

4   Dietrich Bonhoeffer, *Life Together* (Harper and Row Publishers, Inc.), 59.

5   Erik Routley, editor, *Rejoice in the Lord: A Hymn Companion to the Scriptures* (Wm. B. Eerdmans Publishing Co., 1985), 8.

6   It is interesting to note that the practice of equating "unfamiliar" with "difficult" can work in the reverse as well. For example, "The Star Spangled Banner," certainly one of the most familiar songs in the United States, could in no way be considered "easy" to sing, given its range of an octave and one half. The beloved "Silent Night" has something of the same problem.

7   Kenneth A. Myers, *All God's Children and Blue Suede Shoes: Christians and Popular Culture* (Crossway Books, 1989), 23.

8   A clear distinction is made here between the music used in religious traditions where overt movement of the Spirit as an historic, significant, and ritualistic element (such as the Pentecostal denomination) and the Hollywood-esque musical styles that are better suited to a variety show format than the sanctuary. The musical forms of the latter are borrowed from the secular, popular culture. By contrast, the traditional religious music of the Black community, for example, has become *the impetus* for much secular music (rhythm and blues, jazz, etc.) rather than the other way around.

9   The Negro spiritual is an example of this aesthetic.

10 Leonard Bernstein, *The Infinite Variety of Music* (Anchor Books), 50.

11 From a lecture by Steven Pilkington, head of the Church Music Department, Westminster Choir College of Rider University, entitled "Leonard Bernstein: A Lodestar for the Church Musician," May 12, 1994.

12 Pilkington.

13 Ephesians 3:17.

14 Pilkington.

15 Pilkington.

16 See Appendix 5 for examples of seven worship services involving choirs for children, youth and adults. The seventh of these model services uses *Softly and Tenderly Jesus is Calling* as a choral response to the Prayer of Confession.

17 Pilkington.

18 From *The Book of Order*, Presbyterian Church, USA, Chapter 1, "The Dynamics of Christian Worship," W-1.1001.

19 *Book of Order*, W-1.3034.

20 *Book of Order*, W-1.3034.

21 From Ruth Krehbiel Jacobs' notebook, edited by Helen Kemp, as printed in Choristers Guild LETTERS, Vol. XL, Number 6, January 1989.

22 M. Rinckart, *Nun danket alle Gott*, 1636; tr. Catherine Winkworth, 1863.

Appendix 1A
Organizational Aids

AID I A SAMPLE HANDBOOK FOR CHOIRS OF CHILDREN AND YOUTH
The material which follows is taken from a choir handbook given annually to each chorister. Although the information stays essentially the same, the cover is redone each year to reflect any changes in support staff, schedule, etc. The schedule of rehearsals and any special events for the choir year is given. A list of Sunday worship responsibilities could be included on the cover as well.

The Choirs for Children and Youth

PHILOSOPHY—The congregation is the primary choir. All people are given a voice and need the opportunity to learn to use it well. Our music ministry is designed to provide both regular and special opportunities for church members and those in the community without a church home, to express their faith through song. The very best time to begin to make a joyful noise is as a child. Thus, in weekly worship services, our choirs for children and youth take their turn presenting carefully selected and rehearsed anthems and hymns. But the idea of praise and service also includes spiritual development. Each rehearsal has the overall goal of Christian education. Music is our tool. In this regard, our work is different from school or community singing groups. In addition to performance, the choirs' focus is that of praising God and leading people in worship. All are welcome to find a place in the music program. As the noted hymnologist and composer/arranger Alice Parker has said, "Singing is a primary gift of God. It gives us a way of communicating with each other that words alone cannot come close to."

GOALS—The children and youth are trained in the development of their musical skills in a graded program of reading music, ear training, vocal development, pitch acuity, etc. But more than these things, they are developing a sense of Whose they are and what they can become within the context of the Christian faith. Through carefully chosen texts, scriptural and poetic, the basic tenants of the Christian faith are taught. (As every commercial jingle writer knows, we remember what we sing!) With each age group comes the attempt to teach responsibility, professionalism, and commitment via the discipline inherent in achieving high calibre performance standards. Balancing this is a focus on process as equal in importance.

SERVICE AND OUTREACH—The singing and ringing choirs from grade 2 through high school participate in some outreach activity each year to take the great music of the church outside our walls. Several cassette tapes are available by the choirs, including a tape of hymns made by youth to be given to each newly baptized child. In this way, the choristers are given a means by which they may act on their promise made at each baptism, to support the young child in his or her spiritual growth. The music program provides one of the essential elements for a growing congregation: numerous points of entry for potential new members. The music program serves as a valuable means of outreach for the entire church.

STAFF AND SUPPORT—*Biographical information about the music director(s) could be given here.*

The music committee, a part of the Worship, Music and Arts Committee, is made up of several elders of the church and other church members who provide a support system for the entire program. Each year there are many individuals who support the work of the music ministry on a weekly basis as choir parents, helpers and accompanists. The secretary to whom choir matters should be addressed is _____.

FUNDING—The music program is one of many areas supported by the generous pledges of the church members. Staff positions are professional, a large music library is maintained, Orff-Schulwerk instruments, robes, and other supplies for the choirs are paid for by the annual church budget. Only the annual Music Festival is self-sustaining.

It is expected that participants whose families are not pledging members of this congregation will support the program financially. As a guide, comparable class programs, such as those offered at [list here local ballet and music class fees] charge [$_ to $_] each year. While participation is not predicated on financial support at this level for those who cannot do so, it is hoped that the church budget will be supported by the families of all children and youth involved in its programs.

The Graded Choir Program

JOYFUL NOISE (K-l)   Wednesdays, 3:30—4:15
JOYFUL NOISE TOO (age 4-5, the pre-Kindergarten year) Wednesdays, 3:30—4:15

These groups are our youngest choristers, and are primarily preparatory groups. While actual Sunday morning responsibilities as a choir are minimal, these children begin to learn about worship and what is expected of them when they sing in a worship service. The musical focus is on finding the true singing voice, increasing the singing range, and learning to match pitch. Music literacy readiness activities based on manipulative games create an enthusiasm for future musical growth. Movement and use of simple percussion instruments with an improvisatory focus round out the rehearsal time. Orff-Schulwerk (after the German composer Carl Orff) is used with each of the children's choirs. It is an approach to music education based on experiential learning. From time to time, the Joyful Noise program utilizes a weekly "music bag" drawing. The bag is filled with items of interest to the young musician. Each chorister takes home the bag at least once. The Joyful Noise choirs sing in worship several times each year, and parents are invited to several "Open House" rehearsals.

CAROL CHOIR (grades 2-3)   Thursdays, 4:00—5:30

At this age, the children are ready to begin a regular pattern of participating as a choir in worship, which they do every 6 to 8 weeks. They also begin the Service Award Program, a means by which the church acknowledges the chorister's gift of time and talent. A special Chorister Cross is worn, at first on a black ribbon, then changing colors each year and adding beads indicating years of service and other activities choristers may choose to accomplish.

Musical skills are expanded upon, with beginning emphasis on transferring rudimentary notation to the written page. During the one and one half hour class, time is given to improvisation at the Orff-Schulwerk instruments, to movement exploration and to the use of hand signals as a means of learning to sight sing. They begin to use a folder and cubby, and practice worship decorum. The children have two classes during this time frame: their choral rehearsal and a music enrichment class. The Carol Choir sings in worship every five to six weeks.

CELEBRATION SINGERS (grades 4-5)   Thursdays, 4:00—5:30

More intensive vocal challenges and worship responsibilities are introduced at this age level. They sing in worship every four to six weeks and when singing at the 11 entire service of worship, seated together as a choir. Increased emphasis is placed on the learning of musical terminology and literacy development with the goal being usable sight singing skills. The voice is ready for more challenging repertoire and the ear is ready for some part singing. Work in the Orff-Schulwerk and in hand signals is continued and a handbell segment is a part of each week's one and one half hour schedule. The Service Award Program, described under Carol Choir, continues. Celebration Singers have two classes within this one and one half hour time frame, alternating with the Carol Choir for the choir segment and the music enrichment class. Handbell ringing is included as a part of this instruction. The Celebration Singers sings in worship every four to five weeks.

ALLELUIA SINGERS   Wednesdays, 4:55—5:45

Our middle school choir is scheduled just after the Alleluia Ringers, the handbell choir for this age group, and precedes the supper, fellowship, and confirmation class (8th grade) which make up The Wednesday Connection designed for middle school students. This choir sings music in unison, two and three parts, with particular attention given to the changing voices of both boys and girls of this age. Studies show that it is best to sing through the voice change in order that the muscles do not atrophy. With careful attention to the musical, physical and social needs, the Alleluia Singers prepares young people for the more intensive challenges of the senior high choir. The Service Award Program, described under Carol Choir, continues. The middle school choir sings in worship every three to four weeks.

SENIOR HIGH CHOIR   Sundays, 5:00—6:15

This choir is the culmination of the work of the multiple choir program. Many of the young people in this choir have sung with us since they were in pre-school. All high school students are welcome to join at anytime, however. The Service Award Program, described under Carol Choir, continues. The senior high choir sings in worship every two to three weeks.

Procedures

ATTENDANCE AND ABSENCES—A choir is a team effort in every sense of the word, so an individual absence effects the whole group. Likewise, with our very limited rehearsal time, punctual presence at rehearsals and on Choir Sundays is vital. The vocal warm-ups and listening exercises which are done at the beginning are crucial to a successful choral rehearsal. In a handbell choir, missing people means missing bells, thus it is expected that if an absence is anticipated, a substitute will be called from the list provided (excluding the youngest bell choir, grades 4-5).

In the event of absence, please contact us. This may be done by calling the church office or the appropriate choir parent. Their names and phone numbers appear on the inside cover of this handbook. The Youth Choir has a "sign out" book to record anticipated absences.

There are no "excused" or "unexcused" absences. We assume that choristers want to be in the program and therefore grant the next year's Service Award Ribbon (grades 2 through high school) on the basis of 75% attendance at rehearsals and on choir Sundays. Since leading worship is a primary feature of this musical training and because children generally want very much to participate with their choir on these days, the calendar is provided early each semester to advise families of these Sundays.

ATTIRE ON SUNDAYS—Each choir wears a vestment, the youngest children using smocks until grade 2. Shoes should be polished, obvious hair ornaments and jewelry should be avoided, as they call attention to the individual rather than the choir as a whole. Parents are asked to encourage the proper care of the vestment and to assist where appropriate.

SUNDAY RESPONSIBILITIES—Choirs from grade 4 and older sit together for the entire worship hour. Please do not request to be dismissed early. When individual choristers get up and leave after singing, it gives the impression that what we do is merely for show, or performance, instead of being an integral part of the experience of worship. When everyone remains in the service, leading the hymn singing, listening to the scripture, focusing on the sermon, participating in the prayers, our contribution is more meaningful to us, individually, as well. Please plan accordingly on the Sunday mornings your choir sings.

CANCELLATION OF REHEARSALS—If, due to weather a rehearsal must be canceled, radio stations __ AM and __ FM will announce it. Each choir also has a telephone chain to disseminate information quickly. This will be distributed early in the year.

DROP OFF/PICK UP—Place here pertinent information regarding any safety procedures. Youngest choirs are dismissed together and taken to meet their rides. The older children are expected to use the safety procedures explained to them at choir and **reinforced by you at home. Additionally, we ask you to let us know with a form (enclosed)** if your child is in a carpool and with whom, and always advise us of occasions when s/he will be going home with someone else.

ENTERING THE BUILDING AND THE SANCTUARY—Choristers are reminded that their only entrance and exit on rehearsal day is the door [by the playground]. This is a security precaution as well as an important consideration for noise control. Especially during office hours, the staff appreciates your cooperation. Additionally, we ask that parents reinforce the concept of the sanctuary as the room **where we worship. Food and drink, running, yelling, climbing over the pews are not allowed.** Choirs rehearse in the sanctuary the week prior to singing in worship. We enter the space as a group and in our time there, try to help instill a sense of reverence.

CARPOOLS—We have included a form to aid in organizing carpools. Even if you don't need one, please fill it out, since you may be able to help another child make it to rehearsal.

AN INVITATION—Children involved with music often have parents who want to be as well! Contact the church office to make your interest known.

AID II CHOIR PARENT DUTY ROSTER

ON CHOIR DAYS:
1. Assist arrival and dismissal of children as appropriate.
2. Place first names on upper right corner of all handouts, place in cubby.
3. Address envelopes for absentees and enclose any handout sent home that day; if no handout, address and send a "we missed you" card.

4. Update service awards as completions are made.
5. Enter rehearsal 5 minutes before dismissal to take roll, hand out papers.
6. Take attendance (date the box for each rehearsal. "A" = absent. Mark Sundays with a different color.) Fill out registration cards for new members.
7. Mark roll poster as well as attendance cards in office.
8. Leave anything to be mailed on the counter in the work station.

ON SING-IN-CHURCH SUNDAYS:
1. Call extra person(s) to help robe children and to sit with them during the service, as appropriate to age. Help rehang robes afterwards and see that children who leave the service get to church school classes.
2. Help get children seated in pre-service rehearsals, hand out bulletins, hymnals, music, etc. Help calm children while other choirs are rehearsing if more than one choir is in the room. Assist in getting children lined up and ready to enter the sanctuary.
3. Take attendance.

THROUGHOUT THE YEAR:
1. On both regular rehearsal days and service Sundays, your arrival 10-15 minutes before that of the choristers is crucial.
2. Always provide a substitute if you must be absent.
3. Keep a current master list of your choir members with birth dates. Add carpool information as necessary.
4. Record information changes on above list and on original registration forms, attendance form and service award grid.
5. Send birthday cards; advise director of approaching birthdays, prior to rehearsal if possible.
6. Let the secretary know of any changes in registration.

IN THE FALL (delegate as you wish):
1. After third rehearsal, organize a phoning tree for your group. Update as necessary.
2. Assign robes, inform director of any cleaning needs, find someone to mend as necessary. (Sewing group here at church?)
3. All choirs except youth: make roll poster using photograph of each child. Arrange for a parent to photograph your choir, individually and collectively.
4. Make name card (5" x 7" index card) with first name of each chorister for use on rehearsal chair and in sanctuary.
5. Grade 2 and older: Assign a cubby to each chorister and write out a list of names and cubby number.

END OF THE YEAR:
1. Carol Choir and older: prepare new beads and new ribbons for service award program, as per separate instructions.
2. Think through the year and make suggestions for next year.

AID III A SAMPLE ATTENDANCE CARD

Made of 3" x 5" card stock, this little card tracks four years of choir attendance. The cards for each member of a particular choir are joined together by a ring through a hole punched in each upper left corner.

Attendance is indicated by either the date, or an A if absent. In the case of a Sunday service responsibility, a diagonal line is drawn to provide two sections. One represents the weekly rehearsal prior and other, the service date itself.

Because a single card lasts so long, it is prudent to reinforce the hole. If the cards are arranged in seating order, it is a simple matter for attendance takers to look at the empty chairs and know who is missing. This is especially helpful in the case of substitute choir parents.

NAME - LAST, FIRST, MIDDLE																	CHOIR		
ADDRESS						ZIP											PHONE		
	YR.				YR.				YR.				YR.						
SEPT.																			
OCT.																			
NOV.																			
DEC.																			
JAN.																			
FEB.																			
MAR.																			
APR.																			
MAY																			
JUNE																			

AID IV A SAMPLE REGISTRATION CARD WITH SERVICE AWARD GRID

This card is updated each year but not replaced. Notice that the reverse side contains a history of the chorister's ribbons and beads earned each year in the Chorister Service Award program. In this way if the cross is lost, the beads and ribbon colors may be accurately replaced.

CHOIR REGISTRATION

NAME_____ PHONES (HOME)_____

ADDRESS_____ (WORK)_____

BIRTH DATE ___/___/___ PARENT(S) NAME(S) _____
mo. day yr.

SCHOOL_____GRADE_____

INSTRUMENTS PLAYED? HOW LONG?_____

OTHER ACTIVITIES/HOBBIES _____

Office use only: indicate current program year in appropriate place(s)

JNT_____ JN_____ CC_____ CS_____ AS_____
HS_____ Bells_____ Bach_____

AID V A SAMPLE SERVICE AWARD PROGRAM

The service award program described below begins at grade 2 (seven or eight years old) and continues through high school. It involves the Guild Cross, available to members of Choristers Guild, various colored ribbons, 1/8" wide, representing years in the program, and beads which the chorister may choose, or not, to earn. Based on the model of scouting badges, the program acknowledges the time and effort of the individual chorister.

For example, Matthew began the choir program in his pre-kindergarten year and has stayed with it. He is now finishing first grade, his third year of choir. In the spring of that year at the annual service award ceremony, Matthew is presented his Chorister's Cross on a black ribbon signifying his first year in the Service Award program. It also has three tan beads, representing each of the three years he has already participated in choir. A year from now, assuming he has 75% attendance at rehearsals and worship responsibilities, the black ribbon is removed and the cross is then strung on a green one. The three beads remain, but since Matthew missed only two rehearsals, he is given a small blue bead. He also attends church school regularly and gets a small red bead for that. Matthew did not choose to complete the hymn study project but he did come to a special Young Musician's class during the summer and so earns a bead for the one activity but not the other.

Ashley did not become involved at the church until she was in grade 6. At that time, she entered the choir program and wore a Guild Cross on a black ribbon, just like Matthew, except that she had no beads, since she just joined the program. However, she rings in the handbell choir, therefore, she wears a burgundy ribbon along with the black one representing the singing choir. At the Service Award ceremony in the spring, Ashley moves up to the green ribbon for singing choir. She chooses not to continue with handbells, so the burgundy ribbon remains (rather than moving to the next color for bell choir, or removing the burgundy ribbon). She brought in a new member who stayed all year, and gets a large red bead for that accomplishment. She completed the hymn study and chose also to play her violin in the Young Artists' Recital and thus receives beads for each of those activities. She also attends church school regularly. Thus in the course of one year, this active first year chorister changes a ribbon color, and recieves four beads.

Clearly, it is unlikely that any two choristers' beads and ribbons will be identical. Each cross gives a picture of each choristers' involvement. Many choristers have beads nearly all the way up each side of the ribbon, others choose less aggressive involvement with their choir membership.

Beads may be earned for a wide variety of activities, as noted above. Some other suggestions are: choir officer or section leader, singing a solo or playing an instrument in worship, helping with younger choirs, keeping a neat notebook, careful music markings according to instructions, acting as choir librarian, working on some special project to help the music program or the worship or service life of the congregation, etc. No matter which beads are given, all should be earned, not given out like a treat.

The cross belongs to the chorister after four years in the service award program. If the chorister moves prior to that time, we suggest that the parents help us with the expense of giving the cross to their child. At high school graduation, the cross, all of its old beads and any new ones are kept on the final years' ribbon colors and presented to the chorister with some degree of ceremony. The Cross will be worn again each time the choir alumnus returns home to sing during the college-age years. The seniors gather for a photo and handshakes and goodbye hugs which are all a part of the graduation process.

At least one minister is present at the service award ceremony, and the choir parents are involved as well. If the program is so large that stringing and unstringing beads by a few people is unworkable, have each chorister fill out a form stating any new beads, and the new ribbon colors (once 75% attendance has been verified). The choristers, assisted by parents as necessary, then go from station to station, turning in last years' ribbons, getting new ones plus any beads earned during the past choir season. A large supply of wide eye tapestry needles is necessary. Plastic "zippered" sandwich bags labled with each chorister's name, will help keep beads together until they are re-strung on the new ribbons. The choristers then return the updated cross to their cubby or choir robe hanger, or some central location. (They do not get tangled if stored in individual plastic bags or on individual robe hangers.)

Each cross is labeled with the chorister's name on the back with narrow white tape. On the reverse side of the registration card, a grid is kept and updated to record the latest ribbon colors and all of the beads earned over the years. In this way, if a cross should be mislaid, it can be reconstructed accurately. If a chorister leaves the program for some reason other than moving, reuse the cross if need be, but store the ribbons and beads in a labled plastic bag in the event of the chorister's future return. The chorister should be told that this is being done.

CHOIRISTER SERVICE AWARD PROGRAM										
Program Year										
Singing Choir										
Bell Choir										
Bach Choir										
Perfect attendance										
Two absences										
Special Events*										
Soloist										
New Member, summer choir										
Choir Officer										
Choir helper										
Hymn study										
Accompanist										
Church School										
*list special events:										

AID VI A SAMPLE VESTMENT AND VOICE CHARTING CARD

Unlike the other cards described above, this 5" x 7" card is new each year. Its purpose is two-fold:

1) to keep adequate track of the child's size, particularly height. This is useful in assigning a robe and in forming seating charts.
2) to monitor the child's developing voice and musicianship.

DATE ———————— Name of Choir ————————————————

Name ————————————————————— Grade ———— Age ————

Height ———————— Robe # ———————— Folder # ————————

Range

Best tone

Pitch Acuity: poor ———————— fair———————— good ———————— excellent ————————
Sight Reading: poor ———————— fair———————— good ———————— excellent ————————

Appendix 1B
Teaching Tools

Instructions for making RHYTHM BLOCKS

24 TOTAL FEET OF 2 X 4 WITH THE FOLLOWING CUTS:

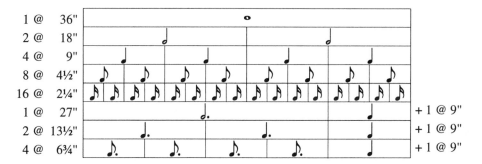

1 @	36"							
2 @	18"							
4 @	9"							
8 @	4½"							
16 @	2¼"							
1 @	27"							+ 1 @ 9"
2 @	13½"							+ 1 @ 9"
4 @	6¾"							+ 1 @ 9"

1.   Sand well
2.   Draw note values and corresponding rests on opposite side with indelible marker
3.   Cover with a varnish

or

Paint first, then draw on note values

I first saw these rhythm blocks used in 1968 by Melvin Gallagher who taught young children for many years in Hawaii. They worked so well that I made a set and have adapted their use with great success in my own teaching.

Instructions for making a SOLFEGE LADDER

This idea came from a book called "Are You Open on Saturday and Sunday" by E. Lowell Rogers (see Bibliography). On one side of the key tags is written a number from 1 through 7 and on the other side DO RE MI FA SO LA TI. Make the ladder long enough for at least one and one half octaves of the diatonic scale to be hung. The base is a large, restaurant size can, with two holes to bolt in the 1x1. Fill the can ½ full with plaster of paris for stability.

Diagram of Hand Signals for Solfege

Do

Ti

La

Sol

Fa

Mi

Re

Do

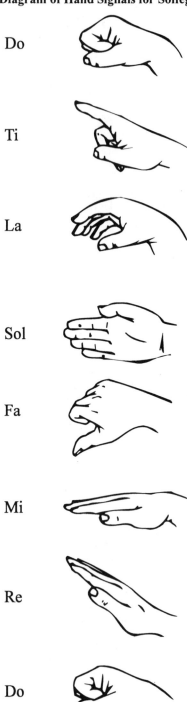

Weekly Rehearsal Planner

Name of choir _____ Rehearsal date _____

Preparing for worship on _____ Anthem _____

Hymns (note descants, free accomp. etc.): _____

_____

_____

Other service music: _____

_____

Other anthems to be covered and dates of use in worship: _____

_____

Areas of focus:
(In each of the following categories, write in specific goals for that particular rehearsal)

1. Vocal Development _____

2. Literacy Skills_____

3. Movement Activities _____

4. Ear Training _____

5. Theological or Scriptural Focus _____

6. Decorum Goals _____

7. Announcements _____

Rehearsal Sequence: _____

(List here in order in which the rehearsal will incorporate the above goals, for example: 1, 4, 2, 3, 5, 6. Review the sequence again prior to beginning the next rehearsal.)

This is but one example of a weekly rehearsal planner. The important thing is to be able to set goals and judge whether or not they are being met. If, for example, a particular number representing one of the stated goals has not been used in several weeks, this should be noted and corrected in the next rehearsal.

Appendix 2A

Auditioned Church Choirs for Children and Youth

In the mainline Protestant church I serve, we began a successful auditioned choir almost by accident. Just two years into building our children's choir program, a colleague in another area church and I decided to hold a "summer arts week" in which music more demanding than usual would be prepared during an intense two week period in August. This project naturally attracted children who were eager for a musical challenge. It was a multi-age group of grades 5—8, and typically, in a children's choral program that was just beginning, only girls signed up. Our goal: to sing the second movement duet of J.S. Bach's Cantata #78, *Wir eilen mit schwachen doch emsigen schritten*, in German, for the second annual Bach Festival to be held the following spring. Our "Bach Choir" was successful in achieving its musical goals, and it disbanded immediately following the festival. But the congregation wanted more.

Thus, the decision was made to regroup the following January in anticipation of the next Bach Festival, this time without the choristers from the other church. The requisite for membership in the Bach Choir was chiefly interest and commitment to both this, the "extra-mile choir," *and* the regular choir. In order to audition, each person must have completed one full year in the regular choir.

The key elements for admission to the choir were enthusiasm and desire reflected in excellent attendance and behavior, pitch acuity, and musical ear. Children with marginal music reading ability were always accepted into the group, with the understanding that this area would be worked on individually as well as in rehearsal. Those with a less-than-great musical ear were encouraged to continue with my help, their efforts in developing their musicianship so that their audition would be successful. For three years the group was made up only of girls, in fact, it was open only to girls (a policy I would not use again) and increased its age span as junior high members entered high school. Then came the year we discovered that the five high school girls in our Bach Choir were required to be on tour with the local public school choir during the same week our Music Festival had been set. The orchestra was hired, the soloists secured, there was no changing of dates. Thus the decision was made to allow boys to audition. By that time, we had "bred" a large, musically eager crew of boys in grades 5—8 who jumped at the opportunity. From that point on, the Bach Choir has been co-ed.

For the first eight years, this auditioned group sang only for this special festival, rehearsing as an auditioned group once a week beginning in January. As interest and opportunities arose, the Bach Choir began weekly rehearsals for the entire program year. In its eleventh year, it underwent a major reorganization due to two primary factors: 1) that original crew of boys were now tenors and basses and wanted to be back in an auditioned group; 2) girls who had begun in grade school were now in high school, in a much greater proportion than before, so that the sound of the group was that of a young women's chorus rather than that of a children's choir. Our solution to both of these factors was to divide the Bach Choir into two divisions: Grades 5—8, treble voices only; and Grades 9—12, a mixed voice ensemble.

These talented musicians represent 85% of the non-auditioned choirs, and nearly all of them are active in other areas of the church's life as well, serving as officers in the fellowship groups, deacons and elders. The experiences of these young people as children in this musically challenged group became the nucleus of our successful (non-auditioned as well as auditioned) high school choir today. All those not in Bach Choir are encouraged to come for voice and musicianship classes, and to audition for the Bach Choir if they think they would like to work that hard. Everyone who has made the effort eventually gets into the group and very few have "given up." Over the years several singers capable of the auditioned choir have opted not to join because of schedule overload.

Each year for many years, I asked the Music Committee to assess the value or problems of having an auditioned choir. I brought up the issue of exclusivity and each time the discussion led to the same decision: keep the Bach Choir. The most crucial concept in the decision to have an auditioned choir is the non-negotiable requirement of active membership in the non-auditioned choir for their age group. On only one occasion did a student test me on this issue, attending faithfully the first four Bach Choir rehearsals but always having an excuse for 'regular' choir; the student was dropped from the Bach Choir after a warning that one more absence would make her ineligible to continue.

Over and over again, we remind this group that their primary responsibility is to their regular choir. This is the group, which with all of their fellow choristers, prepares music for Sunday morning worship (rather than for special occasions, the primary domain of the auditioned choir) and which must not be weakened in any way by the existence of the Bach Choir.

Appendix 2B

Establishing an Inner-city Choir, Sponsored by a Suburban Church

I am indebted to Marcia Wood, Administrative Director of the Trenton Children's Chorus, for her help in preparing this synopsis of its development and structure.

How We Began

In 1989, Nassau Presbyterian Church decided to organize a chorus for children in the inner city of Trenton, one half hour south of Princeton. We had three goals:

1. to provide traditional choral training and performance experience to children who otherwise would not have these opportunities;
2. to provide a way for the adults and children of our own congregation to cross the cultural barrier between white suburbia and black inner city;
3. to connect with other churches of this denomination (and others) by sharing this outreach project with them.

We began with several strengths:

1. a congregation with the necessary will, resources and potential volunteer base to initiate the project;
2. a well established church-sponsored after school program in Trenton that served potential chorus members;
3. a skilled children's choir director who conceived the project, and, who had previous experience teaching inner-city children.

The first task was to visit church and community leaders in Trenton, explain the project and listen to their advice. Working in partnership with congregations in the geographical location we wished to serve has been vital to the success of the Trenton Children's Chorus. These churches have provided rent-free rehearsal space, opportunities for the chorus to perform, a local and continuous contact with families in their neighborhood, and in one instance, the use of a bus. Congregations in the inner-city as well as other suburban locations have taken up unsolicited special offerings which have made it possible to invest in risers, uniforms and other capital equipment.

Recruitment and Training of Support Staff

Using the support system model explained elsewhere in this book, we recruited choir parents and designed an award program. We hired additional music support staff, an accompanist and assistant director. Dedication to the project and interest in working with the particular problems of an urban setting were important criteria in our hiring choices as was musical training.

Our volunteers have occasionally been parents of the singers, but usually are church members or college students. The volunteers have found it helpful to meet together often—weekly during the first year or so. This enabled us to clarify expectations of attendance, behavior and appearance in order to be consistent and firm each week at the rehearsals. We designed and redesigned the awards program to fit the particular needs of these children, emphasizing their responsibility to be present and on time each week, to notify us ahead of time in case of absence, and to respond to notices sent home. It is extremely helpful to visit existing inner-city programs and classrooms and to offer to all staff, training by someone with experience in teaching inner-city children.

Recruitment and Selection of Choristers

During the summer, we visit vacation church schools, day camps, and enrichment programs in the city, offering a demonstration rehearsal, talking about the requirements for membership and the opportunities awaiting our choristers. Wearing the colorful Chorus polo shirt at each site, we hand out a simple brochure explaining who, what, where and when, with a tear-off registration form. These are also left in churches.

Recruitment is a never ending task. Word of mouth and contact with the local school music teachers are key factors. Several of these teachers send us children they identify as interested. These are our most successful choristers musically and in terms of longevity. The children who "drop in" (usually those who live in the neighborhood) have been less successful, despite our efforts to explain the goals and rules of our organization and foster growth in each child.

Our rules are few and simple: pay attention to the director (the choir parent, the bus driver, etc.); don't talk during rehearsal; participate fully. Hitting or fighting is prohibited. Attendance is required. On occasion, we must ask a child not to come back because of failure to abide by the rules. This policy decision was difficult to make since some of the neediest children are the most disruptive. We have come to understand that in our once-a-week rehearsal format, it is not likely that we will be able to dramatically change these negative behaviors despite our desire and earnest efforts to do so. We opt instead to reach those with whom we have a chance to make a difference.

About one third of the children recruited each year drop out before year's end. This abnormally high attrition is once again, connected to the particular problems of the inner city. Many of our children have poor support systems at home, attributable to the unique problems of poverty. Many move in with other relatives, or move away very suddenly. Phones are disconnected routinely. We try to follow through with those who drop out, as well as with those whom we have not invited back, but this is often difficult. It is important to point out that some of our attrition is due to efforts of a child's family to place him/her into what they perceive as a more advantageous educational environment. Usually a private school, we have lost children because the chorister can no longer get to rehearsal since our bus and van routes cannot accommodate the change.

Structure

Currently, the Trenton Children's Chorus consists of two choirs: a training unit of second through fifth graders, and a group of fifth through eighth graders who are invited to participate following their success in the training choir. A number of these older students participate, as well, in the auditioned choir outlined on pages 137—138. Rehearsals are held one afternoon a week; performances every two months or so. This schedule and organization is the result of experimentation until we discovered what worked for this particular group—its singers, its staff and volunteers.

Transportation is the #1 obstacle to an inner-city venture, particularly on a weekday afternoon. (Many organizations prefer Saturday or Sunday meeting times for this reason, an option not open to us.) To deal with the transportation problem, our training choirs are divided between two different churches, so that members can walk to and from rehearsals. Since the older choir meets in only one place, we must provide transportation for the majority of singers. The church bus and a pair of vans pick up from schools and after-school programs. We dismiss late enough in the day so that some parents are able to be on hand to meet their children. The others are taken home by our bus, or by one of our staff.

Commitment is the #2 obstacle: Even more than suburban children, our singers need to learn to work toward long-term goals. Performances are held frequently and intentionally spaced so that each becomes an obtainable, "within sight" reward. Proper rehearsal decorum and attendance are measured in these smaller segments (with visual and verbal reminders), rather than over the course of the year. In this way, a child who has not earned the privilege of performance in one concert may begin immediately to work towards the next one. Applause is a powerful reward.

Opportunities

In addition to programs and concerts for church and community organizations, the Trenton Children's Chorus has had opportunities to join with choirs from the sponsoring churches: children's choir festivals—local and out of state, concerts with community choruses and orchestras, director's workshops and professional organization conferences, musical productions, and, a professional opera production have all been part of our brief history. These occasions become a way to encourage relationships between families in the sponsoring church and families of the chorus, as well as to increase exposure in the larger community.

Each May, we hold a final concert, awards ceremony and supper to which family, church members and friends of the Chorus are invited. Families bring a dessert to share. We are fortunate to have several parents who are willing to cook up fried chicken for a crowd. This opportunity provides valuable time for the staff to connect with the parents and grandparents, most of whom we do not see on a regular basis (as one might with families of the children's choir at our church). We reinforce our goals, recruit for the fall, compliment the choir's work, let the kids show off, and sing together. It is a wonderful end of the year celebration.

Financial Support

We receive partial funding from the annual budget of our own church and from one of the Trenton churches. This second congregation completely sponsors one of the training choirs. A long term goal is to spread that idea to other churches until we have a network of training choirs all over the city.

Two annual fundraisers for our church's inner-city ministries are held in Princeton. Support within and outside of the church membership is generated for these events, through newspaper, radio, word of mouth, etc. Various formats for fundraising have been used: Madrigal Dinners in December, a spring Festival of Choirs, celebrity speakers, etc.

We also look to corporate resources. We sought and received a grant from a downtown Trenton bank to underwrite an annual spring "Festival of Children's Voices" held in the auditorium of the New Jersey State Museum. As we grow, we will approach other local private and government organizations for support which normally requires organizations such as this to seek not-for-profit incorporation.

A small but important source of funding comes from dues which are $10 annually per family. It is important not so much as income but because it exacts a commitment from the family of the chorister and opens a line of communication with them.

Ongoing costs include a salary for musical assistants, materials, snacks, and transportation (bus driver, gas). Office expenses are absorbed by our church. We are able to use the extensive music library at the church but purchase secular music for performance as well. Uniforms, risers, chimes, Orff instruments, and other major equipment needs are purchased as possible. Both the Musical Director and the Administrative Director, though professionally trained, volunteer their time to this project. This is a weakness in our current structure and threatens its long term viability.

Ongoing Projects

The Synod of the Northeast (Presbyterian Church, USA) has honored a yearly grant request to fund an October weekend Chorus retreat. Eligibility for this overnight camping adventure is based on rehearsal effort and attendance in the earliest weeks of the choir season. The retreat gives us an opportunity to further reinforce these goals and to spend a concentrated amount of time developing musical skills.

Two choristers are selected each spring to be the recipients of a scholarship to *Albemarle,* the two week coed music camp of the American Boychoir School here in Princeton. Those selected for this experience pledge to return to our choir the following fall in order to share their learning with the group. Funds for camperships are solicited in co-operation with the church's after school program (which attempts to send each of its children to a summer camp of some type).

In all fundraising, we are careful to note that efforts between outreach groups must be coordinated, that soliciting such funds must not be done at the risk of jeopardizing the overall pledging to the church budget, and that every well has a bottom. Communication between church staff, the stewardship committee, and all program chairpersons is essential.

Musical Considerations

The best way to achieve success with an inner-city chorus is to grow it up, just as a multiple choir program in a church would be built. We are looking toward the establishment of pre-school groups in the future. This will enable us to take advantage of the optimal point for teaching musical skills that are particular to early childhood.

Most of our choristers do not have the opportunity for private instrumental instruction, although several participate in school orchestras or bands. Sight reading instruction appears to be non-existent except as we teach it. Part singing has been a particular challenge in these early years since the ear has not been well trained. We anticipate seeing a dramatic change in due time as our younger children take their place in the older choir.

Many of our choristers are exceptionally talented vocally and delight in the opportunity to sing in a different way from the traditional "gospel music" production used in their own churches and some of the schools. We do use this way of singing occasionally, when it fits the style of a particular song, but not regularly. We opt instead to build the true singing voice, using repertoire from European, contemporary, and traditional American sources. Our philosophy is that a sound is never wrong, only different, and various styles of music can be sung in various ways. The children enjoy finding what their voices can do and respond quickly to nuance of tone quality, less so to nuance of melody (e.g., if, in two phrases there is a slight melodic change in the second, that is more difficult for these children to process and reproduce, either by rote or visually, than learning an altogether different phrase from the first). We attribute this fact to our having begun work with our choristers at age 10 and older, well past the brain's time table for processing such nuance efficiently.

As is true of many ventures, we who began and manage the Trenton Children's Chorus have been the recipients of so very much in return. The smiles, the laughter, the wonderful singing are weekly reminders that the work is worth the effort. We are convinced that we currently have at least one "baby Jessye Norman" in our midst and that given the opportunity, and a lucky break, some of these youngsters may have a career in music.

Each Tuesday afternoon, we see the results of our firm but loving discipline as the children become responsible singers. We learn their strengths as well as their weaknesses, and they get to know ours. We are becoming faces they trust, though the road is long towards eliminating fears and prejudices. We have confirmed that "disadvantaged" applies equally to children in suburbia—that a loving home is the best home. Our congregation is enriched by our budding connections with those from a culturally different environment. We hope that getting to know one another through making music together will be a bridge towards understanding and tolerance.

Appendix 3

Exemplary Anthems for Children's Choirs in the Church

In conducting a search for the finest in sacred choral literature for children, these selections are intended only as *examples* of the many equally fine anthems available. This list, attempts to balance literature of: composers living and dead, folk melodies, various publishers, diverse age and ability levels, seasonal and general texts and, accompaniments ranging from pianistic to suitable for organ as well as other instruments. Where either piano or organ is acceptable, the word keyboard is used.

All of these selections contain: 1) a memorable melody, 2) well crafted text underlay, 3) solid theology, 4) accompaniments which do not overwhelm the voices. They do not sound as if anyone could have written them. There are specific further features of each piece as to its individual merits, but the above mentioned qualities are assumed.

The anthems are organized into three groups. Among the first two, there are pieces on which very young or inexperienced singers may join on refrains, or other small segments. These are notated with *.

In the case of youth choirs, where the voicing is 2 part mixed, SAB or SATB, senior high choir is assumed, although middle school choirs with lowered voices will find suitable materials here as well. Note that mixed voice music is listed in all three categories, depending upon difficulty.

Group I

For early elementary and/or less experienced choristers: unison, or mostly unison with brief two-part sections.

Come and Sing
(unison with keyboard, opt. bells)
Gordon King
Choristers Guild CGA-338

Dear Lord, Lead Me Day By Day*
(unison with flute and keyboard)
Philippine melody, arr. Marshall
Choristers Guild CGA-637

Feed My Lambs *(transpose to D, rather than D flat, as written)*   Natalie Sleeth
(unison with 2 flutes and keyboard)   Carl Fisher CM 7777

God of Earth and God of Sea
(unison with flute and keyboard)
Margaret R. Tucker
Fred Bock Music Co. BG2081

Jesus Hands Were Kind Hands
(unison with flute and keyboard)
arr. Page
Choristers Guild CGA-485

Jesus, Jesus, Light From Light
(unison/2 part equal, keyboard)
Carl Schalk
Augsburg 11-2438

Lord Jesus, Be My Song*
(unison with keyboard)
Kevin Kosche
Choristers Guild CGA-678

Lord, Take My Hand and Lead Me (unison, with SA or SAB section, keyboard)	arr. T. Beck Concordia 98-2489
Psalm 98* (unison with keyboard)	Jane Marshall Choristers Guild CGA-427
To the Glory of Our King (unison with keyboard)	Robert Leaf Choristers Guild CGA-173
Until We Rest in Thee (unison treble with SATB, organ, opt. congregation)	Sue Ellen Page Choristers Guild CGA-504
A Waiting Carol (unison with keyboard, flute or recorder, drum)	Helen Kemp Choristers Guild CGA-555
A Winter Night* (unison with keyboard)	John Erickson Choristers Guild CGA-483

Group II

For choristers with increased ability, generally grade 4 and older. Most of the treble pieces in this section work well with inexperienced middle school choirs, as well as with elementary singers. Some SATB music is included as well.

And God Shall Wipe Away All Tears (unison with keyboard)	Eleanor Dale Hinshaw HMC 1284
As the Angels Said (unison with keyboard)	Robert Leaf Augsburg 11-2433
Bless the Lord, O My Soul (unison, brief divisi with keyboard)	Ruth Watson Henderson Hinshaw HMC 1171
Clap Your Hands, Stamp Your Feet (unison with keyboard)	Ronald A. Nelson Augsburg 11-0649
Come, Let Us Sing (unison/2 part with keyboard, two synthesizers, opt.)	Jody W. Lindh Choristers Guild CGA-478
Da Pacem Domine (4 part canon at 5th, unaccompanied)	Franck, arr. Goetze Boosey OC2B6187
Day By Day (three part treble or mixed with keyboard)	Martin How Hinshaw RSCM-506
Everywhere I Go* (unison/2 equal parts with keyboard)	Natalie Sleeth Choristers Guild CGA-171

Ezekiel Saw the Wheel
(SA with keyboard)

arr. Warren Williamson
Tetra/Continuo TC1132

Fear Not Good Shepherds
(3 part canon with keyboard)

Gregg Smith
G. Schirmer 12303

Fill the House of God*
(unison/2 equal parts with keyboard)

Robert Leaf
Broadman 4560-65

Flocks in Pastures Green Abiding
(unison with keyboard and two flutes, opt.)

J. S. Bach
Oxford Old Master Series

For Hard Things
(unison or SAB with keyboard)

Jane Marshall
Choristers Guild CGA-618

From the Rising of the Sun
(unison with keyboard)

Robert Powell
Choristers Guild CGA-463

God Who Touchest Earth With Beauty
(unison/2 part with keyboard)

Jacqueline Hanna McNair
Broadman 4560-48

He That is Down Need Fear No Fall
(unison with keyboard and flute)

Ralph Vaughn Williams
Oxford U-50

Higher Than the Heavens
(unison, two part with congregation, organ)

Ronald A. Nelson
Choristers Guild CGA-671

How Can I Keep From Singing?
(SATB with keyboard)

arr. Jeffrey Honoré
Choristers Guild CGA-567

The Incarnation
(SA with keyboard)

Ronald A. Nelson
Mark Foster

Jubilate Deo
(six part unison canon, unaccompanied)

Praetorius
Boosey 6350

Keep Your Lamps
(SATB, unaccompanied, three congas, opt.)

arr. Andre Thomas
HMC-577

Love, Joy and Peace
(two part mixed with keyboard)

Jane Marshall
Choristers Guild CGA-503

My Jesus is My Lasting Joy
(unison, keyboard, opt. string quartet accomp. available)

Buxtehude, arr. Bitgood
Gray, GCMR 2727

O Still Small Voice of Calm
(SATB with keyboard)

arr. Austin Lovelace
Belwin-Mills DMC 8097

Praise, Praise, Praise the Lord! (SATB with percussion)	Cameroon Processional Song, arr. Ralph Johnson Earthsongs, Anton Armstrong Choral Series
Praise the Lord, Our God, Forever (3 voices, equal or mixed with keyboard)	Mozart, arr. Ehret Fred Bock, B-G0464
Prayer For the Earth (2 equal parts with keyboard, opt. handbells)	Russian melody, arr. Hopson Augsburg 11-1745
Ride On Now, O King! (unison/descant, keyboard with opt. barred percussion)	Helen Kemp Choristers Guild CGA-54
Sing Praise, Alleluia (SAB with keyboard)	Emily Crocker Jenson 423-19090
Sing Praises to Our God (2 part treble with keyboard)	Robert Powell Concordia 98-2813
So Gentle The Donkey* (unison/SA with descant, keyboard)	John Barnard Oxford T 115
A Star, A Song (unison with keyboard)	Hal H. Hopson Choristers Guild CGA-167
Three Spirituals for Changing Voices (SAT or SATB, unaccompanied)	arr. Robert W. Thygerson Heritage Music Press #H6509
To Us Emmanuel (unison with descant, keyboard)	John Horman Hope A-605
What Does the Lord Require? (SATB with keyboard)	Allen Pote Hope A 684
When In Our Music God is Glorified (SATB with two horns and keyboard)	Stanford, arr. Dede Duson Alliance AMP 0011

Group III

Pieces contain elements which, to sing well in their entirety, will require more skill than those in previous categories. Geared to upper elementary and older choristers, the level of difficulty within this group is wide.

All Praise to God, Who Reigns Above (unison/2 equal with keyboard)	Vulpius, arr. Lenel Concordia 98-1142
All Things in Him (2 equal voices, canon)	Gerhard Krapf Concordia 98-2428

Alleluia, O come and Praise the Lord   J. S. Bach/setting: J. Hill
(unison/two part with keyboard)   Choristers Guild CGA-174

Cantate Domino   Rupert Lang
(3-4 part treble with synthesizer or organ)   Boosey OCTB6536

Dona Nobis Pacem   Richard DeLong
(SSAA, unaccompanied)   Alliance AMP 0021

Donkey Carol   John Rutter
(unison/two part with keyboard, 2 flutes, opt.)   Oxford T 111

Great Gettin' Up Mornin'!   arr. Mary Goetze
(3 part treble, unaccompanied)   Boosey OC3B6182

Have Your Lamps Gone Out?   arr. Malcolm Dalglish
(SAB with hammer dulcimer or piano)   Plymouth HL-403

I Shall Not Be Moved   arr. Alice Parker
(SATB, unaccompanied)   Lawson-Gould 51545

Jesus Name of Wondrous Love   Robert Powell
(2 part mixed with keyboard)   Concordia 98-2473

Jubilate Deo (1934)   Benjamin Britten
(SATB with organ)   Faber Music Ltd.

Little Child, O Babe Most Holy   G. Foxworth/setting: R. Powell
(unison/two part with keyboard)   Concordia 98-2516

Long, Long Ago   Carlisle Floyd
(unison, 2 equal voices with piano)   Boosey 5648

Non Nobis Domine   William Byrd
(3 part treble canon or SAB canon, unaccompanied)   Oxford 40.023

A Prayer of St. Richard of Chichester   L. J. White
(unison/descant)   Oxford # 44.033

Psalm 150   David Willcocks
(SSAA)   Oxford (Gordon V. Thompson Music) G-231

Saw Ye My Savior?   traditional, arr. David N. Johnson
(SATB with sop. solo; possible for children's choir)   Augsburg 11-1531

Seek to Serve   Lloyd Pfautsch
(2 part, equal or mixed)   Hope APM 003

Serenity   Charles Ives
(unison with organ)   Peer International, for Associated Music Publishers
                     from *Five Songs by Charles Ives,* compiled by Barbara Tagg

There is No Rose   Jim Leininger
SSAA with flute and handbells   Alliance AMP 0011

Extended Sacred Choral Works, with Annotations

A Selected List

In this context, "extended" indicates longer than the usual anthem length of two to four minutes. This list is by no means intended to be comprehensive, rather to give the reader a place to begin. All of these works have been successfully performed by children's choirs in the church. It goes without saying that the solos, duets, and the cantus firmus sections of the many Bach cantatas have historically been performed by children's voices in the church, as well as the concert hall. I owe a debt of thanks to my colleague, Dr. Kenneth B. Kelley, Director of Music at Nassau Presbyterian Church, Princeton, NJ, for his cheerful assistance in helping to assemble this compilation.

Amahl and the Night Visitors   Gian Carlo Menotti
SATB chorus, soloists   G. Schirmer
In addition to the boy treble in the lead role, children can be a part of the shepherd's chorus singing either or both the soprano and alto lines. This works well visually as well as chorally.

A Ceremony of Carols   Benjamin Britten
SSA and Harp   Boosey and Hawkes
Try combining upper elementary trebles with middle and high school trebles. Always interested in making his music accessible to less experienced musicians, Britten employed extensively the devices of canon and triads.

Chichester Psalms   Leonard Bernstein
SATB, boy treble   Boosey and Hawkes
Bernstein's original scoring was for boychoir and men. The treble parts, therefore, are accessible to children's voices, especially if performed with the reduced scoring of harp, organ and percussion, instead of the full orchestration. In particular, the second movement treble part with the boy solo is effective with children's voices. The text for the upper voices is Psalm 23, while the men's voices sing by contrast, Psalm 2, "Why do the nations rage?" Each movement may be performed separately from the whole.

Christmas Cantata: Welcome, Thou King of Glory   Vincent Luebeck
Two sopranos (or SA)   Concordia
Male voices are used ad libitum. The work is scored for two violins and continuo.
Flutes, recorders, oboes or clarinets may be substituted for the violins. In German,
English translation printed and usable.

The Christmas Story   Carl Orff and Gunild Keetman
Unison/two part trebles   Schott
Traditional carols set with Orff-Schulwerk accompaniment by the full instrumentarium
including recorders. "Judicious changes in the orchestration may be made, to suit
prevailing conditions." Spoken narration, other speaking parts, and a few solos.

Coming Forth Into Day   Libby Larsen
SATB and 2 part treble choir   E.C. Schirmer
With orchestra. Soprano and baritone soloists. Texts by Jehan Sadat, widow of Anwar
Sadat. The texts reflect the tensions and tragedies of the war torn Middle East as well
as the joys of childhood and family.

Creation's Praise   Ruth Watson Henderson
Two choirs of treble voices   Gordon V. Thompson Music
A challenging piece for children and youth trebles. Try combining all of the trebles
from upper elementary school through high school as Choir I (SSAA with much in
unison and thirds), and adult women as Choir II (SSA, much in triads.) Scored for
piano 4 hands, orchestration available.

Hodie   Ralph Vaughan Williams
SATB, treble choir, soprano, tenor, baritone soli   Oxford
Orchestration is full, keyboard reduction is usable in performance, but not preferred.
Performed with spoken narration. The children's choir is unison/two parts with an
occasional third part.

La Fiesta de la Posada   Dave Brubeck
SATB and unison treble choir   Shawnee Press
A staged production of the traditional Mexican *posada*. Adult soloists (SATB), piano,
two guitars, two trumpets, string bass and percussion. Scores for "Mariachi orchestra"
are available.

Lauda Sion   Dietrich Buxtehude
SAB Harmonia-Uitgave   C.F. Peters
With two violins and continuo. Accessible to a good high school choir; or adult choir
with children singing the soprano line, adult women on the alto; tenor and bass on the
same part. The Latin text, *Lauda Sion Salvatorem*, is for the second Thursday after
Pentecost or Corpus Christe. It would be appropriate for the time between Pentecost
and Advent.

Little Birthday Mass, A   Derek Holman
SSA and piano or harp   Boosey and Hawkes LCB-243
Written for a women's chorus, the piece would work well for ages 12 and older.
Throughout, varied vocal textures and much imitative writing are used, in both mixed
and common meters. The musical material of the Kyrie is reworked in the Agnus Dei.
Several tiny solo selections occur in the Gloria.

Make a Joyful Noise   Laurie Altman
SATB and 2/3 part treble choir   Unpublished
This is an extended work commissioned by Nassau Presbyterian Church, Princeton,
NJ. It is scored for jazz quartet (piano, bass, drums, vibraphone) and cello with solos
for soprano and baritone. At the time of this printing, the work is unpublished but
available from the composer who may be contacted through Westminster Conservatory, (609) 921-7100. The text is from Psalm 150 and Matthew 25:31-46.

Mass   Igor Stravinsky
SATB   Boosey and Hawkes
Scored for double wind quintet, children's voices work well on the treble parts
throughout, or only in the Gloria and Sanctus sections.

Mein Herz Ist Bereit (My Heart is Prepared)   Johann Vierdanck
Two equal treble parts   Walton Music Corp.
Scored for two violins and cello, this lovely and accessible piece of just under four
minutes could be used during Advent. In this edition, it is possible to perform the work
with keyboard alone. The text is Psalm 57:7-11.

Mass in C   Sigismund Neukomm
Two equal voices, keyboard or strings   Boosey and Hawkes LCB-247
Neukomm was a student of Michael Haydn, and this setting of the mass is a lovely
example of that classic style. The Benedictus, a chamber duet, could stand on its own
sung by full choir as a Palm Sunday (or Advent) anthem. The logical writing of this
period creats a superb learning tool for part singing, and this work is particularly
charming and accessible to children. Edited by Douglas Townsend, the full score and
instrumental parts (strings) are available on rental.

Misa Pequeña para Niños   Francisco Nuñez
Treble unison, two and three parts, piano   Boosey and Hawkes LCB-256
Opportunities for teaching literacy and listening concepts abound in this Spanish mass.
A missa brevis by virtue of its abbreviated texts, all five sections contain either simple
homophony or canon for the multiple parts (up to three). The Dorian mode of the Gloria
changes to Mixolydian through the use of inversion. The opening 16 measures of the
Señor, ten piedad, (Kyrie) are a cappella as is the final movement *Cordero de Dios*
(Agnus Dei). Everything else is accompanied by piano, which often creates rhythmic
contrast and dissonance with the voices.

Missa Brevis   Nancy Telfer
SSA   Lenel Music
This shortened mass setting has exciting changing meters and rhythmic motifs. It is unaccompanied.

Missa Brevis in C Minor   Imant Raminsh
Three part treble   Plymouth Music Co.
Keyboard accompaniment and optional oboe. The soprano solo may be done well by a high school girl. Very accessible to upper elementary voices, the work follows many of the devices used by Benjamin Britten in his compositions for children.

Missa Brevis in D   Benjamin Britten
Three part treble with organ   Boosey and Hawkes
More rhythmically challenging than Ceremony of Carols, this exciting piece will be sung well as a follow up to that more familiar work.

Missa Iona   Donald Fraser
Double SATB and 3 part children's choir   unpublished
With organ, harp and strings. The text is English and Latin. A recording of this work is available through the American Boychoir School, 17 Lambert Dr., Princeton, NJ. 08543

Noye's Fludde   Benjamin Britten
Soloists and chorus of animals   Boosey and Hawkes
Originally scored for youth, the opera is often cast with adults in the large solo roles and children as the animals. The original casting, however, is accessible to well trained high school students. The opening Animal chorus parts ("Kyrie eleison") are placed low to mid-range, and are difficult to sing beautifully by young children and still be heard. To avoid belting, add middle school and high school students, or have all of the animal entrances sung an octave higher than written.

The Passion of Our Lord according to St. Matthew   J.S. Bach
Double SATB, Children's choir, orchestra
Children can easily handle the *cantus firmus* in the first movement. More difficult is the two part treble section in movement 33. Often sung by soloists or by the women of Choir 1, children's voices offer a wonderful contrast to the adults of Choir 2. Of the various editions, I prefer the translation by Robert Shaw, published by G. Schirmer.

Psalm 150   Benjamin Britten
Two part   Boosey and Hawkes
Britten wrote in his notes: "The instrumentation of this work is largely left to the choice of the conductor, according to the availability of the instrumentalists. What are essential are 1) a treble instrument—Recorder, Flute, Oboe, etc.; 2) some sort of drum; 3) a keyboard instrument...as for the voices, it is really essential to have two parts." This piece works well with middle school students, changed voices doubling the alto line in most places, dropping out in what might be termed "distinctly treble" passages.

Psalmkonzert   Heinz Werner Zimmermann
Five part mixed choir, unison children   Concordia
Baritone soloist, three trumpets, vibraphone, and string bass. The children sing the
cantus firmus, "Now Thank We All Our God."

Saint Nicholas Mass   Benjamin Britten
SATB and two part children   Boosey and Hawkes
Orchestra, tenor soloist. The children should be at a distance from the adult choir ("a
gallery choir" it is termed) and with a separate conductor. Very accessible to upper
elementary and middle school trebles.

Symphony of Psalms   Igor Stravinsky
SATB   Boosey and Hawkes
From the composer: "The choir should contain children's voices, which may be
replaced by female voices (soprano and alto) if a children's choir is not available."
Another possibility would be to use children's voices on the opening alto solo, then
combine with women (or senior high girls) for the rest of the work. The text is built on
Psalm 38:13-14; Psalm 39:2-4, and the entire Psalm 150.

Appendix 4

Recommended Hymns for Young Children

This list is intended as a guide to choosing hymns particularly appropriate for inexperienced singers, approximately age nine and younger. There are many fine hymns not included in this list because the range, the melody, or the text are "too big." They will, of course, be learned in time. Criteria used in the selection of the hymns below include:

1. Text—*or part of a text*, such as a refrain or single verse—which is for the most part, accessible to the child's understanding;
2. Melody which lies mostly within the range middle D to the D above—*or which has a refrain in that range*;
3. Melody which avoids numerous wide intervals.

Although most have stood the test of time, many of these hymns were written in the latter half of the 20th century and may be found in numerous hymn books published since 1978. Many of them can be arranged as anthems. Take care to select a key which will be in a median range for these young voices.

HYMNS OF PRAISE

All Creatures of Our God and King	Lasst Uns Erfreuen
All Praise to God for Song God Gives	Sacred Song
For the Beauty of the Earth	Dix
All Things Bright and Beautiful	Royal Oak
We Plow the Fields and Scatter	Wir Pflugen
Come, Ye Thankful People Come	St. Georges Wisdom
Sing to the Lord of Harvest	Steurlein
Earth and All Stars	Dexter
Guide Me, O Thou Great Jehovah	CWM Rhondda
Now Thank We All Our God	Nun Danket
All People That on Earth Do Dwell (Psalm 100)	Old Hundredth
My Shepherd is the Lord (Psalm 23)	Joseph Gelineau, 1963
God of the Sparrow	Roeder
Lord of Our Growing Years	Little Cornard
Of the Father's Love Begotten	Divinum Mysterium
Praise the Lord, God's Glories Show	Llanfair
From All That Dwells Below the Skies (Psalm 117)	Lasst Uns Erfreuen
Let Us With a Gladsome Mind (Psalm 136)	Monkland
Praise the Lord! His Glories Show (Psalm 150)	Llanfair
Praise My Soul, the King of Heaven	Praise My Soul
Sing Praise to God Who Reigns Above	Mit Freunden Zart

ADVENT

Come, Thou Long Expected Jesus	Stuttgart
O Come, O Come, Immanuel	Veni Immanuel
People, Look East	Besancon
Prepare the Way	Bereden Väg För Herran

Lift Up Your Heads, Ye Mighty Gates	TRURO
Savior of the Nations, Come	NUN KOMM

NATIVITY

Born in the Night, Mary's Child	MARY'S CHILD
In Bethlehem a Babe Was Born	ISCOVERY
That Boy-Child of Mary	BLANTYRE
The Snow Lay on the Ground	VENITE ADOREMUS
'Twas in the Moon of Wintertime	UNE JEUNE PUCELLE
O Little Town of Bethlehem	FORREST GREEN
O Come All Ye Faithful	ADESTE FIDELES
Hark, the Herald Angels Sing	MEDELSSOHN
Joy to the World!	ANTIOCH
While Shepherds Watched Their Flocks	WINCHESTER OLD
Once in Royal David's City	IRBY
All My Heart This Night Rejoices	BONN (FRÖHLICH SOLL)
Angels We Have Heard on High	GLORIA
On This Day Earth Shall Ring	PERSONENT HODIE
Away in a Manger	AWAY IN A MANGER
Good Christians Friends, Rejoice	IN DULCI JUBILO
Welcome, Child of Mary	NU ZIJT WELLECOME
Infant Holy	INFANT HOLY
To Us in Bethlehem City	BETHLEHEM CITY
The First Noel	THE FIRST NOEL
Go Tell It on the Mountain	GO TELL IT ON THE MOUNTAIN

EPIPHANY

Angels From the Realms of Glory	REGENT SQUARE
Bring We the Frankincense of Our Love	EPIPHANY SONG
Midnight Stars Make Bright the Sky	HUAN-SHA-CH'I

PASSION AND DEATH

All Glory, Laud and Honor (lines 1 & 2 repeated between verses as refrain)	ST. THEODULPH
Come to the Place of Grief and Shame	ST. CROSS
Jesus Walked This Lonesome Valley	LONESOME VALLEY

RESURRECTION AND ASCENSION

Jesus Christ is Risen Today	EASTER HYMN
Ye Sons and Daughters of the King	O FILII ET FILIAE
The Strife is O'er	VICTORY
Christ the Lord is Risen Again	CHRISTUS IST ERSTANDEN
Christ the Lord is Risen Today!	LLANFAIR
Good Christians All Rejoice and Sing	GELOB SEI GOTT
Thine Is The Glory	MACCABAEUS
This Joyful Eastertide	VRUCHTEN
Hail the Day That Sees Him Rise	LLANFAIR

O Sons and Daughters Let Us Sing	O Filii et Filiae
All Hail the Power of Jesus' Name	Coronation
Rejoice, the Lord is King	Darwell's 148th

PENTECOST

Breathe on Me, Breath of God	Trentham
The Lone, Wild Bird	Prospect
Spirit of the Living God	Living God

LIFE IN CHRIST

Jesus Loves Me! This I Know	Jesus Loves Me
Seek Ye First	Lafferty
I'm Gonna Live So God Can Use Me	I'm Gonna Live
Cuando el Pobre (When a Poor One)	El Camino
Come Christians Join to Sing	Madrid
When Morning Gilds the Skies	Laudes Domini
Who is He in Yonder Stall?	Resonet in Laudibus
Lord, I Want to be a Christian	I Want to be a Christian
My Hope is Built On Nothing Less	Solid Rock

THE CHURCH'S HISTORY/UNITY/FELLOWSHIP/MISSION

Christ Is the King! O Friends, Rejoice	Gelobt sie Gott
For All the Saints	Sine Nomine
I Sing a Song of the Saints of God	Grand Isle
Lift High the Cross	Crucifer
God of Grace and God of Glory	CWM Rhonda
O God of Love, O King of Peace	Quebec

LORD'S SUPPER/WITNESS

Let Us Talents and Tongues Employ	Linstead
Let Us Break Bread Together On Our Knees	Let Us Break Bread
Come We That Love the Lord	Vineyard Haven

Parents, church school teachers and other adults in the congregation may be interested in ways to help children learn the hymns of the faith. Here follows a notice that might be placed from time to time in the worship bulletin, or used as a handout from choir or through the church school. Dividing this material into several notices placed as inserts in the weekly worship bulletins may result in more of it being read.

Informal Ways You Can Help Children Learn Hymns

Hymns are the "folk heritage" of the church. They are handed down, new ones are written and together they form a corporate cornerstone for stating our faith. Alice Parker has said, "Singing is a birthright, a primary gift of God." To sing hymns to the best of ones ability takes some training and experience. Here are some ways that you can help.

During the week:

1. Tell your child your favorite hymn. Ask about his/her favorites.
2. If you do not have a recording of hymns of the faith, consider an investment in this. Playing it in the car or home will do much to unconsciously teach the words of the faith, as well as ingrain a proper singing tone in the ear.

For Sundays:

1. Have your children (as appropriate to their ability) be responsible for looking up all the hymns for the service. Help them see that our hymnal is carefully organized. *(Perhaps an outline could be given here of the organization of the hymnal used by this congregation.)* You will notice that the hymnal is really a companion to the Bible, telling the story of God's love for us through the ages, shown most clearly in the life of Christ. But the hymnal does not stop there. It goes to tell us how to respond to God's initiative with us, how to be a Christian in the world.
2. Help younger children learn to follow the word route for each stanza. *(In many hymnals, these are clearly marked with a number on each beginning line to aid the eye.)*
3. Encourage readers to go silently over the words of one or more stanzas prior to singing the hymn.
4. Teach children to point to the notes highest on the "system, " the blocks of notation, usually in four voice parts, moving horizontally across the page. This may be done best at the organ introduction. Point out that the note heads higher on the page are correspondingly higher in their voices, etc.
5. Younger children will be able to sing refrains or brief sections of hymns whose words/melody repeat on each verse. We try to use these frequently to aid our younger worshippers. Point these place out at the organ introduction.
6. Readers will be able to check the information at the top of each hymn. If your child is in choir s/he will learn to look for information: Who wrote the words (text)? Who wrote the tune? Did the same person harmonize it? Which is older, the words or the music? What is the name of the tune? What is the meter of the text?
7. Encourage your child to look in the various indexes for information about each hymn. There are many of these. Having practice at using them is central to understanding and remembering how they work. The worship service time may be useful in this regard.
8. Encourage your child's attempts at singing—anything! Be sure the voice they use is a true singing voice, not shouting or belting which is damaging to the instrument.
9. Consider purchasing a copy of our hymnal for your home.
10. Set a good example: hold the hymnal up so that your face looks forward, not towards the floor (unless of course you are sharing the hymnal with a child!) Ask your child to notice how the worship leaders hold their hymnals.

In days gone by, hymns were included in the singing of table grace, at family gatherings, as well as at worship which was often more frequent than it is today. We encourage your family to help preserve this wonderful heritage.

Appendix 5

Models for Worship Planning
Involving Choirs for Children and Youth

The careful planning of the corporate worship life of the congregation, in partnership with the clergy, is at the heart of the church musician's role. Chapter 8 discusses at length the need to allow ample time for planning worship services in which the various components complement and support one another. This Appendix contains:

1. an example of a form which can be used by the church musician to keep track of the direction and specific content of each worship service as planning progresses.

2. seven model services which are considered in terms of their scripture lessons, anthems, and sermon topic. Suggestions for other elements, such as the Call to Worship, a psalm, or a children's worship bulletin, are included as well. These particular services were all planned jointly by clergy, musicians, and Christian educators for a mainline Protestant church. They are not based on lectionary readings. Excerpts of anthem texts are given to aid the reader in connecting the text to the scriptural reference. A specific order of the worship elements is not suggested, except in the case of the last service. All publication information for the resources used is given, either in a footnote, or in Appendix 3, Exemplary Anthems.

(See also a model worship service conceived, prepared and lead by senior high students with guidance from the youth minister and choir director. It is found in Chapter 4.)

Worship Planning

Today's date: _____

Date of worship service _____ Preacher: _____ Hour: 9:15, 11:00, (10:00)

Special service components or other information (Lord's Supper, baptism, new members, Confirmation, stewardship, minute for mission, soloist, etc.) _____

Scripture on which sermon is based: *(synopsis on reverse)* _____

Other scripture lessons: _____

Hymns *(descants, free accompaniments, instruments, etc.)* _____

Introit: _____ Choir _____

Anthem: _____ Choir _____

Offertory: _____ Choir _____

Benediction Response: _____ Choir _____

Prelude: _____

Postlude: _____

Special info: (necessary transpositions or modulations to connect one musical event to another; logistical reminders so that the drama of worship is not interrupted, etc.) _____

_____

Need to Contact: _____

(sound room, custodian, clergy, choir, church school teachers, other staff, etc.)

Further meetings _____

Service I

*This service was planned around the theme of trusting in God, and the evidence
of that trust as shown to the Israelites in the desert, and through the years to our own
day. The presence of an African-American soprano as the guest soloist in a primarily
white congregation provided not only the splendid rendition of the solo, but her
particular presence as a Black woman singing about God's care for the whole world
added immeasurably to the service.*

Suggested Readings:
  Old Testament   Exodus 16:1-18
  New Testament   Luke 7:1-10

Sermon Text: *"When the people of Israel saw it, they said to one another, 'What is
it?" Exodus 16:15*

Suggested Hymns:
  Lord of Creation   SLANE
  O God of Bethal   DUNDEE
  Guide me, O Thou Great Jehovah   CWM RHONDDA

Suggested Anthems:
  Children of the Covenant (after Old Testament lesson)   Sue Ellen Page
  Unison treble, with organ, opt. synthesizer   CGA-495
*"Children of Israel, wandering in the wilderness, not knowing where the journey
would take them. But trusting in God to lead them on; by donkey, across the vast
desert they came: Children of the Covenant, pilgrims of the promise of God." (text
by Eric Johnson)*

  I Will Trust in the Lord (Offertory)   Spiritual, arr. Undine Smith Moore
  SATB, divisi, a cappella   Augsburg 11-2505
"I will trust in the Lord 'til I die...."

  He's Got the Whole World in His Hands   Spiritual, arr. Margaret Bonds
                                                Theodore Presser 15100360
*(Sung by soloist or advanced treble choir as Benediction Response—seat congrega-
tion)*

Suggested Call to Worship:
*Psalm 95: 1-7, set metrically by Christopher Weber in "A New Metrical Psalter"
(see bibliography). Using the tune Duke Street, the children's choirs begin alone, a
cappella, verse 1, the mixed voice choirs join in parts on verse two, then the organ
and the congregation join on verse three.*

Suggested Children's Bulletin:

THE WHOLE WORLD

Find the place in the service of worship bulletin where *He's Got the Whole World in His Hands* will be sung. Do you know this spiritual about God's love? Make a list of words or pictures of people or things that are in God's hands. Listen carefully to find out which ones are in the song.

BREAD FROM HEAVEN

The reading from Exodus takes place after the Israelites had escaped from the pharaoh in Egypt. As you remember, they did not have time to take a lot of food with them. God said to Moses, "I am going to rain *bread from heaven* from you, and each day the people shall go out and gather *enough for that day.*"

On three plates, draw enough food for you for one day. Don't draw more than you need.

To find out what happened when the Israelites tried to save bread for another day, read Exodus 16:20. UGH! On the fourth plate, draw food that the Israelites tried to hoard for another day. Show what happened to it.

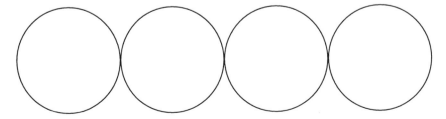

MAKE THE CONNECTION

In the service this morning, there will be both baptisms and confirmation. Place the words from the list here in the correct places to find out the connection between the two rituals.

older	congregation	promises
responsibility	baby	Jesus

When a ( ) is baptized, the parents and the ( )

promise to teach the child about God and ( ).

When the child is ( ) (about 13), the child takes those ( )

as her or his own. Now a member of the church, she or he has the ( )

of continuing to learn about and serve God.

Service II

Planned around the theme of the Good Shepherd, this service will be particularly appropriate for use in congregations where Advent is not limited to the theme of waiting and preparing. In this service, all anthems are sung by children's choirs. (The adult choir could be present to lead the hymns, but take a week off from singing an anthem, in order to allow more time to prepare a major work for the Christmas season.)

Suggested Readings:
Old Testament   Isaiah 40:9-11
New Testament   John 10:1-18

Sermon text: *"He will feed his flock like a shepherd, he will gather the lambs in his arms, he will carry them in his bosom, and gently lead those that are with young."*
Isaiah 40:11

Suggested Hymns:
While Shepherds Watched Their Flocks   CHRISTMAS
Savior, Like a Shepherd Lead Us   BRADBURY
O Come, O Come Emmanuel   VENI EMANUEL

Suggested Anthems:
Oh, Come Away   Traditional French, arr. Helen Kemp
Unison, canon, unaccompanied   from Canons Songs, and Blessings
                                                    (see Bibliography)

Holy Manger	Traditional French, arr. John Horman
unison, keyboard and flute	Choristers Guild CGA-468
Little Lamb	Gregg Smith
unison, piano 4 hand	E.C. Schirmer
Long, Long Ago	Carlisle Floyd
SA, piano	Boosey and Hawkes 5648

Suggested Prayers:
At the confession of sin: Almighty and most merciful God; we have erred and strayed from Thy ways lost sheep...

Suggested Psalm: Ps. 23
The Lord's My Shepherd SEARCHING FOR LAMBS
Children's choir in alternation with congregation.

Services III and IV
Planned as a two part sermon series in Lent, these services explored God's steadfast love shown to us in two particular ways: "The One Who Is There Already" and "When We are Left Behind." Care was taken when planning the services to include time for the children's choir to prepare with the preacher. This helped them focus on what would be said and how their anthem would play a part in proclaiming and explaining that message to the people.

Part I "The One Who is There Already"
Suggested Readings:
Old Testament Genesis 41:54b - 42:1-4; Exodus 1:1-7
New Testament John 14:1-4

Sermon text: *"...Joseph was already in Egypt." Exodus 1:5*

Suggested Hymns:
O God, Our Help In Ages Past ST. ANNE
What a Friend We Have In Jesus WHAT A FRIEND
Lead On, O King Eternal LANCASHIRE

Suggested Anthems:
Song for Beginnings (sung by two choirs, grades 2 - 5) Kevin Riehle
Unison, with descant Choristers Guild CGA-493
"Come, my children, I will teach you of the goodness of the Lord. God, your guardian, never sleeping, never slumbering, gives the word: I will keep you as the apple of my eye." Adapted from Ps. 17, 22, 34, 121

I Will Arise (sung by senior high choir) Traditional, arr. Parker/Shaw
SATB, a cappella Lawson-Gould 905
"I will arise and go to Jesus, He will embrace me in His arms. In the arms of my dear Savior, Oh! there are ten thousand charms..."

Suggested Response to Scripture:
>After Old Testament Lesson   Of The Father's Love Begotten, vs. 1
>After New Testament Lesson   Of The Father's Love Begotten, vs. 3

Part II: "When We Are Left Behind"

Suggested Readings:
>Old Testament   II Samuel 18:24-19:4
>New Testament   John 13:31-38

Sermon text: " Blessed be the God and Father of our Lord Jesus Christ, the Father of mercies and God of all comfort, who comforts us in all our affliction, so that we may be able to comfort those who are in any affliction with the comfort with which we ourselves are comforted by God. "
II Corinthians 1:3-4

Suggested Hymns:
>Praise to the Lord, the Almighty   LOBE DEN HERREN
>Seeking Water, Seeking Shelter   PSALM
>For the Beauty of the Earth   DIX

Suggested Anthems:
>David's Lamentation *(after Old Testament Lesson)*   William Billings
>SATB   Peters 66336
>*"David the King was grieved and moved. He went to his chamber and wept. And as he went, he wept and said: "O my son, would to God I had died for thee, O Absalom, my son." II Samuel 18:32-33*

Hope Completes the Trilogy   text: Fred Pratt Green, vs. 1-2,
(To be sung at some point after the sermon)   sung to FOREST GREEN
                                               (arr. by director to fit group)

"Though love is greatest of the three, and Faith one step behind. Its hope completes the trilogy, Lest Faith and Love be blind: For hopeless Love is blind with tears, and hopeless Faith with rage, But Hope has seen beyond our fears God's juster, kindlier age. "

Suggested Congregational Psalm: Psalm 46
>(God is our refuge and strength, a very present help in trouble...*Spoken or sung responsorially.)*

Service V
Planned for Palm Sunday, the children's choirs grade five and younger were involved. Kindergarten and grade one children joined the four year olds on the Introit which moved directly into the opening hymn and palm parade. This was led by the fifth grade church school class. The anthem "Ride On, King Jesus," sung by the adults, keeps the Palm Sunday theme, but personalizes its significance by the use of the first

person pronoun. The 2nd and 3rd graders must wait with the 4th and 5th graders until after the sermon to sing their anthem (sometimes difficult for this age to do) because its text is about the events which will occur later in the week. The sermon must move this service from the drama of "Hosannas" on Palm Sunday to the anticipation of "Crucify Him" at the end of the week. The careful placement of this tender anthem made it a most memorable worship experience for chorister and congregation alike.

Suggested Readings:
Old Testament   Psalm 118:4, 22-29
New Testament   Matthew 21:1-11

Sermon Text: "The *stone which the builders rejected has become the chief corner-stone. This is the Lord's doing, it is marvelous in our eyes." Ps. 118:22-23*

Suggested Hymns:
All Glory, Laud, and Honor (preceded by introit, below)   St. Theodulph
(Vs. 1 begins as a solo by a child or youth, unaccompanied, organ only entering at "the people of the Hebrews," followed by singing the full hymn, choirs and congregation.)
Hosanna, Loud Hosanna   Ellacombe
Alone Thou Goest Forth, O Lord   Bangor

Suggested Anthems:
Who Comes Riding On a Donkey's Back? (Introit)   text: Fred Pratt Green
(This poem was spoken alternating solo speakers with the full group, and accompanied by several children playing a simple ostinato. This served not only to provide a background of sound for the poem, but to establish the pitch the soloist needed for the upcoming hymn. Immediately following the call to worship, the solo singer began the opening phrase of the first hymn, as above.)

Ride On, King Jesus   Spiritual, arr. L.L. Fleming
SATB, a cappella   Augsburg 11-0541
"Ride on, King Jesus. No man can hinder you. Ride on, King Jesus, Ride to me. When I looked around me to find someone who's gentle and kind, someone to show me the way, I look to Jesus and pray."

A Lenten Love Song *(sung after the sermon)*   Helen Kemp
Unison   Choristers Guild CGA-486
"Now Jesus went into the garden, the garden of Gethsemane. He went there sad and very weary, to be alone and pray... `My God, I am so sorrowful, is there no other way?'"

Suggested Prelude and Postlude:
March on *Lift Up Your Heads*   A. Guilmant
Toccata in G minor   Gabriel Pierne

Suggested Psalm (spoken or sung responsorially as the call to worship):
Psalm 24:7-10 *"Lift Up Your Heads, O gates! and be lifted up, O ancient doors! that the King of glory may come in..."*

Service VI

This service was planned as a festival service focusing on the life together of this particular congregation, given us by God, in worship, in outreach, in fellowship. The celebratory mood was enhanced by combined choirs, in which the senior highs joined the adults for two movements of "The Peaceable Kingdom" by Randall Thompson. The combined children's choirs sang the unison choir part of "Until We Rest in Thee," which includes a congregational verse, with soprano descant.

Suggested Readings:

Old Testament	Isaiah 55:6-13
New Testament	Philippians 1:3-11

Sermon Text: *"Now to him who is able to keep you from falling..."*

Suggested Hymns:

Holy, Holy, Holy	NICEA
I Sought the Lord	FAITH
God of our Life	SANDON
Now Thank We All Our God	NUN DANKET

Suggested Choral Music: *(All or portions of the texts are given, with scriptural source as applicable.)*

Ye Shall Have a Song *(Introit)*	Randall Thompson
SSAA and TTBB, a cappella	E.C. Schirmer

"Ye shall have a song, as in the night when a holy solemnity is kept, and gladness of heart, as when one goeth with a pipe to come into the mountain of the Lord." Isaiah 30:29

Until We Rest in Thee (Response to scripture lessons)	Sue Ellen Page
SATB, unison choir of children,	Choirsters Guild CGA-504
congregation, organ	

"We have no rest until we rest in Thee. We have no peace until Thy peace we see. We need no home save in Thy loving care. Thy church is ours, O God, in Christ to share." Text by the Rev. Cynthia A. Jarvis

Offertory—Song of Devotion	John Ness Beck
Solo (or unison choir of advanced trebles, in lower key)	G. Schirmer

"I thank my God for every remembrance of you..." Philippians 1:3-11

For Ye Shall Go Out With Joy *(Benediction Response)*	Randall Thompson
Double Choir of SATB	E.C. Schirmer

"For ye shall go out with joy and be led forth with peace. The mountains and the hills shall break forth into singing, and all the trees of the fields shall clap their hands." Isaiah 55:12

Suggested Children's Bulletin:

NAME THE COMPOSER

Complete the following sentences with information from the hymnbook or the worship bulletin.

The first hymn [Holy, Holy, Holy] has a descant to be sung with the fourth stanza.

Who wrote the descant? _____

(Listen carefully. Who is singing the descant?) _____

_____

Find the anthem in the worship bulletin. Who wrote the words or text? _____

_____

Who wrote the music? _____

_____

The middle hymn, "God of Our Life," was written for the 50th anniversary of the Shadyside Presbyterian Church in Pittsburgh.

Who wrote the words? _____

_____

The last hymn [Now Thank We All Our God] was translated from the German.

Who translated it? _____

GO OUT WITH JOY

Following the benediction at the end of the service of worship today is a benediction response. It is taken from Isaiah 55:12, the Old Testament Lesson for today.

The benediction response is: "For ye shall go out with joy." In the frame below, draw a picture of our congregation leaving the church building joyously.

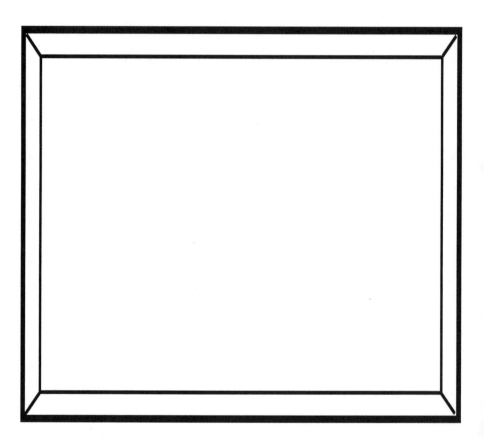

ILLUSTRATE A VERSE

Isaiah 55.10
Draw pictures above the words in circles. Then read the verse silently to yourself
using your pictures instead of the words.

"For as the   and the

$\qquad$ rain $\qquad$ $\qquad$ snow $\qquad$

come down from heaven, and do not return there until they

have watered the   making it bring forth and sprout,

$\qquad$ earth $\qquad$

giving   to the sower, and   to the eater,

$\qquad$ seed $\qquad$ $\qquad$ bread $\qquad$

so shall My Word be that goes out from My mouth; it shall not return empty."

Service 7

The staff decided to use several recurring images of God in this service: God's hands and the realization that we are inscribed *upon them [all three hymns, the Old Testament Lesson]; God's continual calling us back [choral response after the prayer of confession, the assurance of pardon, the second and third hymns]; the use of the word "through" regarding times of trouble—God's strengthening and sustaining of us, not leaving us in trouble, or circumventing difficulty, but leading us through it [both anthems, the second and third hymns, both scripture lessons]. The parables of the lost sheep and gold coin were read to further reinforce these themes. For this sample service, the order of worship is given in its entirety. The title and mood of the prelude help to prepare the rest of the service. Material in italics is informational only, and did not appear in the order of worship. See footnotes, Appendices and bibliography for more information.*

Prelude and Silent Meditation   Psalm Prelude   Herbert Howells
                                        (Based on Ps. 23:4)

Call to Worship   Psalm 100[4]   Hal H. Hopson
     Choir:

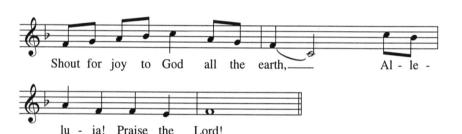

Shout for joy to God all the earth,___ Al - le - lu - ia! Praise the Lord!

> Leader: *(spoken)* Know that the Lord is God. God made us, we belong to the Lord; we are God's people, and the sheep of God's flock.
> All: (Sing above refrain)

Hymn[5]   Come and sing to God our Savior   UNSER HERRSCHER
     vs. 1 (sung a cappella and antiphonally by the adult choir and the senior high choir)

> *(Adults)* Come and sing to God our Savior. Let us make a joyful noise.
> *(Youth)* For the Lord is our salvation, And the source of all our joys.
> *(Both)* Lord, we come into this place, Singing songs of love and grace.

vs. 2 All
You are mighty, great and glorious, Sovereign over all that is.
All the worlds are your possession, Earth and sky and all that lives.
All are firmly in your hand, Peoples, planets, sea, and land.

vs. 3 All
Worship, honor, love we bring you, Prayers of thanks and hymns of praise.
You have named us your possession, You, our guide for all our days.
Shepherd God whose ways are true, Hear us as we worship you.

Prayer of Confession (Preceded by silent prayer)
> Gracious God, in whom we live and move and have our being, hear our prayer.
> Let our cries come to you. For we like sheep have gone astray; we have all
> turned to our own way
>> in selling out to soulless living;
>> in squandering your gifts so freely given;
>> in ignoring Christ's call to follow;
>> in neglecting those in need.
>
> In your mercy and compassion forgive us, O God, and lead us in the way of
> righteousness and peace; through Jesus Christ, we pray. Amen.[6]

Choral Response   Softly and Tenderly Jesus is Calling[7]   Will L. Thompson

Promise of the Gospel   Isaiah 44: 21-22
> *"Remember these things, O Jacob, and Israel, for you are my servant; I*
> *formed you, you are my servant; O Israel, you will not be forgotten by me.*
> *I have swept away your transgressions like a cloud, and your sins like mist;*
> *return to me, for I have redeemed you." Friends, this is the good news. In*
> *Jesus Christ, we are forgiven. Believe in the promise of the Gospel and go*
> *in peace.*

Congregational Response   GLORIA PATRI

Old Testament Lesson   Isaiah 49: 1;12-16a
Anthem   How Can I Keep From Singing?   Trad. American,
                                                              arr. Jeffrey Honoré

(Senior High Choir)
> *"...No storm can shake my inmost calm, while to that Rock I'm clinging.*
> *Since Love is Lord of heaven and earth, how can I keep from singing?"*

New Testament Lesson   Luke 15:1-10

Sermon *"Even these may forget, yet I will not forget you." Isaiah 49:15b*

Hymn   My Shepherd is the Living Lord   RESIGNATION

Offering
Suggested Offertory
> *One of the many settings of Psalm 121—"I lift up my eyes to the hills"*
> *Adult Choir*

Doxology
Affirmation of Faith
The Prayers

Hymn   How Firm a Foundation   FOUNDATION
Benediction
Benediction Response
> *(Verse two, lines three and four, of the last hymn, sung a cappella, in canon*

*by the two choirs: "I'll strengthen you, help you, and cause you to stand,
upheld by my righteous, omnipotent hand.")*

Endnotes

[1]   From *The Hymns and Ballads of Fred Pratt Green,* Hope Publishing Company, Carol Stream, Illinois. p. 20.

[2]   Two metrical versions are found in *Singing Psalms of Joy and Praise,* Fred R. Anderson, The Westminster Press, p. 34, and sung to UNSER HERRSCHER; and *A New Metrical Psalter,* Christopher L. Webber, p. 96, sung to DIADEMATA.

[3]   Green, p. 20.

[4]   Since this was used as a (brief) Call to Worship, only the antiphon was used. *Psalm 100* by Hal H. Hopson, Hope Publishing Co., #HH 3934. Carol Stream, Illinois 60188, 1988   Reprinted with permission.

[5]   Text by Fred Anderson, from *Singing Psalms of Joy and Praise.* (See bibliography.)

[6]   Prayer by the Rev. Elsie Armstrong Olsen, Associate Pastor for Youth, Nassau Presbyterian Church, Princeton, NJ.

[7]   Sung by high school girls, they got their pitch for the unaccompanied opening from the first hymn. By singing both of these successive musical elements in Bb major, there was a subtle connection between the two, without making an issue of it.   And since they occurred within a few moments of each other, keeping them in the same key was easy on the ear. (A related key would accomplish the same thing.) Senior high girls were chosen to sing this response, since vocally the sound was just right. But more particularly, we wanted these young women to be the vessel by which a particular image of God was evoked: that even more steadfastly than a loving mother calls and welcomes her children home, God's son calls us back. "If you are weary, come home!" The arrangement of this response is found in Chapter 8, in G major.

Selected Bibliography

Musical Resources

Note: Musical Resources include books and articles from periodicals. In some cases, choral repertoire is cited in this bibliography (rather than in the Appendix of Exemplary Anthems). These are collections which fulfill particular pedagogical functions and are listed here as invaluable resources for the musician who works with children and youth.

Voice Training

Alderson, Richard. *Complete Handbook of Voice Training.* West Nyack, NY: Parker Publishing Company, 1979.

Collins, I. H. "The Child Voice." *Choristers Guild LETTERS,* 23 (1981): 63-65.

Cooksey, John M. *Working with the Adolescent Voice.* St. Louis: Concordia, 1992.

Ehmann, Wilhelm and Haasemann, Frauke. *Voice Building for Choirs.* Chapel Hill: Hinshaw Music, 1981.

Gackle, M. Lynn. "The Adolescent Female Voice: Characteristics of Change and Stages of Development." *Choral Journal,* 31(8), 17 -25.

"The effect of selected vocal techniques for breath management, resonation, and vowel unification on tone production in the junior high school female voice." *Dissertation Abstracts International,* 48(04), 862A. 1987.

Haasemann, Frauke, and Jordan, James M. *Group Vocal Techniques.* Chapel Hill: Hinshaw Music, 1991.

_____. *Group Vocal Techniques: The Vocalise Cards.* Chapel Hill: Hinshaw Music, 1992.

Jennings, Kenneth. *Sing Legato: a Collection of Original Studies in Vocal Production and Musicianship.* San Diego: Neil A. Kjos, 1982.

McKenzie, Duncan. *Training the Boy's Changing Voice.* New Brunswick: Rutgers University Press, 1956.

Swanson, Frederick J. *The Male Singing Voice Ages Eight to Eighteen.* Cedar Rapids, IA: Laurance Press, 1977.

Vale, Walter S. *The Training of Boys' Voices.* London: The Faith Press, Ltd, 1932.

Vennard, William. *Singing: The Mechanism and the Technic.* New York: Carl Fischer, 1967.

Repertoire

Chapman, Sandra. "Selected Choral Literature for Junior High Choirs." *Choral Journal* 31(7), 23-29.

Choral Music For Children: An Annotated List. Reston, VA: Music Educators National Conference, 1990.

Feierabend, John. *Book of Bounces.* Simsbury, CN: First Steps in Music, 1994. (First in a series entitled "First Steps in Music.")

Fahrer, Alison and Jarry, Paul A. editors. *Repertory Library: Vocal Music.* Cincinnati: Canyon Press, Inc., 1970.

Goetze, Mary. *Simply Sung. Folk Songs Arranged in Three Parts for Young Singers.* New York: Schott, Inc., 1984.

Hawkins, Margaret. "An Annotated Inventory of Distinctive Choral Literature for Performance at the High School Level." *Monograph No.3, ACDA.*

Kemp, Helen and John. *Canons, Songs and Blessings: A Kemp Family Collection.* Garland, TX: Choristers Guild, 1990.

Kemp, Helen. *Of Primary Importance, Vol. I and II.* Dallas: Choristers Guild, 1989, 1991.

_____ . *Where in the World: Folksong Warmups From Many Lands.* Minneapolis: Augsburg Fortress. 1989.

McCray, James. "A Survey of Published Magnificats for Treble Voices." *Choral Journal* 28(8), 5-11.

Stultz, Marie. "Selecting Music to Improve and Inspire Your Children's Choir: An Annotated List." *Choral Journal* 34(5), 35-40.

Wedel, Eva. "Music in Worship: A Selected List for Children's Choirs." *Choral Journal* 31(4), 45-47.

Conducting

Busch, Brian R. *The Complete Choral Conductor: Gesture, and Method.* New York: Schirmer Books, 1984.

Christiansen, Helga. *Better Choir Singing.* Garland, TX: Choristers Guild, 1973.

Decker, Harold, and Herford, Julius. *Choral Conducting: A Symposium.* Englewood Cliffs, NJ: Prentice-Hall, Inc., 1973.

Decker, Harold, and Kirk, Colleen J. *Choral Conducting: Focus on Communication*. Englewood Cliffs, NJ: Prentice-Hall, Inc., 1988.

Garretson, Robert L. *Choral Music: History, Style, and Performance Practice*. Englewood Cliffs, NJ: Prentice Hall. 1993.

Gordon, Lewis. *Choral Director's Rehearsals and Performance Guide*. West Nyack, NY: Parker Publishing Company, 1989.

Green, Elizabeth A. *The Modern Conductor*. Englewood Cliffs, NJ: Prentice-Hall, Inc. A Division of Simon and Schuster, 1987.

Halliday, John R. *Diction for Singers*. Provo, UT: Brigham Young University Press, 1970.

Marshall, Madeline. *The Singer's Manual of English Diction*. New York: Schirmer Books, 1953.

McElheran, Brock. *Conducting Technique for Beginners and Professionals*. New York: Oxford, 1989.

Meek, Charles J. *Conducting Made Easy for Directors of Amateur Musical Organizations*. Metuchen: Scarecrow Press, 1988.

Moe, Daniel. *Basic Choral Concepts*. Minneapolis: Augsburg Publishing House, 1968 and 1972.

_____ . *Problems in Conducting*. Minneapolis: Augsburg Publishing House, 1968 and 1973.

Pfautsch, Lloyd. *Mental Warmups for the Choral Director*. New York: Lawson-Gould Music Publishers, Inc., 1969.

Poe, Frances R. *Teaching and Performing Renaissance Choral Music: A Guide for Conductors and Performers*. Metuchen, NJ: The Scarecrow Press, Inc., 1994.

Webb, Guy B., editor. *Upfront! Becoming the Complete Choral Conductor*. Boston: ECS Publishing, 1993.

Willetts, Sandra. *Upbeat Downbeat: Basic Conducting Patterns and Techniques*. Nashville: Abingdon Press, 1993.

Age Specific Materials

Andress, B. *Music Experiences in Early Childhood*. New York: Holt, Rinehart, and Winston, 1980.

Andress, B., and others. *Music in Early Childhood*. Wash. DC: Music Educators National Conference, 1973.

Feierabend, John. *Book of Bounces.* Simsbury, CN: First Steps in Music, 1994. (First in a series entitled "First Steps in Music.")

_____ . *Music for Little People.* New York: Boosey and Hawkes, 1989.

_____ . *Music for Very Little People.* New York: Boosey and Hawkes, 1986.

Herman, Sally. *In Search of Musical Excellence: Taking Advantage of Varied Learning Styles.* Dayton: Roger Dean Publishing Company, 1994.

Heyge, Lorna Lutz, and Sillick, Audrey. *Kindermusik for the Very Young. Years I and II.* Music Resources International, 1988.

Pre-School and Primary Roundtable. *Choristers Guild LETTERS,* 40 (1988-1989): 1-9.

Youth Choir Roundtable. *Choristers Guild LETTERS,* 42 (1990-1991): 2-9.

Specific Schools of Music Education

Abramson, Robert M. *Rhythm Games for Perception and Cognition.* 1973.

Bacon, Denise. *45 Two-part Amercian Songs for Elementary Grades.* Wellesley, MA: Kodaly Center of America, 1973.

Birkenshaw, L. *Music for Fun, Music for Learning.* New York: Holt, Rinehart, and Winston, 1974.

Burnett, Millie, *Melody, Movement and Language. A Teacher's Guide of Music in Game Form for the Pre-School and Primary Grades.* R and E Research Associates, 1973.

Carley, Isabel McN., editor. *Orff Re-Echoes I and II.* Cleveland Heights, OH: American Orff-Schulwerk Association, 1977, 1986.

Erdei, Peter and Komlas, Katalin. *150 American Folk Songs to Sing, Read and Play.* New York: Boosey and Hawkes, 1974.

Findlay, Elsa. *Rhythm and Movement: Applications of Dalcroze Eurythmics.* Evanston, IL: Summy-Birchard, 1971.

Frazee, Jane. *Discovering Orff: A Curriculum for Music Teachers.* New York: Schott, 1987.

Hackett/Jensen. *A Guide to Movement Exploration.* Peek Publications, 1966.

Henneburger, Judith. *Musical Games and Activities to Learn By.* Garland, TX: Choristers Guild, 1976.

Herald, Marlene and McCormick, Eloise. *Introducing Joyful Sunday (Book I) and Another Joyful Sunday (Book II): An Instructional Guide to Creative Teaching in Church School Classes.* Tarzana, CA: Fred Bock Music Company, 1978.

Locke, Eleanor G. *Sail Away.* New York: Boosey and Hawkes, 1989.

Music For Children: Orff-Schulwerk American Edition, Volume I, II, III. New York: Schott Music Corporation, 1977, 1980, 1982.

Nash, Grace, and others. *Do It My Way: The Child's Way of Learning.* Sherman Oaks, CA: Alfred Publishers, 1977.

Nelson, Esther. *Movement Games for Children of All Ages.* Sterling Publishers, 1975.

Ramseth, Betty A. *That I May Speak.* Minneapolis: Augsburg Publishing Co.

Suzuchi, Shinichi, et al. *The Suzuki Concept.* Diablo Press, 1973.

Wisbey, Audrey S. *Music as the Source of Learning.* University Park Press, 1980.

Youth and Children's Choirs

Bartle, Jean Ashworth. *Lifeline for Children's Choir Directors.* Toronto: Gordon V. Thompson Music, Revised and Expanded edition, 1994.

Choral Journal, March 1989 and 1994: Entire issues devoted to choral work with children.

Church Music for Children: A Complete Choir Education Program. I Pre-Elementary: II Younger Elementary: III Older Elementary: IV Combined Elementary. Nashville: Cokesbury, 1994.

Farrior, Christine Bordeaux. *Body, Mind, Spirit, Voice: Helen Kemp and the Development of the Children's Choir Movement.* Greensboro: C.B. Farrior, 1993.

Fortunato, Connie. *Children's Music Ministry.* Elgin, IL: David Cook Publishing, 1983.

Heyge, L., Mathia, C., Robinson, L., and Sillick, A. *God's Children Sing.* Richmond, VA: Musikgarten, 1995.

Jacobs, Ruth Krehbiel. *The Children's Choir, Vol. I* (Vol. II by Nancy Poore Tufts). Philadelphia: Fortress Press, 1960 and 1965.

_____. *The Successful Children's Choir.* Tarzana, CA: H.T. FitzSimons Co., 1948.

Kemp, Helen. *Music in Church Education with Children*. Garland, TX: Choristers Guild, 1970.

_____ . *Of Primary Importance, Vol. I and II*. Garland, TX: Choristers Guild, 1989 and 1991.

McRae, Shirley W. *Celebrate! A Practical Guide For the Use of Orff Techniques and Materials In the Church*. Minneapolis: Augsburg, 1984.

_____ . *Directing the Children's Choir: A Comprehensive Resource*. New York: Schirmer Books, 1991.

Phillips, Kenneth. *Teaching Kids to Sing*. New York: Schirmer Books, 1992.

Pojhola, Erkki. *Tapiola Sound*. Ft. Lauderdale: Walton Music Corporation. 1992, 1993.

Rao, Doreen. *Choral Music Experience, Vol. 1—5*. Oceanside, NY: Boosey and Hawkes, 1987, 1988.

_____ . *We Will Sing! Choral Music Experience for Classroom Choirs*. New York: Boosey and Hawkes, 1993.

Rottermund, Donald, editor. *Children Sing His Praise*. St. Louis: Concordia, 1985.

Schott, Sally, co-ordinator. *Sing!* (Textbook for high school singers.) Chapel Hill: Hinshaw Music Textbook Division, 1988.

Sheehy, E. *Children Discover Music and Dance*. New York: Teachers College Press, 1968.

Swears, Linda. *Teaching the Elementary School Chorus*. West Nyack, NY: Parker Publishing, 1985.

Thompson, Rebecca, with Blacka, G., and Naifeh, S. "Pathways to More Effective Rehearsals." *Choristers Guild LETTERS*, 44, 1-10.

Yarrington, John. *Building the Youth Choir: Training and Motivating Teenage Singers*. Minneapolis: Augsburg Fortress, 1990.

Sight Reading and Musicianship
Bertalot, John. *Five Wheels to Successful Sight-Singing*. Minneapolis: Augsburg Fortress, 1993.

Fenton, William A. and Johnson, Sarah O. *Choral Musicianship: A Director's Guide to Better Singing*. Lebanon, IN: Houston Publishing, Inc., 1990.

Herman, Sally. *Building a Pyramid of Musicianship*. Curtis Music Press, 1988.

Houlahan, Michael and Tacka, Philip. *Sound Thinking: Music for Sight-Singing and Ear Training*. New York: Boosey and Hawkes, 1990.

Rogers, E. Lowell. *Are You Open on Saturday and Sunday? An Innovative Approach for Teaching the Language of Music*. Phoenix, AZ: Dick Jones Publishing Co., 1976.

Roth, Robert N. and Nancy L. *We Sing of God: A Hymnal for Children*. Teacher's Guide, A Book of Hymns, Rudiments of Music Worksheets. The Church Hymnal Corporation, 1989.

Telfer, Nancy. *Successful Sight Singing: A Creative, Step by Step Approach*. San Diego: Neil A. Kjos Music Company, 1992.

General Teaching Pedagogy

Bruner, Jerome. *The Process of Education*. New York: Random House, 1960.

Gardner, Howard. *Art, Mind and Brain*. New York: Basic Books, 1982.

_____. *The Unschooled Mind: How Children Learn and How Schools Should Teach*. New York: Basic Books, 1991.

Gardner, Howard. *Multiple Intelligences: The Theory in Practice*. New York: Basic Books, 1993.

Harmin, Merrill. *Inspiring Active Learning: A Handbook for Teachers*. Alexandria: Association for Supervision and Curriculum Development, 1994.

Healy, Jane. *Endangered Minds: Why Children Don't Think and What We Can Do About It*. New York: Touchstone (Simon and Schuster), 1990.

Highet, Gilbert. *The Art of Teaching*. New York: Random House, 1950.

Johnson, D. W. et al. *Circles of Learning: Cooperation in the Classroom*. Edina: Interaction Book Company, 1990.

MacDonald, R.E. *A Handbook of Basic Skills and Strategies for Beginning Teachers*. New York: Longman, 1991.

Montessori, Maria. *Spontaneous Activity in Education (1917)*. Cambridge, MA: Robert Bentley, Inc., 1964.

Moody, W., editor. *Artistic Intelligences: Implications for Education*. New York: Teacher's College Press, 1990.

Theological and Liturgical Resources

Alston, Wallace M., Jr. *The Church*. Atlanta: John Knox Press, 1984.

Bradshaw, Paul F. and Hoffman, Lawrence A., editors. *The Changing Face of Jewish and Christian Worship in North America*. Notre Dame: University of Notre Dame Press, 1991.

Bonhoeffer, Dietrich, translated by John W. Doberstein. *Life Together*. San Fransisco: Harper and Row, 1954.

Doran, Carol and Troeger, Thomas H. *Trouble at the Table: Gathering the Tribes for Worship*. Nashville: Abingdon, 1992.

Hoffman, Lawrence A., and Walton, Janet R., ed. *Sacred Sound and Social Change: Liturgical Music on Jewish and Christian Experience*. Notre Dame: University of Notre Dame Press, 1992.

Huck, Gabe. *How Can I Keep From Singing? Thoughts About Liturgy for Musicians*. Chicago: Liturgy Training Productions, 1989.

Johansson, Calvin M. *Discipling Music Ministry: 21st Century Directions*. Peabody, MS: Hendrickson Publishers, Inc., 1992.

Keifert, Patrick R. *Welcoming the Stranger: A Public Theology of Worship and Evangelism*. Minneapolis: Fortress Press, 1992.

Lectionary Text Years A,B,C; Various Occasions and Occasional Services; Lesser Feasts and Fasts. New York: The Church Pension Fund, 1978-83.

Lewis, C.S., *An Experiment in Criticism*. New York: Cambridge University Press, 1961.

Lovelace, Austin C. and Rice, William C. *Music and Worship in the Church*. Nashville: Abingdon Press, 1960.

Myers, Kenneth A. *All God's Children and Blue Suede Shoes*. Wheaton, IL: Crossway Books, 1989.

Newbigin, Lesslie. *The Gospel in a Pluralist Society*. Grand Rapids, MI: William B. Eerdmans Publishing Co., 1989.

_____ . *Truth to Tell: The Gospel as Public Truth*. Grand Rapids, MI: William B. Eerdmans Publishing Co., 1991.

Niebuhr, H. Richard. *Christ in Culture*. New York: Harper and Brothers. 1951.

Our Heritage of Hymns, I and II. Garland, TX: Choristers Guild, 1986 and 1989.

Old, Hughes Oliphant. *Worship*. Atlanta: John Knox Press, 1984.

Routley, Erik. *Church Music and the Christian Faith*. Carol Stream, IL: Agape, 1978.

Spong, John Shelby. *Rescuing the Bible from Fundamentalism: A Bishop Rethinks the Meaning of Scripture*. San Fransisco: Harper, 1991.

Stevik, Daniel B. *The Crafting of Liturgy: A Guide for Preparers*. New York: The Church Hymnal Corporation, 1990.

White, James F. *Protestant Worship: Traditions in Transition*. Louisville: Westminster/John Knox Press, 1989.

Wuthnow, Robert. *The Struggle for America's Soul: Evangelicals, Liberals, and Secularism*. Grand Rapids, MI: William B. Eerdmans Publishing Co., 1989.

Related Resources
The Arts in Worship and Education; Arts Education

The Arts in Communication of Faith. United Methodist Church, Nashville, TN: Graded Press, 1969.

Bernstein, Leonard. *Leonard Bernstein's Young People's Concerts*. Newly Revised and Expanded Version, ed. Jack Gottlieb. New York: Anchor Books, Doubleday, 1962, 1970, 1992.

Brueggemann, Walter. *The Prophetic Imagination*. Philadelphia: Fortress Press, 1978.

Bryans, Nina. *Full Circle: A Proposal to the Church for an Arts Ministry*. Thomas House Publications, 1988.

Chapman, Sandra. "Ensuring the Future of the Arts: School/Community Partnerships." *Choral Journal*, 34(4), 23-29.

Gastler, Bernard. "Children's Choir/College Partnerships: Unlikely But Successful Bedfellows." *Choral Journal*, 34(4), 31-36.

Little, Sara. *To Set One's Heart—Belief and Teaching in the Church*. Atlanta: John Knox Press, 1983.

Ward, Wendy. *Gift of God—Gift to God: Living the Word Through Artistry*. Philadelphia: Geneva Press, 1984.

Related Resources
Miscellaneous
Bock, Fred and Lois. *Creating Four-Part Harmony: Effective Ideas for Ministers of Music.* Carol Stream, IL: Hope Publishing Company, 1989.

Calahan, Kenneth L. *Effective Church Finances: Fundraising and Budgeting for Church Leaders.* San Francisco: Harper Publishing Company, 1992.

Covey, S. R. *The Seven Habits of Highly Effective People.* New York: Simon and Schuster, 1989.

Duckert, Mary. *Together at the Table: Children in the Congregation.* Philadelphia: The Geneva Press, 1981.

Eskew, Harry, and McElrath, Hugh T. *Sing with Understanding: An Introduction to Christian Hymnology.* Nashville, TN: Broadman Press, 1980.

Furnish, Dorothy Jean. *Experiencing the Bible with Children.* Nashville: Abingdon Press, 1990.

Hammer, Richard. *The Church Guide to Copyright.* Matthews, NC: Christian Ministry Resources, 1990.

Hanson, Richard Simon. *Worshiping with the Child.* Nashville: Abingdon Press, 1988.

The Hymnal 1982 Companion. Glover, Raymond F., general editor. New York: Church Hymnal Corporation, 1990.

Lovelace, Austin C. *Hymn Notes for Church Bulletins.* Chicago: G.I.A., 1987.

Mapson, J. Wendell, Jr. *The Ministry of Music in the Black Church.* Valley Forge: Judson Press, 1984.

Orr, N. Lee. *The Church Music Handbook for Pastors and Musicians,* Nashville: Abingdon Press, 1991.

Parker, Alice. *Melodious Accord: Good Singing in Church.* Chicago: Liturgy Training Corporation, 1991.

Routley, Erik. *The Music of Christian Hymns.* Chicago: G.I.A., 1981.

Schalk, Carl, editor. *Key Words in Church Music: Definition Essays on Concepts, Practices, and Movements of Thought in Church Music.* St. Louis: Concordia, 1978.

Sharp, Timothy W. "The Decade of the Hymnal 1982-1992: Choral Piety and Belief, Hardbound." *Choral Journal,* 31(9), 31-44.

Stulken, Marilyn. *Hymnal Companion to the Lutheran Book of Worship.* Philadelphia: Fortress Press, 1981.

Sydnor, James Rawlings. *Hymns and Their Uses.* Carol Stream, IL: Agape, 1982.

Westermeyer, Paul. *The Church Musician.* New York: Harper and Row, 1988.

Wilson, Marlene. *The Effective Management of Volunteer Programs.* Boulder: Volunteer Management Associates, 1976.

Young, Carlton R. *The Companion to the United Methodist Hymnal.* Nashville: Abingdon Press, 1993.

Video Tapes
An Annotated List

Body, Mind, Spirit, Voice: Developing the Young Singer. Helen Kemp. One on one classroom encounters with elementary age children. St. Louis: Concordia #VHS-87MZ0236, 1985.

The Children's Choir with Doreen Rao and the Glen Ellyn Children's Chorus. Produced by the American Choral Directors Association, 1988. (See address under Organizations, below.)

The Chorus, a Union of Voices. Traces the heritage of choral music from its origins to the present day. Explores the diversity of modern choral music and shows many different types of choral musical effects. Script by Ronald Kenetchy. Educational Audio Visual, Inc. Pleasantville, NY: 1985.

Contemporary American Music and the Children's Choir. A lecture by Gregg Smith and performances by the Los Angeles Children's Chorus, the St. Louis Children's Chorus, the Bach Choir of Nassau Presbyterian Church, Princeton, NJ, and the Phoenix Boys Choir. From the National Convention of the American Choral Directors Association, 1991. (See address under Organizations, below.)

Daily Workout for a Beautiful Voice. Charlotte Adams. The Charlene Archibeque Choral Series Video #1. Santa Barbara: Santa Barbara Music Publishing, 1991. (805) 962-5800.

The Glory of Gospel: The Nation's Best Choirs. Produced by Merav Ozeri with The Black Music Caucus, New York Chapter. Reviews the roots of the spirituals which contained inflections, quartertones and extended syllables found only in African song. A four-part series, it includes performances by choirs from the U.S. Air Force Academy, Rutgers State University, Mt. Nebo Baptist Church, among others. New York: Marvid Productions, 1989.

Group Vocal Technique. Frauke Haaseman and James M. Jordan. Designed as a companion to the book by the same title. Contains vocal group exercises performed by an adult community choir, two high school choirs, and the Westminster Choirs. Chapel Hill, NC: Hinshaw Music, 1989.

Guiding the Uncertain Singer. Mabel Stewart Boyter, music educator and church musician. This tape addresses the teacher's needs regarding pitch matching. Garland, TX: 1991.

Howard Swan, produced by the American Choral Directors Association. Reviews the history of American choral music in the first half of the twentieth century and discusses the present state of choral music in both church and school. 1988.

Jester Hairston, produced by the American Choral Directors Association. An interview with the noted African-American conductor about his early training in music and his career. 1988.

Harlem to Haarlem: Story of a Boy Choir. Traces the Choir on tour from New York to the Netherlands, particularly on the work of one boy, as well as director Walter Turnbull. Includes concert performances. New York: WABC-TV, 1979.

Leonard Bernstein's Young People's Concert with the New York Philharmonic. Written and hosted by Leonard Bernstein, produced by Roger Englander. A series of 25 Sony Classical video cassettes released by the Smithsonian Institution via mail order, and also available from the Leonard Bernstein Society, 25 Central Park West, Suite 1Y, New York, NY 10023.

Master Class Series, Vol 2, Part 1, Practical Presentations. Margaret Hillis, conductor of the Chicago Symphony Orchestra, on the art of choral singing, with members of the Chicago Symphony Orchestra Chorus. Chicago: Master Class Productions, 1985.

Music in Early Childhood. This 1/2 hour public television documentary provides parents and educators with information about musical child development from birth through the early elementary years. It features the work of John Feierabend and The National Center for Music and Movement in the Early Years. Simsbury, CN: First Steps in Music, 1991.

Musical Encounter, 10. The Human Instrument. Aimed at the primary and intermediate grade school audience, it presents a program of choral literature ranging from classical pieces to pop music. Lincoln, NE: Great Plains National Instructional Television Library, 1988.

Musical Encounter, 19. The Chorus Show. Aimed at the primary and intermediate grade school audience, it presents a program of choral music and takes a view backstage to experience auditions. Lincoln, NE: Great Plains National Instructional Television Library, 1988.

Robert Shaw, Vol. 1, 2, 3. Shaw works with the Robert Shaw Festival Chorus in preparing and performing the following: Vol. 1—Brahms *German Requiem*; Vol. 2—Beethoven *Missa Solemnes*; Vol. 3—Berlioz *Requiem.*

Sing and Rejoice: Guiding Young Singers. Helen Kemp. Classroom performance demonstrations and techniques. St. Louis: Concordia #VHS87MZ0231, 1985.

Singing and Growing, I—A Sound Foundation, and II—New Singing Skills. Harvey K. Smith, Director, Phoenix Boys Choir. Using boys from the Choir, Smith explores the essential elements of fine choral singing. Statesville, NC: Video Teaching Aids, Inc. (704)872-6141.

Sounds, Scores and Signals I and II. Jane Marshall. What kind of sound do you hear? What is the content of sound? Getting to the sound through score study. What signals do we send to get the sound, manually and in rehearsals? Includes video, sample marked score, chart of pure vowel sounds and bibliography. Garland, TX: Choristers Guild, 1991.

Biblical Resources
An *Annotated List*

Anderson, Fred. *Singing Psalms of Joy and Praise.* Developed for use by the author for his congregation, the metrical settings use inclusive imagery for God. Philadelphia: The Westminster Press, 1986.

Batchelor, Mary. *The Children's Bible in 365 Stories.* A valuable companion to the Bible, not intended as a substitute for it. Batavia, IL: Lion Publishing, 1985.

Bucke, Emory Steven, editor. *The Interpreter's Dictionary of the Bible, An Illustrated Encyclopedia.* In four volumes. Identifies and explains all proper names and significant terms and subjects in the Holy Scriptures, including the Apocrypha. New York: Abingdon Press, 1962.

Eaton, John H. *The Psalms Come Alive, An Introduction to the Psalms Through the Arts.* Explores the Psalms through the arts: poetry, architecture, music, dance and drama. London and Oxford: Mowbray, 1984.

Meeks, Wayne A., general editor. *The Harper Collins Study Bible, New Revised Standard Version.* A comprehensive yet approachable resource containing study guides for both the Old and New Testaments plus the Apocryphal/Deuterocanonical Books. Also contains information about the books of the Bible in several traditions, a timeline and numerous color maps. Harper Collins, New York, 1993.

Miller, Patrick D., Jr. *Interpreting the Psalms.* Organized in two parts: General Approaches, which notes the poetic features of the Psalms as an aid to understanding. This is followed by the exposition of ten selected Psalms. Philadelphia: Fortress Press, 1986.

Routley, Erik. *Exploring the Psalms.* "The purpose of this study is not to provide a detailed commentary, but rather to introduce a reader to the Psalms as a basis for his devotions and as a door through which he will come to a special kind of understanding of the Old Testament and of our Lord's teaching." (From the Preface.) Philadelphia: The Westminster Press, 1975.

Weber, Christopher. *A New Metrical Psalter.* Attempts to follow the original texts as presented in the Book of Common Prayer, 1979. Normal English word order and phrasing have been given a high priority; with inclusive language and standard meters with suggested tunes. New York: The Church Hymnal Corporation, 1986.

Weiser, Artur. *The Psalms, A Commentary.* From The Old Testament Library. Includes all of the Psalms. An extensive introduction provides background for the commentary on each. London: SCM Press Ltd. 1982.

Young, Robert. *Young's Analytical Concordance to the Bible.* "Designed for the simplest reader of the English Bible" according to the author, it contains around 311,000 references. Arranged by word, the concordance allows the user to find specific scriptural references. Grand Rapids, MI: Wm. B. Eerdmans Publishing Company, 1964.

Organizations and Periodicals

The American Boychoir Presser Treble Choral Music Study Center. 19 Lambert Drive, Princeton, NJ 08540

American Choral Directors Association. National Headquarters and *The Choral Journal.* P.O. Box 6310, Lawton, OK 73506

American Guild of Organists: National Headquarters and *The American Organist.* 475 Riverside Dr., Suite 1260. New York, NY 10115

American Orff-Schulwerk Association. National Headquarters and *The Orff Echo.* P.O. Box 18495, Cleveland Heights, OH 44118

Association of Anglican Musicians and *The Journal.* Communications Office. P.O. Box 164488, Little Rock, AR 72216-4488. FAX 501-372-2512

Association of Disciple Musicians (Disciples of Christ). Homeland Ministries, P.O. Box 1986, Indianapolis, IN 46206

Association of Lutheran Church Musicians and *Cross Accent.* P.O. Box 16575, Worchester, MA 01601

Baptist Sunday School Board of the Southern Baptist Convention. Church Music Dept., 127 9th Ave. North, Nashville, TN 37234

Black Music Research Journal. Columbia College, 600 South Michigan Ave. Chicago, IL 60605. FAX (508) 741-1218

The Canadian Music Centre. 20 St. Joseph Steet, Toronto, Ontario M4Y 1J9. (416) 961-1660

Choir and Organ. 4th Floor. Centro House, Mandela St. London NWI ODU. FAX (071) 288- 8532

Choristers Guild. National Headquarters and the *LETTERS.* 2834 W. Kingsley Rd. Garland, TX 75041

Chorus! For and About the Choral Music Enthusiast. P.O. Box 2318, Duluth, GA 30136

Chorus America, Association of Professional Vocal Ensembles. 2111 Sansom St. Philadelphia, PA 19103. FAX (215) 563-2431

Creator, the Bimonthly Magazine of Balanced Music Ministries. P.O. Box 100, Dublin, OH 43017. FAX (614) 777-7346

Dalcroze Society of America and *The American Dalcroze Journal.* c/o Dr. Julia Schnebly-Black. University of Washington, 2871 45th Ave. NE, Seattle, WA 98105

The Fellowship of American Baptist Musicians. 1600 Tall Tree Drive, Trenton, MI 48183

The Fellowship of United Methodists in Worship, Music and Other Arts. National Headquarters and *Worship Arts.* P.O. Box 24787, Nashville, TN 37202. FAX (615) 340-7006

Foundation for Music-Based Learning and *Early Childhood Connections.* P.O. Box 4274 Greensboro, NC 27404-4274

The Hymn Society in the United States and Canada. Headquarters and *The Hymn.* Texas Christian University, P.O. Box 30854, Fort Worth, TX 76129

International Federation for Choral Music and *International Choral Bulletin.* Dr. Michael J. Anderson, University of Illinois, Department of Performing Arts (M/C 255) 1040 West Harrison, Chicago, IL 60607

International Society of Children's Choral and Performing Arts, Ltd. Education Division. The Kennedy Center for the Performing Arts. Washington, D.C.

International Society of Music Educators and the *Journal of Music Education.* Administrator, ISME International, Music Education Information and Research Center, University of Redding, Bulmershe Court, Redding RG6 18Y, United Kingdom. FAX 44-734-318846

The Liturgical Conference, "an independent voluntary not-for-profit membership association concerned with the renewal of life and worship in the Christian church." *Liturgy*, a journal of pastoral liturgy. 8750 Georgia Ave. Silver Spring, MD 20910-3621

The Moravian Music Foundation and the *Moravian Music Journal.* 20 Cascade Ave. Winston-Salem, NC 27107

Music Educators National Conference. 1806 Robert Fulton Dr., Reston, VA 22091

The Ontario Choral Federation. 100 Richmond Street East, Suite 200, Toronto, Ontario M5C 2P9 (416) 363-7488

Organization of American Kodaly Educators and the quarterly periodical, *Kodaly Envoy.* Music Department Box 2017, Nicholls State University, Thibodaux, LA 70310. FAX (504) 443-4927

Pastoral Music. 225 Sheridan St., NW, Washington, DC 20011-1492. FAX (202) 723-2262

Presbyterian Association of Musicians, and *Reformed Liturgy and Music.* 100 Witherspoon St. Louisville, KY 40202-1396

The Royal Candian College of Organists. 12 St. Clair Avenue West, Toronto, Ontario M4V 1L7 (416) 929-6400

The Royal School of Church Music. Addington Palace, Croydon. England CR9 5AD, or, 40 Foxhall, Middlesex, NJ 08846 (Chorister Training Scheme, published 1977)

United Church of Canada, 85 St. Clair Avenue East, Toronto, Ontario M4T 1M8 (416) 925-5931

United Church of Christ. National music group being formed, 1994. Chairperson is Arthur Clyde, U.C.C. Hymnal Commission, (216) 736-3721

Church of the Nazarene—Worship and Music Office, P.O. Box 419527 Kansas City, MO 64141

Church of Jesus Christ, Latter Day Saints, Head of Music Division, Michael Moody, 50 East N. Temple St. Salt Lake City, UT 84150, (801) 240-2551

Reorganized Church of Latter Day Saints. Worship Office, Peter Judd, Independence MO (816) 833-1000

Seventh Day Adventist—International Adventists Musicians Association. P.O. Box 476 College Place, WA 99324

The Yearbook of American and Canadian Churches, Abingdon Press. Lists over 300 associated denominations and is available by writing to 475 Riverside Drive, New York, NY 10115

Index